Women of the Northern Plains

Women
of the
Northern Plains

Gender and Settlement
on the Homestead Frontier,
1870–1930

BARBARA HANDY-MARCHELLO

MINNESOTA HISTORICAL SOCIETY PRESS

Publication of this book was supported in part with funds provided by the Ken and Nina Rothchild Endowed Fund for Women's History.

www.mnhs.org/mhspress

The Minnesota Historical Society Press is a member of the Association of American University Presses.

Manufactured in the United States of America

10 9 8 7 6 5 4 3 2 1

♾ The paper used in this publication meets the minimum requirements of the American National Standard for Information Sciences—Permanence for Printed Library Materials, ANSI Z39.48–1984.

International Standard Book Number 0-87351-521-8 (cloth)

Library of Congress Cataloging-in-Publication Data

Handy-Marchello, Barbara.
  Women of the Northern Plains : gender and settlement on the homestead frontier, 1870–1930 / Barbara Handy-Marchello.
    p. cm.
  Includes bibliographical references and index.
  ISBN 0-87351-521-8 (hardcover : alk. paper)
  1. Rural women—North Dakota—History—19th century.
  2. Rural women—North Dakota—History—20th century.
  3. Rural families—North Dakota—History—19th century.
  4. Rural families—North Dakota—History—20th century.
  5. Frontier and pioneer life—North Dakota.
  6. Sex role—North Dakota—History.
  7. North Dakota—Rural conditions.
  8. North Dakota—History.
  I. Title.
HQ1438.N9H36 2005
305.43'63'09784—dc22
2004021947

Women of the Northern Plains

Acknowledgments

I am grateful to the many people who helped bring this book to completion. First of all, to my mother, Carolyn Pickard Handy, who taught me to love study and learning and to persist in both, but to enrich study by working and playing outdoors.

Great teachers taught me to use reason in pursuit of a solution, to conduct research, and to make words respond to my ideas. I hope I have proved worthy of their efforts. David Danbom, who guided my master's thesis, remains my adviser and friend. His comments on portions of this book guided me toward stronger conclusions. It has been my great good fortune to study with Linda Kerber and Malcolm Rohrbough, who supervised the research and writing of my dissertation, from which this book has grown. Linda has patiently read and reread portions of this book, supplying comments and encouragement at every stage.

Colleagues David Rowley, Anne Kelsch, Marcia Wolter Britton, Virginia Heidenreich, Janet Daly, Mary Jane Schneider, and Birgit Hans offered encouragement, asked the right questions, made useful comments on various stages of the manuscript, and never let me doubt that I would complete the project. Kathy Jellison, Steve Reschly, Deb Fink, and Claire Strom provided the collegial environment that nurtured my interest in the social history of agricultural societies.

Londa Ingebretsen, Gwen Fraase, Bobby Hoffman, Connie Kingsley, Norma Nelson, and many other women talked about their lives on the farm as we shared meals and friendship. They offered me the opportunity to reflect on my research in the context of their lives and helped me to locate the truth in the data. Students Jodi Nelson and Heidi Dyrstad enriched my research with their contributions. I am grateful for their generosity.

. . .

Many archivists directed me to important documents or helped me gain access to research materials. I am especially indebted to John Bye of the North Dakota Institute for Regional Studies at North Dakota State University and to Sandy Slater of the Elwyn B. Robinson Department of Special Collections at the University of North Dakota, whose interest in gathering rural women's history was of tremendous help as I conducted this research. Sarah P. Rubinstein has been a wise, generous, and patient editor. I thank her for maintaining faith in this project over such a long period and for her good counsel.

Finally, I am happy that I share my life with Marty Marchello. He made possible the research and writing of this book through his constant support and devotion.

Women of the Northern Plains

Introduction

"Will you trust me, Katie dear—
Walk beside me without fear?
May I carry, if I will,
All your burdens up the hill?"
And she answered with a laugh,
"No, but you may carry half."

MRS. V. K. WILCOX

In 1905, the *Annual,* a farm journal published by the Farmers' Institute of the North Dakota Agricultural College, printed a poem by Mrs. V. K. Wilcox that she had read, along with a speech titled "Home Making," at the Tri-State Grain Growers Convention. The poem tells the story of Katie Lee and Willie Gray, two children who play together and grow up to marry and raise a family. Willie farms and Katie raises the children, but he turns to her for farming advice—for which she draws on the experts at the agricultural college—and he tries to ease her work by purchasing the best equipment for her. Willie always assumes the lead, offering her his strength as they climb the hills of life together. Katie reminds him, time and again, that he carries half the load and she happily carries the other half, noting, "labor halved is earthly bliss."[1]

Mrs. Wilcox subtly makes several points in this poem. Though Willie is clearly devoted to Katie and their marriage seems to be overwhelmingly happy, he constantly needs reminding that he carries only half the burden. The social construction of female subordination blinds him to the *fact* of Katie's contributions, of which he is obviously aware but has no means of evaluating. Wilcox also dramatically entwines the family and the farm into a single economic and social unit—what is today called the "family farm"—revealing a woman's perspective on farming

3

and marriage: a woman married to a farmer is also a farmer whether she plants and harvests or not. Finally, Wilcox notes that the butter Katie churns and sells in local markets brings in enough money to interest Willie when they are unable to keep up with mortgage payments. In North Dakota, successful farming cannot depend solely on wheat; diverse crops drawing on both fields and barnyards—on both men's and women's labor—and sold in markets that rise and fall at different times of the year provide better financial security for farm families.

Katie Lee and Willie Gray are not far from the historical reality of farm couples in North Dakota, but this truth may not be apparent at first glance. Patriarchal family relationships and community structures were the cultural norms of most of North Dakota's early settlers, and farm women seem to have occupied a position subordinate to their husbands and to other men in the community. Pioneers brought with them cultural attributes that placed patriarchal systems of marriage at the center of society. However, these systems were moderated by both custom and law, and an examination of the historical records indicates that "partnership" might be a better descriptor than "patriarchy."

Dakota Territory's marriage laws (later preserved by the State of North Dakota) assumed that matrimony created an equal partnership under the leadership of the husband. According to the Civil Code of Dakota Territory, the marriage relationship entwined a woman and a man in "obligations of mutual respect, fidelity and support." The law declared that the husband must support the wife unless he is unable to; then she must support him from her own property. Though the distance between law and reality cannot always be bridged, the law required that either partner in a marriage assume responsibility for support when necessary. Marriage and family stability depended on the economic contributions of both husband and wife.[2]

The second section of the marriage code defined the marriage relationship in patriarchal terms: "The husband is head of the family." Thus, the mutuality of the first section is modified by sex hierarchy. The tension between these two sections demonstrates another aspect of farm life: though women's work was essential to successful farming, women were expected to remain subordinate in the private domain of farm and home as well as in the public political arena. The marriage code was written by men who lived in relationships that informed their writing of the law. They were the heads of their own families and, if they farmed, were well aware of the significance of women's economic contributions to the farm's stability.[3]

Wheat was the main crop on northern plains farms, and early settlers fully expected that wheat would sustain the family and bring wealth to those who worked hard and managed their farms well. However, when wheat failed to meet that promise, a complex of economic activities utilizing farm resources, especially women's work areas of poultry and butter production, served to sustain the family and maintain its hold on the farm.

When settlers first turned the sod to plant wheat and other small grains in the early 1870s, the soil was wonderfully fertile. Nevertheless, years of extensive agriculture brought about decreasing fertility, which combined with capricious weather patterns and unstable prices to make wheat farming an unreliable source of income. Those who successfully risked buying land, who arrived with a little capital, or who settled early enough to improve and expand their farms before 1900 were prepared to take advantage of the combination of good crops and high prices that characterized the "Golden Age of Agriculture." They became comfortable, even wealthy. But for most first-generation farm families, the good years between 1900 and 1920 were merely a respite from the hard times that preceded and followed the two "golden" decades.[4]

The instability of wheat farming made women's productive activities on the farm central to the family's survival and success, not peripheral, not "pin money." Some women brought to Dakota marketable skills that they used to supplement farm income, and most women raised poultry and milked cows to provide food for the family and a surplus for sale or trade. Women's productive work yielded only a small portion of the income derived from the farm, but it was steady and substantial enough to meet the basic needs of the family no matter the condition of crops or agricultural markets.

Anthropologist Peggy R. Sanday proposes that women's status in a community rises in accordance with their productive activities, but that productivity alone may not be sufficient to improve the overall status of women. Sanday's theory works very well in analyzing the condition of North Dakota farm women. While the first generation of European

American farm women may have enjoyed the respect of their families and communities, they did not gain additional political or economic rights as a result of their work. Furthermore, by the time they retired from their farms in the 1920s, agricultural institutions and the influence of an increasingly industrial society had worked some changes in the social construction of farm women's roles, changes that emphasized reproductive (or household) labor and mothering and in the process obscured the historical contributions of pioneer farm women.[5]

The political, economic, and social orders that prescribed the subordination of women were not at all unusual for this generation of American women. Any other gender arrangement would have been striking enough to draw considerable attention. But the historical subordination of women generally—and in agricultural history specifically—has obscured the significance of women's partnership in the successful settling of northern plains farms. If subordination is conceived of as a social construction, it is easier to understand what factors were put in place to maintain it, why it did not exist at the personal level, and how it worked to hide the role of women in farming.

Several factors maintained women's subordination. Those who immigrated to Dakota from midwestern states, from several northern, central, and eastern European nations, and from Syria continued to follow their cultural traditions concerning the marriage relationship. Further, the major European immigrant groups—Germans, Black Sea Germans, and Norwegians—as well as Yankee Americans frequently asserted the superiority of men in public and private arenas. In addition, local Christian congregations, while giving women a prominent public position, denied them leadership in religious matters and any official voice in church business. Finally, professional agriculturists, who became increasingly involved in all aspects of farm life in the early years of the twentieth century, confirmed and enhanced the subordination and invisibility of farm women in order to create in agricultural families a social structure matching that of their urban, middle-class counterparts.

Pioneer farm families, however, could not afford to maintain the subordination of women in their homes or communities. Women (and often their husbands) routinely challenged institutional and rhetorical subordination with their work in the community and home, in groups and as individuals. The significance of their economic, political, and social roles, especially during hard times, coexists in tension with the social order of the late nineteenth and early twentieth centuries.

The work of the women in this study took place in a context of maturing farms, growing families, evolving communities, and changing markets. The actual timing for these developments varied for each family, though approximate settlement dates for different parts of the state can be established. The process was under way in the Red River Valley, in the state's eastern portion, by 1870; the last homesteaders claimed their land in the western counties just before the United States entered World War I. The settlement pattern was generally east to west, aided by the Northern Pacific and Great Northern Railroads, but a south-to-north migration beginning around 1885 occurred in the central counties, while another pattern resulted from Canadians moving in from the north.

As families settled, they moved through similar stages. At first they lived in crude shelters while breaking grass-bound sod and expanding crop acreage. They soon acquired draft stock, milk cows, and poultry. Settlers found markets for their crops and labor, relying on a combination of grain sales, off-farm work, and trade of surplus eggs, butter, and garden produce to generate enough income to maintain the family and improve the farm. If they managed to remain on the farm through the first few years, they eventually built a barn, expanded the house, and began to acquire more land and better equipment. For the earliest settlers, the uncertainty of farming the northern plains was complicated by distance from markets and trade centers. Later settlers had fewer difficulties finding necessary supplies of equipment and food in nearby towns and enjoyed improved access to markets via grain elevators and railroads.

State agencies offered technical support to farmers soon after statehood in 1889. The commissioner of agriculture and the North Dakota Agricultural College sent professionals into farming communities to discuss improved agricultural and homemaking practices. These professionals had little interest in the economic role of farm women or in their ability to generate income from farm resources. Instead, professional agriculturists in accordance with national programs sought to teach farm women "scientific" homemaking and childcare. At the same time, North Dakota's dependence on wheat began yielding to diversified crops, and the advent of commercial creameries shifted control of the farm dairy to men. Women, still seeking a reliable source of income from their own labor, invested more time and effort in their poultry flocks.

Farm women's participation in settlement extended beyond the farm to community affairs. Both formally and informally, both collectively and individually, women assumed leadership roles in establishing new communities. Rural churches offered women the strongest and most visible standing in community affairs. Having created these powerful social and economic positions in the church, farm women were able to shape their communities according to their own moral and cultural standards.

In common with farm women in other places and times, work, family, and community were the three foundations of women's experience on northern plains farms. The nature of work was determined by distant markets in industrial cities; family concerns were shaped by frequent pregnancies and large families, by the recurring, necessary absence of men or the death or desertion of husbands, and by the pull of cities on farmers' children; communities grew to meet the needs of families for social gatherings, for communal worship, and for ordering rural society through the establishment of schools and other institutions. The organizations that emerged in communities built by pioneer farm families on the northern plains bear the mark of women's interests, labor, and thought.[6]

The resources for this study are products of these institutions. Interviews, memoirs, and government records, especially those of agricultural agencies, reveal the lives and work of pioneer farm women and, taken together, form a rich body of evidence describing the many roles they played. I relied most heavily on interviews with first-generation pioneers conducted by the Work Projects Administration's Writers' Project employees in 1939 and 1940. There are three groups of interviews: the Pioneer Biography Files, the Ethnic Group Files, and the Hard Wheat Files. The interviewers asked consistent questions about immigration, farming, and families. Some people answered with the least possible energy; others spoke at length about their experience as pioneers. These records in general provide information on families, housing, and nearby market towns, on the ways pioneers managed to survive the first years when they had only small quantities of crops to sell, and on how their farms eventually grew large enough to sustain their families. The interviews are limited by the interviewer's skill in eliciting answers from the subjects and by the subject's ability to remember accurately and to express in English the nature of his or her experience. More men than women were subjects of interviews. In spite of these limitations, the interviews demonstrate a remarkable consistency in experience across classes, ethnic groups, and regions of the state and give voice to many pioneers who did not have the time to write their own life stories. Another set of interviews or responses to inquiries was collected by chapters of the North Dakota Federation of Women's Clubs between 1938 and 1953. Through the Pioneer Mother Project Records, the Women's Clubs offered farm women another opportunity to record their personal histories. To this collection I was able to add an interview I conducted with Magdalena Job, who arrived in North Dakota as a young woman in 1914 and happily agreed to talk about her early years on the northern plains just a few months before her death at the age of ninety-five.[7]

Memoirs are another important source for this study. Diaries, a traditional source of women's history, are rare among farm women of the northern plains. While very few women kept diaries for lack of time, lack of writing materials, or lack of interest, several wrote memoirs or family biographies. These books are lively, intimate, and emotionally honest. They show women at their daily labor giving life to the statistics that agricultural agencies compiled for their reports. The memoirs hide little about family dynamics, revealing how the stress of starting a new farm often wore away at family affection, but they also demonstrate settlers' strength, persistence, faith, and pride. Women's memoirs of their pioneer lives link the comfort and intimacy of the home and family to the seasons and markets of the agricultural economy.[8]

A third important resource is found in the various government documents of agricultural production. The federal decennial census chronicles land ownership and crop and livestock production for the year before the census is taken. In other words, the records are for the year ending in "nine" instead of "zero." An additional agricultural census was taken in 1885. The census is not a static document; questions about crops and production differ from year to year, making it difficult to assess change in these statistics over time. Census takers occasionally made mistakes in their records, and sometimes farmers were reluctant to be honest about crops and income. Despite these well-known limitations, the federal census provides the best long-term record of farm production for individual farms (up to 1885), for townships, for counties, and for states.

The State of North Dakota also took an interest in recording statistics of agricultural production. The commissioner of agriculture and labor collected figures yearly from county assessors, but these statistics are notably inaccurate. Assessors complained that they were not paid sufficiently for the job, and the records reflect their lack of interest in the work. However, the commissioner's biennial reports include narratives about agriculture (including dairy) and labor, selected letters from farmers and professional agriculturists, and statistics on seasonal hired workers that are not available anywhere else.

The North Dakota Agricultural College (NDAC) at Fargo created several types of records about its efforts to improve farm practices and family life. The Experiment Station (a federal agency operating in association with the college), the Farmers' Institute, and, later, the Extension Service published advice for and articles by farmers, presented traveling programs, and wooed farmers' children to the NDAC's agricultural and domestic science programs. Having more direct contact with farmers than did other agricultural agencies, NDAC employees noted women's role in the farm family and economy and looked for ways to include women's interests in their publications and programs.

Farm women who immigrated to North Dakota continued to farm as they and their mothers had elsewhere, raising garden vegetables to feed their families, crops to sell or trade, and small livestock for eggs, milk, and meat. Farming was central to their family's economy and fashioned the framework in which their personal and community relationships were formed. As such, the patterns of their lives were not very distinct from those of farm women in other places and other times. On the other hand, the soil, climate, and settlement patterns of North Dakota created a secondary framework that distinguishes this group of pioneer women from other groups and from their contemporaries in states to the east, south, and west.

I have examined the records and voices of North Dakota pioneer farm women within the context of farm women's history, which has bloomed brightly over the past twenty years, amending these women's earlier invisibility in historical writing and making apparent the centrality of women's productive and reproductive farm work in the past and present all over the world. Historians, anthropologists, and sociologists who study farm women tend to agree on four basic points. First, women's and men's work on farms was (and still is) inextricably linked, though in particular times or in certain cultures there was a tendency to designate tasks as properly "male" or "female." Second, bankers, economists, government agencies, agricultural academics, community leaders, and sometimes family members devalued women's contributions to farm income. This process had its foundation in European cultural systems and became more widespread with the industrialization of western nations. Third, scholars agree that farm women had important public roles in rural communities. Their leadership and labor made education, local medical care, churches, companionship, social welfare, and economic and political activities possible. Fourth, scholarship on farm women depends implicitly on listening to their voices and trusting their assessment of the family and the farm as an indivisible unit. My research reinforces these points while examining, first, how women from so many different cultures carried out their roles on northern plains farms during an era of rapid industrialization in the United States, and, second, how various agencies, operating on the assumption of women's frailty and subordination, sought to devalue and hide the work that was so obviously important to their families and communities.[9]

Records created by farm women, by Writers' Project interviews, and by agricultural agencies tell us a great deal about how marriage and children and butter and egg production framed the lives and work of pioneer farm women, but there is more. This is the story of women whose accumulated knowledge and native intelligence enabled them to make decisions about farm crops and investments and about their family's safety, security, and future. For some, the burdens became overwhelming: they forced their families to give up the land and move to a place they considered more acceptable, or they succumbed to terrible fears and were hospitalized or committed suicide, or they never thought of North Dakota as home. For others, the rewards of settlement more than repaid their work and investment. They moved into comfortable houses and saw their children succeed. They had sufficient leisure to enjoy the sheer beauty of "wheat fields, trees and wildflowers and flaming sunsets," the peaceful moments in the barn in the company of the quiet cows, and the fun of a wedding or a dance. All of these women built the foundations of today's rural communities and are the foremothers (often literally) of the present generation of farm women, whose work remains at the center of farm and rural life.[10]

1

Dakota
The People, the Place, the Times

... here was a beauty spot with wheat fields,
trees and wildflowers and flaming sunsets.
ROSA SIGURDARDOTTIR GUDMUNDSON

In 1869, Paul Hjelm-Hansen visited the Red River Valley, located on the eastern edge of northern Dakota Territory. Writing in Norwegian newspapers, Hjelm-Hansen described a prairie that "resembles a green ocean whose waves are formed by the tall grass.... There is nothing to behold except the green ocean." Though some settlers would find the absence of forests, mountains, and oceans to be shortcomings in the North Dakota landscape, most expected that the grasslands would yield easily to wheat cultivation.[1]

Wheat would, indeed, become "king" in North Dakota. As one pioneer recalled, "In those days, wheat was everything." The cultivation of wheat required turning over and destroying perennial grasses with deep root systems adapted to native soil conditions and the uncertain climate. Wheat, an annual grass, requires cultivation of the soil and adequate rainfall to meet its single growing season needs. It is meant to be harvested for sale in the market as well as to meet a large part of local human food requirements, so a crop had to be gathered every year. Unlike its wild cousins, wheat has no long-term protection system against drought, hail, and frost.[2]

North Dakota's wheat fields lie west of the prairies and east of the High Plains in the northernmost tier of states. North Dakota straddles the ninety-eighth meridian, which defines the eastern edge of the Great Plains. Most of the state is grassland, ranging from the tallgrass prairies along the Red River to the mixed-grass plains along the Missouri. Deciduous forests cover the extreme northeastern corner of the state, and badlands—canyons and rock outcroppings—break out of the grasslands in the southwest. Climatic conditions differ in North Dakota's three major topographical divisions: the Red River Valley, the Drift Prairie, and the Missouri Plateau. Moving west, rainfall diminishes and the soil becomes thinner and, in places, rocky and dotted with boulders.

All of North Dakota is considered semi-arid, even the Red River Valley, which technically lies in the humid Central Lowlands. This designation means that no part of the state is arid or humid, but that moisture conditions might be too wet, too dry, or just right during any given growing season. Most moisture (77 percent) comes in the form of rain during the growing season, but such precipitation is unpredictable. The state's average annual rainfall is around 17.3 inches, but totals are highest in the Red River Valley and lowest in the slope country west of the Missouri River. In any area and in any given year, however, rainfall may be inadequate or overabundant. Periodic droughts mark the region's history, the severest occurring from 1885 to 1889, in 1910 and 1917, and from 1929 to 1936. Dangerous prairie fires flare up during drought years, especially in spring and fall, when native grasses and wheat stubble are dry. Though droughts are perhaps the most discouraging of weather patterns, excessive rainfall can be just as devastating to crops.[3]

At the beginning of the settlement era, the uncertainty and irregularity of Dakota's climate sparked an intense debate over the country's suitability for agriculture. Railroad companies, town speculators, and the territorial government rained praises on the semi-arid land. Jay Cooke and Company, financial backers of the Northern Pacific Railroad, published a pamphlet in 1871 to encourage the sale of railroad bonds. Dakota's climate, it declared, was like Iowa's—farmers could expect forty bushels of wheat to the acre and adequate rainfall. However, some experienced residents with fewer stakes in the territory's future painted a different picture. Colonel William B. Hazen, stationed at Fort Buford in the slope country near the confluence of the Missouri and Yellowstone Rivers, wrote a lengthy letter to the *New York Tribune* in 1874 stating that the Dakota climate was both too cold and too hot for comfort and that its rainfall was far too short for commercial agricul-

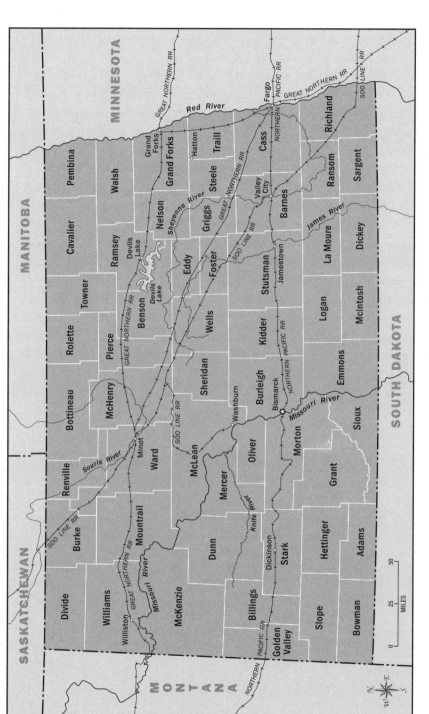

North Dakota

ture. He predicted that famine awaited those who would try to farm western Dakota.[4]

Actually, both sides were right—some of the time. Weather statistics for any given year could support either argument. The semi-arid nature of Dakota's climate means that rainfall was, and remains, irregular. West of the Missouri, farmers could count on a growing season with adequate rainfall for crops every once in a while, maybe even two or three years in a row. To the east of the plains, in the Red River Valley, farmers could depend on one or two excessively dry (or wet) years from time to time. Those who chose the Drift Prairie between the two border regions were caught in a game of chance.

Seasonally, air temperatures vary wildly from a record 60 degrees below zero to a record 121 degrees above zero (all temperatures Fahrenheit). The yearly mean temperature, the lowest in the forty-eight contiguous states, is 40 degrees. The final freezing temperatures are usually expected near the end of May; the first of the fall, around mid-September. Frost can appear on a growing crop even in summer, however, and many Barnes County settlers remembered 1888, the year they experienced frost every month.[5]

Daily life on the northern plains was complicated by weather extremes.

The Drift Prairie is also known as prairie pothole country. Mosquitoes breed with abandon in the shallow, still waters of the prairie wetlands. These mosquitoes do not carry malaria, but they inspired homesteaders' reports of constant battles with insects. Grasshoppers invaded the area periodically, completely destroying crops in the worst years. The 1880 agricultural census noted that several counties of Dakota Territory reported no wheat crop due to grasshopper damage.[6]

The grasslands support a variety of large and small animals, migratory waterfowl, and songbirds. Few settlers would take advantage of wild protein resources as the Indians had, but the trees and wild fruits growing along the rivers would be important sources of fuel and food. Some settlers would also have access to soft lignite coal lying near the surface in the Missouri Plateau.[7]

Hjelm-Hansen saw oceans of grass, apparently unoccupied. His oversight, whether innocent or purposeful, was typical of Europeans and Yankee Americans who promoted settlement. In fact, the Great Plains had been occupied by agricultural peoples for centuries before the Homestead Act offered "free" acreage to those who would live on and cultivate the land. The northern plains were home to the Mandan, the Hidatsa, the Arikara, and the Chippewa (Ojibwe). Bands of Dakota, Lakota, and Cheyenne moved through the area on hunting and trading trips and occasionally to make war.

The Mandan and the Hidatsa had lived in permanent villages along the Missouri River and its tributaries since the early eighteenth century; the Arikara moved into the area a few decades later. They hunted seasonally to supplement their crops of corn, beans, squash, and sunflowers. They gathered the fruits of the chokecherry, plum, grape, and saskatoon that grew along the riverbanks. They lived in large earth lodges that housed several generations of related men, women, and children.[8]

The Chippewa resided at the northern end of the Red River Valley and slowly moved into the Turtle Mountains along the Canadian border. They hunted buffalo on the plains and adopted some of the customs of plains peoples. The Chippewa were also strongly influenced by the French and English fur traders with whom they traded and intermarried by the middle of the eighteenth century.[9]

The Fort Laramie Treaty of 1851 began the process of assigning parcels of land to various plains tribes. According to land tenure theories, land defined by boundaries and secured by title organizes relations among people. The relations may be equal or hierarchical, but once regulated by law, they are meant to be orderly. After Indians were given the land as their own territory, it was then possible—and legal—for the government to take it away. Though the process made little sense to Native Americans, who had not previously conceived of land as divisible or as privately owned, securing Indian rights to the land was, ironically, the necessary first step toward European American settlement on the plains.[10]

In 1867, the first reservation in northern Dakota Territory was set aside for several bands of Dakota at Devils Lake. Fort Totten was established nearby to provide military assurance that the Dakota would remain peaceful. They had been hunters, but the buffalo soon disappeared from the region. They came to the reservation voluntarily, but with few options.[11]

Fort Berthold, originally located west of the Missouri between the Heart and Yellowstone Rivers, became the reservation of the Mandan, Hidatsa, and Arikara. In 1870, President Grant, by executive order, greatly reduced the size of the reservation. By 1874, about 2,100 members of the three tribes resided at Fort Berthold, where they continued to practice agriculture. Though they had been peaceful in their relations with the government and had often provided scouts for the U.S. Army, their circumstances were no better, and sometimes worse, than those of tribes that had been hostile.[12]

A number of Lakota bands were assigned to the Great Sioux Reservation occupying the heart of Dakota Territory, land that was eventually reduced to several smaller reservations. One of these was Standing Rock, partially situated in south-central North Dakota. Among the Lakota were some bands that remained antagonistic toward railroad construction, the army, and European American settlement. Standing Rock became the reservation home of Sitting Bull and his followers when they returned from Canada in 1881.[13]

The Chippewa and the Métis—people descended from Chippewa or Cree women and French or Scottish men—asked for a reservation of twenty-two townships, but the government was slow to respond. Anticipating the formation of a reservation in 1882, Chippewa leaders tried to establish a legitimate claim to the lands they had requested and warned settlers away from the area. Settlers' accounts suggest that the warning served as fair notice and that encounters were peaceful. In 1884, President Arthur issued an executive order reducing the reservation to two townships in Rolette County, the majority of it unsuitable for farming. Most Turtle Mountain Chippewa and Métis remained off the reservation, but disputes over taxation of their farms and property led them to arm and prepare for conflict. Though Rolette County officials called in the National Guard, Governor John Miller withdrew the troops before shots were fired. A similar incident took place in 1891. Following these "troubles," the Chippewa and Métis who remained in the area took up farming alongside their French Canadian, Yankee, and Irish American neighbors.[14]

By the time the federal land office opened in Pembina in 1871 and the government began surveying the northern part of Dakota Territory, people of several different cultures had been hunting and farming, establishing villages, and engaging in trade there for centuries. It was a place of varied human endeavors, though most settlers, like Hjelm-Hansen, would see or understand little of this early activity. The decade-long conflict and threatened violence between government officials and the Chippewa, the real or imagined threats related to the Lakota Ghost Dance in 1890 and 1891, and the memories of the 1862 Dakota War in Minnesota constitute the only unfriendly encounters between Indians and European American settlers in North Dakota. Despite this record of relative peace, many settlers would hold to the idea that they were living in hostile Indian country long after events had proven them mistaken.

In North Dakota, the great difficulty between pioneers and Indians rested in their competing interpretations of the nature and use of the land. Both groups regarded the land as the basis of their economy and their reason for inhabiting this particular part of the continent. Both claimed a right to the land: one by legal title, the other by use and occupation. But their approaches to land use differed widely. John Christianson reported an incident that, while probably apocryphal, symbolizes the conflicting ways in which settlers and natives thought about the land. As Christianson was breaking sod one day, a group of young Indian men followed him, turning the heavy chunks back to their original position, grass side up, covering the exposed soil. Christianson stopped, offered the men some tobacco, and asked why they were undoing his work. They pointed to the broken sod and said, "Wrong side up! Wrong side up!" For Indians, the land's value lay in its grass, which supplied food for deer, elk, bison, and horses as well as prairie turnips, wild fruits, and other plants for people to harvest. European and Yankee settlers, however, believed the land's greatest potential could be released only by breaking it open with a plow and planting in it the seeds of domesticated grasses.[15]

In spite of disparities in worldview, settlers living closest to Indian reservations often enjoyed good relations with their native neighbors. Still, whether friendly or fearful, settlers contributed to the ongoing process of pushing native peoples aside and confining them to shrinking parcels of land through treaties, force, and, finally, farming.[16]

Just as the Fort Laramie treaty drew lines across the "green ocean," politicizing the land without regard to culture or topography, in 1861 Congress drew a new line to establish Dakota Territory. This massive political unit would be broken in two at statehood, divided by another political line running east and west across its middle.[17]

At first, the territory's northern portion did not appeal to settlers. In 1870, there were only 2,400 "civilized" residents (whites and Christian Indians), most huddled in the northeast corner, near the old trading post at Pembina. But when the Northern Pacific Railroad (NPR), supported by land grants and cheap federal loans, crossed the Red River at Fargo in 1872 and pushed on to Bismarck in 1873, it offered transportation for people, freight, and crops as well as some assurance that settlements in the northern part of the territory would eventually develop. In 1874, the federal land office moved from Pembina to Fargo and a second office opened in Bismarck. By 1875, the territory's population had grown to 10,000, with most settlers still clustered in the Red River Valley.[18]

In 1872, the NPR set up its own immigration department—complete with agents in Europe—to sell its extensive lands. In the territories, the company had been granted forty sections (about 25,000 acres) for each completed mile of track. The NPR published pamphlets in several languages—including Swedish and German—offering land along its route at 10 percent down with seven years to pay the remaining debt. The company built "immigrant houses" in the Minnesota towns of Duluth, Glyndon, and Brainerd to provide temporary quarters for those interested in buying railroad land. Despite these efforts, the NPR immigration department saw little success in the northern part of Dakota Territory. After two years, the railroad had sold none of its extensive land holdings there, perhaps because even the company's land commissioner, James B. Power, saw little future in agriculture in Dakota Territory. Traveling along the NPR line in 1872, he observed a parched, desertlike country; he later declared that even the name, "Dakota," had a "faraway sound."[19]

Even this slight interest in Dakota Territory's northern district ended with the panic of 1873. The bankrupt Northern Pacific halted construction at Bismarck; many territorial residents doubted the road would ever be completed. Worse, the existing track did not directly connect Dakota towns and farms with the markets of Minneapolis and St. Paul. Pioneers struggled to survive in the hostile environment with little lumber or machinery and few doctors, schools, or churches. Grasshopper infestations in 1872 and 1874 made them wonder if Dakota would support farming families. The present was difficult; the future was uncertain.[20]

Those who stayed saw an impressive turnabout beginning in 1878, the opening of the seven-year Great Dakota Boom. A combination of good rainfall, peaceful relations with Indians, and flat, fertile land free of tree stumps and ready to be turned by farm machinery encouraged new settlement. The Northern Pacific resumed construction in 1879, and in the next decade other lines—including James J. Hill's St. Paul, Minneapolis and Manitoba (which became the Great Northern in 1889) and the Minneapolis, St. Paul and Sault Ste. Marie (the "Soo line")—connected farm market towns to the great mills and shipping terminals in St. Paul and Duluth via a spider web of rail. More important, perhaps, was the development of improved milling techniques for hard red spring wheat, known as No. 1 Hard, that grew best on the northern plains.[21]

In 1875, the large mills of Minneapolis and St. Paul developed new methods for making flour from hard red spring wheat. The result was a flour high in gluten and superior for baking. Strong demand for high-quality flour milled from No. 1 Hard spurred a 600 percent increase in flour production between 1875 and 1885. During those same years, shipments of wheat on the Northern Pacific increased nearly forty times. The boom was good for the railroads and flour mills headquartered in Minnesota.[22]

During the boom years, Dakota was the talk of the nation. Settlers wrote home encouraging friends and relatives to come out and claim "free" land. Both Dakota Territory and the Northern Pacific Railroad put immigration offices to work publishing "boomer" literature in several languages. Magazine articles featured the great bonanza farms of the Red River Valley. Writing a typical boomer pamphlet for the Burleigh County Pioneer's Association in 1874, Linda Slaughter, wife of a military surgeon stationed at Fort Rice, described the climate as healthful and stated that all kinds of vegetables would grow "with but little trouble."[23]

Boomer efforts, combined with railroad construction and the availability of land, inspired a 1,000 percent increase in the population of the northern part of the territory between 1878 and 1890. Settlers and speculators bought railroad land or claimed 160-acre parcels under the preemption law, the homestead law, and the Timber Culture Act of 1873. In 1877, 232 claims were filed under the three federal land acts. In 1882, the Fargo and Bismarck land offices processed 5,579 claims. What NPR commissioner Power had once seen as a desert was by 1881, in his words, the home of a "thrifty population of nearly 35,000 people."[24]

In the early 1880s, the peak years of the Great Dakota Boom, more acres were purchased under the preemption law than were claimed under the timber culture or homestead laws. While land applied for under the preemption law was purchased outright after the claimant had lived on the parcel for a few months, homestead and timber culture claims required that several conditions be met. The Homestead Act demanded that settlers build a dwelling, live on the parcel for five years, and cultivate part of the land. The Timber Culture Act required applicants to plant a varying number of acres of trees and prove that a portion of those trees survived at the end of eight years. Only after meeting these requirements, presenting the necessary proof, and paying a small filing fee would they receive the patent to their free land. Those who could not afford to wait five years before mortgaging or selling the land could commute their claim by paying between $1.25 and

$2.50 per acre (depending on location) as soon as legally and financially possible.[25]

The boom saw the development of bonanza farms in the Red River Valley. Investors in the bankrupt Northern Pacific—offered railroad lands in exchange for their worthless stock or bonds—put together huge wheat farms, some as large as sixty thousand acres. For a number of years, extensive agriculture made bonanza farms as profitable as farms in humid areas to the east. Most such farms raised nothing but wheat and feed for the draft stock. On the largest farms there were no gardens, beef cattle, or swine: all foodstuffs as well as machinery, lumber, and other necessities were purchased in large quantities at wholesale prices. Bonanzas also occasionally received rebates from the railroad for their wheat shipments. The cost of producing wheat on the bonanza farms was about forty cents per bushel, yielding the owners a profit even in the declining market of the boom years. These farms provided employment for newly arrived settlers, but they also presented an artificially rosy picture of northern plains agriculture. Great profits, it seemed, were to be made from wheat agriculture.[26]

As the acreage devoted to wheat cultivation and the number of bushels harvested both increased during the boom years, the price of wheat dropped. The peak of the boom was 1883, the year that saw the most land claim filings and the most bushels of wheat shipped to Minneapolis. But then wheat prices crashed, dropping to forty-six cents in 1884. Although they revived somewhat after that, the 1890 price was ten cents lower than the 1882 price had been.[27]

By 1890 the boom was over. Claim filings dropped; towns lost significant numbers of residents or disappeared altogether. The population continued to grow at a slower pace, but many settlers became discouraged and left. Historian Elwyn B. Robinson suggests that the boom was terminated not by the low wheat prices nor by the serious drought of 1889 but instead by the end of speculation in Dakota land. When speculators began to lose money, the heady excitement of the Great Dakota Boom faded. Harold E. Briggs, a historian of the boom, attributes its end to several factors: a five-year drought that began in 1885, a slump in railroad construction, and, by 1887, reduced availability of desirable land east of the Missouri. Briggs expresses some agreement with Robinson's speculation theory when he notes that many settlers had come not to build homes but to claim land. As soon as they secured the title, they left, sometimes with cash in hand from a mortgage they would never repay. Although all settlers no doubt felt at least some of these "push" factors during the late eighties, not many would act on them.[28]

A second boom, beginning in 1898, coincided with a period of national economic growth. In North Dakota, railroads again undertook extensive construction projects, doubling the state's total miles of track between 1898 and 1915. Settlers and speculators claimed land in the far western counties of the Missouri slope. Prices for wheat and land rose as claim filings expanded. Those who had survived the devastating droughts, the below-production-cost wheat prices, and the loss of towns and neighbors were positioned to enjoy relatively high wheat prices and good crops following 1900. They invested in fine houses, bigger barns, and improved livestock. During this second boom, state agricultural officials began a long and frustrating effort to encourage farmers to diversify their holdings with livestock, especially dairy cattle.[29]

During and between the exciting boom years, there existed an undercurrent of stability fed by the migration of quiet and determined settlers to northern Dakota Territory. These migrants from eastern and southern states and immigrants from Norway, Sweden, Germany, Iceland, Russia, Canada, and Syria sought homes and farms rather than investments. They were not speculators or clean-handed managers of bonanza farms. They seldom saw Fargo or Bismarck again after they exited the train that brought them to the territory. They came for "free" land, for land at a price, for adventure, for opportunity, to practice their religion openly, or simply because their family and friends were already in Dakota. Most had agricultural experience, but for many of the European immigrants that experience was limited to small farms of perhaps as few as five acres. Others had never worked the land at all: influenced by boomer literature, promotion agents, and letters from friends and family, they "expected to get rich on the prairie."[30]

Many of the early settlers were Yankee Americans with a strong heritage of mobility. They sensed that the continent's interior, which had always been ready to absorb a new generation of speculators, farmers, ranchers, and miners, would soon be settled up. Quickly identifying themselves as the pioneer generation, they sought their fortunes through farming or by selling farmland, seed, equipment, and cattle.[31]

Along with the Yankees came Scandinavians, many on the second or third leg of their slow westward migration. Earlier, Scandinavian immigrants had settled in Minnesota, Iowa, and Wisconsin, but good land was growing scarce there. Norwegians and Swedes continued to immigrate in the early twentieth century because of the challenges they faced buying land at home. Dakota Territory had plenty of land on which to build farms in good wheat-growing country. Scandinavians, primarily Norwegians, came to dominate the Red River Valley and eventually scattered west throughout Dakota.

Around 1885, another settlement pattern developed in central Dakota Territory. Moving north into the area from the rail terminus at Eureka were Black Sea Germans, immigrants whose ancestors in the early nineteenth century had emigrated from several German states into South Russia. Perhaps more than any other ethnic group, the Black Sea Germans made the journey as families. They spoke German dialects but were often called Russians or "Rooshans" in the vernacular of their neighbors. They had practiced wheat agriculture for decades in South Russia and knew how to live successfully on the grasslands.[32]

Each immigrant group arrived in a country that was in some way strange to them. Norwegians could accept the harsh winters but missed the ocean and mountains. Russians understood the grasslands but hated the cold, root-killing winters so different from the mild climate of the Black Sea region. Those who came from Illinois, Wisconsin, and Minnesota cursed the wind and the often rainless sky. Success in their agricultural enterprises would depend on weather, soil, access to markets, and their ability to adjust to new and difficult conditions.

As they adapted to the environment and to the market economy, immigrants from Europe and migrants from the United States sought to maintain their cultures and traditions. Homesteading Germans, Czechs, Danes, Dutch, Ukrainians, Irish, Scots, English, Syrian Christians and Muslims, Russian Jews, New Englanders, midwesterners, and southerners almost immediately established religious congregations and parochial schools to preserve their "Old Country" or "back home" customs and beliefs. Some communities were small, homogeneous, and endogamous, holding tightly to their language and traditions; others grew from a mix of ethnic groups. All of the immigrants negotiated between two cultures, maintaining a fervent attachment to one and an ambivalence leaning toward distrust of the other—at the same time becoming something ethnically distinct from either.[33]

By 1930, when most of the early pioneers had retired and sold their farms or bequeathed them to their children, farm and city folk together numbered 680,845, the largest population the state would ever have. More than 83 percent of North Dakotans were rural, and immigrants from foreign countries and their children comprised 62.5 percent of that figure. The farms they had built on the "green ocean" averaged nearly 500 acres, up from approximately 277 acres at the time of statehood.[34]

When the pioneers arrived, they viewed the prairies and plains of Dakota with differing expectations. Some saw a "veritable Garden of Eden," a place of "great charm before it was put under cultivation." Others were "[stunned] with [the] immensity" of the grasslands and daunted by the task of turning over the sod and making the vast prairies into farms and homes. Even for the most optimistic, survival and success on this frontier depended on coming to terms with the northern plains while building farms, raising families, and creating new communities. This process would demand labor and money as well as the constant renegotiation of social and economic relationships.[35]

2

"My Duty as Wife and Mother"
Marriage and Family

*I think I would find the same thing to do as I did,
if it was what my children and husband wanted.*

CAROLINE GJELSNES

Born in South Russia in 1865, Wilhelmina Geizler immigrated to the
United States in 1885 with her husband, John. At the time of their immigration, she was pregnant with her first child; by the age of thirty-
three, she had given birth to nine children. She raised them in the ordinary fashion of the prairie, teaching the oldest to mind the younger
ones and to manage some simple household tasks while Wilhelmina
worked in the fields. By the age of five, the oldest child, Catherine,
looked after the babies while her parents were out of the house. Wilhelmina taught Catherine to start the fire to heat the noon meal when
the sun reached a certain spot on the floor.[1]

But Wilhelmina Geizler's pattern of working beside her husband in
the field and teaching her children household tasks was interrupted in
April 1898 when a prairie fire approached the farm, threatening the
children she had sent out to bring in the cattle. Wilhelmina ran to help
them and found daughter Annie with her foot caught in a gopher hole
and her clothes on fire. Burning her hands, face, and chest, Geizler tore
off the blazing garments, carried Annie home, and returned to the pasture to fight the fire. Little Annie lived for nine hours, but Wilhelmina
Geizler lived for fifteen days, suffering agonizing pain from her burns.
Neighbors came to help out during the crisis, but Catherine, now thirteen, was soon fully responsible for the household's operation. As she
was dying, Wilhelmina instructed Catherine in the details of housework and childcare; there were seven surviving, younger siblings for
Catherine to feed, clothe, supervise, and train. Finally, Wilhelmina

asked Catherine to be good to her stepmother, knowing that John would undoubtedly remarry in order to keep his family together.[2] Wilhelmina Geizler's death illuminates the multiple threads that wove the fabric of pioneer women's personal relationships. As provider for, teacher of, and guardian to her children, her primary role in the household as mother of nine became the central fact, the most prominent thread, as she instructed her eldest daughter in household economy. Wilhelmina placed this burden on Catherine knowing that John would not, indeed, could not, take over her work. Household duties were the special reserve of women, and Catherine had begun her training many years before her mother died.

Catherine inherited from her mother a legacy of hard work that was also a gift, allowing her to grow up with her siblings in their father's home. They would remain a family because Catherine was able to take on her mother's roles. Affection was the cohesive element in pioneer families, evident in Geizler's courageous risk of her life for her children but also in her admonition that Catherine treat her stepmother kindly. How difficult it would have been for a second wife to step into the role of wife and mother if she faced the children's resentment.

Wilhelmina and John Geizler married, immigrated, claimed three quarter sections of land, and had their first child during the fourteen months between March 1884 and May 1885. Their marriage and their family were created at the same time as their farm, and the farm became the couple's silent partner. The bond between family and farm was both beneficial and tyrannical: land was a powerful benefactor that supported large families over generations, and land was an enemy that drained families of money, health, hope, and sometimes even life. Historian Virginia Scharff suggests that nineteenth-century western women's "quest for domestic security" was at odds with men's "search for secure property." But in North Dakota, many women identified their personal or their family's security with ownership of a productive farm. Farm families expected to prosper through generations linked to each other by their work and presence on the land. While it is apparent that women's and men's strategies for successful farming differed and that women might have preferred fewer acres and fewer children to work them, farming also brought women's and men's work into mutually beneficial partnership. In the emerging culture of the northern plains, land ownership and agriculture shaped the nature of the family and marriage relationship just as the family shaped the land to meet the requirements of production agriculture.[3]

As in most cultures around the world, northern plains settlers generally agreed that marriage was the proper status for adult women, and women like Catherine Geizler spent their youth preparing for marriage and motherhood. The economic advantage of marriage for men who farmed increased the pressure on young women to marry, but Dakota women seldom did so before reaching the age of twenty-one. After completing their schooling, most spent the years before marriage at work as domestics in a nearby town or on a neighboring farm, continuing the education in household management and childcare begun by their mothers. Some taught school during their late teens, but this option was generally available only to English-speaking girls with at least eight grades of education. Many young working women shared their income with their parents and siblings, perhaps helping put younger children through school or assisting with mortgage or tax payments. By the time of marriage they were accustomed not only to supporting themselves and others with the earnings of their labor but also to thinking of family relationships in the context of productive work and multiple sources of income. They had sufficient training in house-, barnyard-, and field work to make them attractive and useful partners to farming men, and they evaluated their options for marriage and the men who courted them on the basis of economic resources as well as on affection and personal attraction.

The experiences of three young women illustrate how economic positioning shaped marriage choices. When a young man who courted Aagot Raaen, the daughter of impoverished Norwegian immigrants, declared that if she did not marry him he would end the relationship, she asked that he wait awhile because her income was so important to her family. He replied, "I have waited as long as I am going to. It is now or never!" Raaen chose her work and family over marriage. Similarly, choices seemed very limited when Rachel Kahn agreed to marry a man who had already immigrated to America and was courting her by mail. "I realized," she wrote, "that I had to take the chance of going to a stranger in a strange land. No other avenue was open to me. I was already eighteen years old and time was against me." While Raaen and

Kahn made decisions with restricted options, Catherine Peterson-Hoyer chose to marry a man who was already successful. Peter Hansen asked Peterson-Hoyer to marry him because he was "tired of batching and decided he would have a cook from then on." Peterson-Hoyer agreed because "Peter had $1000" with which to begin their married life.[4]

In some ethnic groups, the custom of arranged marriages prevailed for many years after immigration. Nina Farley Wishek, commenting on Black Sea German practices from her perspective as a Yankee American, stated that marriage "was not a matter of sentiment, but a business affair to be managed by the elders." Immigrants like Jacob Zimmerman noted that the tradition was brought from the German villages of South Russia, where "love was never considered in marriages." But marriage customs, like many other Old Country traditions, underwent necessary changes in the new communities of the northern plains. Lacking village elders or parents to identify the proper partner, one German Russian immigrant's marriage was arranged by her sister. Having not found a satisfactory job, the young woman re-

Marget and John Bakken and children in front of sod house, Cavalier County, ca. 1895. The adults each hold a tool symbolic of gendered labor.

peatedly returned to her sister's home, where she did not have a useful role. This woman felt that at eighteen she was "not ready" for marriage and, after the arrangement was complete, that her sister had not made a good match because her husband's property consisted of a poorly heated shack. Her expectations for marriage, based on the custom of her Russian village, had not been met. Though she remained partnered with her husband until his death, she described the experience as being "sold . . . off" in marriage.[5]

Dakota women of almost every ethnic group usually married somewhat later than did women throughout the United States. According to the 1890 and 1900 censuses, less than 10 percent of women under the age of nineteen were married. Elaine Lindgren has found that the independent homesteading women of North Dakota had an average age of twenty-seven at marriage while the national average was twenty-two. The few women who report having married before they reached twenty, such as Susannah Preece Bonde at seventeen and Mrs. Douglas Bell at sixteen, tend to be Yankee Americans. Though the average age of marriage for women rose slightly in the 1920s following the national trend, most women still married between the ages of twenty-one and twenty-five. The 1890 and 1900 census reports indicate that by age thirty at least 75 percent of Dakota women were married. The men they married were on average five to ten years older.[6]

While delaying marriage until a woman was in her twenties shortened slightly the average number of childbearing years over the course of the union, premarital pregnancy led to marriage for some younger women. According to community gossip, legal records, and child welfare assessments, premarital pregnancies and illegitimate children were common in rural communities. These records not only permit glimpses through the barrier of privacy surrounding the most intimate of family matters, they also demonstrate the power of neighbors, churches, government agencies, and other institutions to impose standards of acceptable behavior. While all ethnic groups and rural communities disapproved of out-of-wedlock pregnancy and illegitimate children, a pregnant woman who married before giving birth could usually deflect the censure of her neighbors.[7]

The number of recorded illegitimate births in North Dakota tended to run higher than the national average. For instance, in 1928 there were 20.3 illegitimate births per thousand in North Dakota while the national rate was 16.7 per thousand. Though figures are not available until after 1924 and are suspect because the process of registering births was not widely practiced by North Dakotans, the statistics underscore that premarital pregnancy affected a noticeable portion of the population in this predominantly rural state.[8]

The circumstances and solutions surrounding illegitimacy are as varied as the individuals involved. However, the scant available evidence does display some tendencies. In Black Sea German communities, where marriages were often arranged by parents, an unmarried pregnant woman usually found herself at the altar fairly quickly. Nina Farley Wishek noted that in McIntosh County "weddings are always church affairs even though on some occasions it is a compulsory affair." In 1926, a federal child-welfare study found only two illegitimate babies in a county with a "large German-Russian population . . . where marriage customs prevailed." These two babies were surrendered for adoption. The only "early" baby listed among the children born to pioneers who were interviewed by the Writers' Project was that of a Black Sea German woman in McIntosh County who was five months pregnant at the time of her marriage. Her example suggests that the custom of arranged marriage was breaking down among members of the younger generation.[9]

Another reason for the low illegitimate birthrate in Black Sea German families is offered by Pauline Neher Diede, who explained that German Russian girls were kept ignorant of all matters relating to sex and sexuality, "more or less shocked into reality[,] . . . and punished when things went wrong." Girls who became pregnant before marriage would sometimes "be disowned and not allowed into the home ever again." By becoming pregnant, a German Russian girl defied her parents' authority, interfering with their customary right to select her husband by forcing them to approve her choice.[10]

Sheriffs' reports indicate that charges of "bastardy" and "seduction" occurred all over the state. However, criminal charges were filed only when the woman or her parents notified the sheriff. Most families settled on other solutions, though these options were not always satisfactory.[11]

Aagot Raaen left among her papers brief notes concerning some of the solutions her contemporaries employed in cases of premarital pregnancy in Newburgh Township, Steele County. About a "very young" woman who married a man who was not the father of the child she carried, Raaen wrote, "the talk around was that her brother-in-law had got her in a family way when she was staying with them." Whether the girl's relationship with her brother-in-law was consensual is impossible to know, but if he was providing her with room and board she may have felt coerced by her dependent position. Raaen noted that the young woman was a "terrible housekeeper," suggesting that by marrying young she had missed the important training afforded a woman who grew to maturity in the role of an employed domestic.[12]

Other stories are more chilling. In 1876, a pregnant young woman, recently arrived from Norway, was married to a man who "promised not to hold it against her, but," Raaen noted, "he did." In the case of a woman married in 1881 to a man who was not the father of her child, the child died from "neglect." A few years later, a man was forced to marry the woman who was carrying his child. There was also a child born to a woman who would not "own" her daughter and instead gave her to another woman to raise.[13]

Premarital sexual activity, acceptable for young Norwegian farm workers, was condemned in the United States. Abandoned by their lovers, women were forced by their parents to conform to American public standards of sexual behavior by marrying someone, even if the marriage proved disastrous. "Safely" married, these women no longer posed a challenge to public expectations about marriage and motherhood, and as a result their families' privacy was restored. Outcomes of forced marriages—broken promises and child neglect—were private, though they generated community gossip.

When Aagot Raaen's mother, Ragnhild Rodningen, was a young woman, she became pregnant while engaged to a young man who worked on the same Norwegian farm. Although their planned marriage legitimized the pregnancy, the death of her betrothed before they married left Rodningen in an awkward position. When she immigrated to America to join her parents and siblings in Iowa, she found among the Americanizing Norwegians even less acceptance for herself and her child. Her parents ultimately arranged her marriage to an alcoholic who had almost no property and an unpromising future. Thus, a new family was created in much the same way as those in the stories Raaen recorded decades later. Raaen's notes about the young women she knew in Newburgh Township legitimized her mother's experience while criticizing women's sexual independence and the practice of forced marriage in the context of Norwegian American customs and American moral standards.[14]

Forced marriages offered a common solution to the problem of premarital pregnancy. With land the central economic and social focus, the presence of unmarried mothers and fatherless children destabilized a system in which land ownership and the agricultural economy were intended to support a family through generations. A woman's economic role in an agricultural economy was usually linked to a man's— his success at farming was dependent on her field and household labor. Within this economy there were other possible configurations of family, but the fact that men were willing to marry a woman who was carrying another man's child is a strong indicator of the centrality of marriage in a farming community and of the importance of women's labor and management skills to the farm and the household.

Women pregnant out of wedlock who did not marry often hid their pregnancies by leaving the community for the duration and giving up the child for adoption. Others chose to keep their babies and work as domestics in rural or urban households. Maternity homes provided unmarried pregnant women with a place to live and give birth. The Florence Crittenton Home in Fargo, founded and run by the state chapter of the Woman's Christian Temperance Union, was the best and busiest maternity home in North Dakota for many years. The Crittenton Home sheltered women without censure, as suggested in the notes of one admission: "For the same reasons . . . promise of marriage, etc., unfortunate." Workers at the home encouraged women to bond with and keep their babies rather than giving them up for adoption. The home also arranged for work, typically as a domestic, so women could afford to raise their children. The new family often faced some difficulty. In the case of a young Norwegian immigrant who gave birth at the home, the matrons arranged a job for her as a domestic in a farm home and a place for the baby with a Fargo woman. The mother maintained her parental rights by paying $2.50 per week for the child's care.[15]

The unsatisfied demand for domestic workers in both urban and rural homes meant that women, even those with illegitimate children, could always find work and, usually, a place to live. On the other hand, domestics were perhaps more likely to experience out-of-wedlock pregnancy. Taking a job far from home and family increased women's opportunities to make independent choices about sexual activity. Two women who filed paternity suits around the turn of the twentieth century admitted to having freely engaged in sexual activity with one or more men working on the same farm over a lengthy period of time before becoming pregnant. However, the circumstances of domestic employment on a farm may also have isolated young domestics from social and familial systems that would have protected them from imprudent decisions.[16]

Once married, most pioneer women began a period of pregnancy, childbirth, and lactation that lasted up to twenty-five years. Many would have nodded in recognition of Rachel Calof's sentiment that "the most dependable state of affairs I knew during the many years I lived on the prairie was pregnancy." The Pioneer Biographies include lengthy recitations of children's names and birth dates: families of more than nine children were not uncommon.[17]

This fertility can be measured in various ways. Historian Larry Peterson has calculated North Dakota's fertility rate according to the number of children under the age of five per one thousand women aged fifteen to forty-four. His study indicates that between 1880 and 1930 the state's fertility rate ran between 1.3 and 1.5 times higher than the national average. According to the 1890 federal census, North Dakota's birthrate (births per one thousand population) was 36.5, the highest in the nation, which that year averaged 26.9. In 1900, North Dakota's rate was 33.6 while the national rate was 27.2. By 1924, when the State of North Dakota officially began registering births, the birthrate (calculated from registered births) had fallen considerably to 21.5, but for the years 1924 through 1929 it remained above that of the nation as a whole. The decreasing fertility of women in the nineteenth century was mostly the privilege of white, native-born women. Nationally, as well as in North Dakota, immigrant women averaged more pregnancies than those who were native born and white.[18]

These ratios explain why Rachel Calof's "state of affairs" was so "dependable," but they do not detail how many children the average Dakota farm family had. In 1900 and 1910, census takers asked each married woman how many children she had borne and how many were still living. Numbers for three rural townships suggest something about family size (in general and by ethnicity), about the earliest and latest ages for childbirth, and about infant mortality (Tables 1 and 2).[19]

Table 1: Birth Data for Three Townships, 1900			
	Newburgh	Jewell	Montefiore
Number of married women	90	48	22
Age range	17–84	18–67	17–69
Average age	41.2	40.5	39.1
Number of births	433	390	95
Average births per woman	4.8	8.13	4.3
Mode	1 and 2	6 and 7	3
Number of living children	359	255	83
Death rate	17.0%	34.6%	12.6%

Table 2: Birth Data for Three Townships, 1910			
	Newburgh	Jewell	Montefiore
Number of married women	78	38	38
Age range	21–84	20–62	23–69
Average age	43.6	34.5	41.4
Number of births	461	339	234
Average births per woman	4.8	7.4	5.4
Mode	3	12	2 and 3
Number of living children	377	223	166
Death rate	18.2%	34.2%	29.0%

Newburgh Township, located in the northeastern corner of Steele County, was settled, beginning in 1874, almost entirely by Norwegians from the Hallingdal region, many of whom had lived in Iowa before moving to Dakota Territory. Black Sea Germans, most arriving directly from South Russia, began to move into Jewell Township in McIntosh County in the mid-1880s. Montefiore in McLean County was the last of the three townships to see significant settlement. Though early arrivals put down roots in the mid-1880s, the township experienced a population surge between 1900 and 1910. Montefiore residents claimed the United States, Canada, Scotland, Poland, Germany, Sweden, Denmark, and German-speaking Russia as their countries of birth—a miniature version of the state's ethnic mix. Beyond their age and ethnic makeup, the three townships also differed in their populations of women. In Newburgh, where the settlements were established earliest and the population most stable, the women were the oldest of all surveyed and, therefore, more likely to have arrived at menopause and thus to have completed their families (Table 3).[20]

The birth data suggests that ethnicity influenced differences in family size. The Black Sea German women of Jewell Township had given birth to significantly more children on average than the women in the other two townships, and the mode (the number of children reported most often) is highest for Jewell Township. These statistics corroborate anecdotal evidence about Black Sea German families. However, individual women in Newburgh and Montefiore Townships had as many children as did their counterparts in Jewell Township. For example, the woman with the largest family in Newburgh Township in these two census years had given birth to sixteen children. In 1910, at age fifty-one, she still had twelve children at home, the youngest only eight years old.

The death rate of children born to these women is shockingly high. These reported deaths are not necessarily of children under age five: older women may have experienced the deaths of mature sons and daughters. Nevertheless, few women saw all of their babies grow to adulthood, losing them instead to prairie fire, "summer complaint," accidental drowning in wells, and lack of adequate medical care. McIntosh County was hit by a raging diphtheria epidemic in 1897, probably causing a higher-than-average death rate. It is also worth noting that many of these child deaths took place before immigration.[21]

The data collected by the census takers represents only the children born to married women; it does not indicate how many children these women might actually have in their care. For instance, fifty-four-year-old Rosina Schilling had been married in Russia and was widowed after giving birth to ten children, five of whom died before 1900. She emigrated in 1898 and married again a year later, to a widower ten years younger than she. His daughter and son lived with them. It was not uncommon for rural women in the settlement era to raise stepchildren, grandchildren, orphaned neighbor children, or younger siblings.[22]

In her important history of women on the frontier, Julie Roy Jeffrey reported that frontier townships did not have significantly higher birthrates than eastern towns and states and concluded that western women preferred small families. However, statistics indicate that during North Dakota's settlement era, women, particularly Black Sea Germans, had larger families than the national average. Ethnic traditions and immigrant aspirations for family security in an agricultural economy raised birthrates among pioneers on the northern plains. Large families were desirable because of the labor children provided. Parents planned to give their sons land upon marriage, which meant accumulating land while the children were growing. The children worked the expanding acreage, and parents had land to give their sons, thereby keeping their children's families close to home. While this plan seemed feasible during the early years of settlement, by 1939, when many of these immigrant parents were interviewed, they realized that their plans had been thwarted by a depression of agricultural markets and the artificially inflated commodity prices and expectations of the war years. Some, like J. O. Meidinger, father of seventeen children, later regretted having large families.[23]

Table 3: Birth Data for Married Women over 45 in Three Townships

	Newburgh		Jewell		Montefiore	
	1900	1910	1900	1910	1900	1910
Number of women	30	24	14	14	7	17
Number of births	158	183	173	154	32	144
Average births per woman	5.2	7.6	12.3	11.0	4.6	8.4
Mode	8	6	15	8	3	6
Number of living children	119	152	101	92	28	94
Death rate	25.0%	16.9%	41.6%	40.3%	12.5%	34.7%

Recurrent pregnancies and the demands of child rearing, especially in difficult pioneering circumstances, extracted a great toll. Though many women accepted frequent pregnancies as inevitable, they recognized the limitations childbirth placed upon them. Bertha Steigen Bartz, who gave birth to eight children, reported that she was "sick [pregnant] about half the time" and seldom able to get away from home. When Bertha Nystrom arrived in North Dakota and visited her sister, she was shocked to see that "several years of pioneering and the bearing of five children had completely changed her appearance." They cried together that evening, Bertha perhaps both for her sister and for the future she saw for herself in her sister's face.[24]

Family limitation was certainly practiced by some pioneer couples, but few records reveal any efforts to control fertility. Pauline Neher Diede wrote that her mother and other pioneer women "craved more time between births," though they apparently did not have the information or the power in their marriage to effect more comfortable spacing between pregnancies. However, while Diede's mother, Christina Neher, was recovering from birth, the midwife, Frau Jaeger, cared for Christina, her year-old child, and the new baby in her own home and kept a watchful eye on Ludwig Neher. So did Ludwig's brother-in-law, Fred Martin, who urged him to leave Christina at the Jaegers for a while so she would not become pregnant again. Frau Jaeger instructed Christina to nurse the baby to prevent pregnancy. Two months after the birth, Frau Jaeger confronted Ludwig Neher and told him that he must abstain from sexual relations with his wife for a while longer. Both family members and neighbors recognized the need to space births adequately and did not hesitate to interfere in this case.[25]

One pioneer included in his memoir a reference to women's private discussions. After church services, he wrote, men and women socialized in sex-segregated groups, and women's conversations "may have been an opportunity to share personal problems, especially concerning physical well-being and health." His careful wording suggests that during these gatherings women may have discussed contraception as well as treatments for problems related to menstruation, childbirth, and menopause. However, if these women knew of any contraceptive method more sophisticated than abstinence or breast-feeding, there is no indication of it.[26]

Women experienced some desperation about how to limit their fertility. Rachel Calof "felt a growing revolt against bearing more children" but gave birth to two more after a miscarriage nearly took her life. Mamie Goodwater received contraceptive advice from a friend in Wisconsin who wrote, "You know we don't sleep together." Another of Goodwater's correspondents, worried about her forthcoming delivery, wished she had used "George Willard's receipt," a cryptic message that refers to either a contraceptive formula or an abortifacient. In her next letter the same woman described her doting devotion to the new baby, suggesting that her concern was less for raising children than with the difficulties of pregnancy and delivery. In a similar vein, Effie Hanson wrote to a friend that her mother-in-law had attended her recent childbirth and had given her "some medicine to make me vomit." She had no birthing pain and "got out of it easy this time." She added, "I wouldn't mind having a dozen if I could get out of it that way."[27]

Luck and abstinence seem to have been the most widely used means of family limitation. Another alternative was abortion, about which the historical record says little. Three instances, one the subject of community gossip and the others legal cases, involve single women. One woman was said to be "taking stuff" to abort her pregnancy; another was surgically aborted against her will by the doctor who impregnated her; the third died after two men performed an abortion on her. None of these cases appear to involve a person who might be practicing abortion regularly. The paucity of trained midwives also suggests that, while abortions did occur, there was no system for procuring them in most rural communities.[28]

Infant care was extremely difficult under the circumstances of homesteading. Dr. James Grassick underscored the problem of raising healthy babies when he wrote in 1918 that "the soldier living in the trenches has a sixteen times better chance of living one year than has a babe born in the country districts of North Dakota." In protecting their children, women faced limited access to medical care, poor maternal and infant nutrition, lack of childcare alternatives, inadequate housing, and enormous challenges from accidents and disease. Many held a reasonable distrust of doctors, who were often poorly trained, and few had spare cash with which to pay medical bills. Families made decisions about their children's health in the context of maintaining their place on the land and planting and harvesting crops in a timely manner.[29]

The experiences of three families demonstrate the ways in which a commitment to farming shaped such decisions. Julia Gage Carpenter had little breast milk when her son was born, so she fed him cow's milk instead. When the baby became ill and weak, Carpenter took him to a doctor in Aberdeen, South Dakota, who recommended mother's milk. Carpenter hired a wet nurse in Aberdeen, and the child grew stronger. After two months, Carpenter returned to her LaMoure County homestead and resumed feeding cow's milk to the baby, but the child weakened again and eventually died. Though other mothers or widowed fathers might have turned to a neighboring woman for mother's milk,

Carpenter's diary does not reveal the presence of women on nearby claims who may have been able to assist her.[30]

Magdalena Job also fed cow's milk to her infant, as she traveled to meet her husband on their new claim in Montana. Journeying with a horse-drawn buggy, two pigs, some chickens, a milk cow, and her two-month-old son, she reported, "I had the top buggy with the cow tied behind, and I had . . . the kid . . . and when he cries, and I have no milk, I stop and milk the cow. There were no bottles like we have now. I used an eyedropper to feed the baby." She traveled for three days in this manner, laboriously stopping to milk the cow and feed the baby en route. Job had at first refused her husband's request to move from North Dakota to Montana, in part because she was pregnant, but she eventually agreed because in Montana they could get two quarter sections "for nothing."[31]

In the third example, Rachel Calof's eighth child, Celia, became critically ill at seven months of age, and Calof tried "all of the grandmother remedies without success." Abe Calof was busy threshing, and the couple decided he should finish the crop before taking the sick child to the doctor. Fortunately, Celia recovered despite the delay and the doctor's inadequate skills.[32]

These three women were not careless about their children's needs and health, but neither did they chance casting their families' futures to the winds of the northern plains. They chose the security of land or crop for the common good rather than sacrifice the family's future in order to protect its weakest member. Their decisions employed deep-seated, perhaps unconscious, concepts about the importance of farming and land ownership for their children's future.

Violence frequently shattered the peace of pioneer households, even in families remembered as protective and loving. The historical record indicates that most cases of aggression were perpetrated by the household's adult male toward women or children, but there are a few known instances of violence on the part of women as well. Family violence was considered to be a private matter. In two communities where aggressive behavior was known, neighbors did not attempt to intervene. Although Thomas Raaen frequently beat his wife, Ragnhild, knocking out her teeth and causing scars and recurring headaches, he did not experience community censure. Ragnhild sought shelter from her Norwegian immigrant neighbors if he threatened her during the winter when it was too cold to hide along the riverbank, but she did not expect them to interfere. When Thomas was excluded from membership in the Goose River Church, it was for drinking to excess, not for attacking his wife.[33]

Asked if anyone ever tried to help neighboring Black Sea German women who were abused by their husbands, Magdalena Job replied, "Well, that was not my business. We never butted in. We never had any trouble with our neighbors; we were all friends." In spite of cultural differences between these communities and the distance of about thirty years, there exists this similarity: no one wanted to interfere in the private matters of family and home. The boundary separating an angry outburst from unacceptable violence is subjective, and few people were willing to intervene unless the violence was extreme. Successful farming depended on strong neighborly associations. No one knew when he or she might need to borrow equipment or exchange labor; no one could take a chance on being excluded from the social networks farmers called upon in difficult times. Interference in private matters might lead to such exclusion.[34]

Abuse directed toward children appears to have been widespread and not generally considered excessive unless the child suffered permanent damage. Pauline Neher Diede viewed abuse as part of a family's response to hard times or as simply a means of raising well-behaved children. In her Knife River community, the "general abuse of minors in the family . . . was considered discipline according to the Bible," and men beat their wives and children because of the "great demand placed on men just to survive." According to the minister of a Black Sea German Lutheran church, "parents, teachers, pastors and officers deemed it their holy duty to instil into the young respect for law and order." Parents taught their children to respect authority and, when necessary, punished them severely, preferring to "have a dead son than a disobedient one." While Black Sea Germans used religion to excuse or justify aggressive behavior, violence toward children in other communities seems to have been practiced without biblical or philosophical foundation.[35]

Some women, like Mary Madden Collins, did not accept routine violence, instead finding ways to protect their children. Collins kept a rawhide whip in the kitchen and threatened youngsters with it when necessary, but she rarely complained to her husband about their ten children because his punishments were too severe.[36]

One striking case briefly aroused community ire and police interference. At age seven, Margaret Kottke had been sent to work as a servant in the home of Mr. and Mrs. Walter Zimmerman near Granville. On a cold, snowy October day in 1919 she was beaten and then sent to bring in the cows. The Zimmermans later reported her missing and asked neighbors to help search for her. The next day her bruised, dirty body, clad in light summer clothing, was found next to a haystack in the farmyard. Her stomach contained only a few grains of wheat. The initial charge against the Zimmermans—failure to provide proper food and shelter for the child—was later changed to murder, and both were tried and convicted of manslaughter. Newspaper reports indicate shock at the "[i]nhuman treatment" the little girl received. The press identified her as an illegitimate child who had been sent to live first with relatives and then with the Zimmermans after her mother married and had more children. It is not likely she would have been much better off in her mother's home: while the Zimmermans were awaiting trial, Margaret's stepfather, Arthur Kottke, was charged with neglect of his own children. Local newspapers soon tired of the case, and one did not even bother to print the jury's verdict. In death Margaret Kottke received the community's sympathy—her burial was paid for by Granville businessmen—but her death did not spark any discussion among community members about the treatment of children in their own homes or in service positions. There were no editorials or letters concerning the case published in the newspapers.[37]

Though children had few defenses against violence, women looked for ways to protect themselves or to retaliate for the abuse they received. Ragnhild Raaen usually left the house when Thomas was drunk, but on one occasion, in response to his verbal abuse, she threw a pail of cold water in his face and, although he did not offer an apology, he ceased berating her for the rest of that day. Some women had their husbands arrested for assault, as evidenced by the sheriff's records from three counties. In one case, a man spent five days in jail for striking his wife with his hand. Although Linda Gordon has argued that women's attempts to control men's violent behavior might have led to more violence and to increased efforts to subordinate women, it appears that some were able to gain at least temporary respite through resistance.[38]

Elizabeth Pleck has noted that wife beating was widespread in immigrant communities and more accepted by immigrant women than by native-born women. Perhaps the neighbors' reluctance to intervene was based in part on the immigrants' need to prevent social disintegration. So when the Black Sea German settlers of Knife River met for prayer in the Neher household, it may have been the desire for community cohesion that prompted worshippers to admonish a woman who prayed for protection from her husband. These same women, however, occasionally heard "an upright pillar of a woman [who] stood out and directly demanded her human dignity so to be more than to be treated as an ox." Pauline Neher Diede, who heard these women speak, claims that the freedom promised in their relocation to the United States encouraged them to insist on proper treatment in their homes. Though this freedom would be unrealized for some time, the women believed in it, talked about it, and defied physical abuse as much as possible.[39]

North Dakota's liberal divorce law favored women. If a woman decided to end a marriage because of her husband's adultery, extreme cruelty, willful neglect, willful desertion, habitual drunkenness, or felony conviction, she could claim to be the "innocent party" and seek legal possession of the homestead. How well women knew the provisions of the law is not clear, but for those who retained a good lawyer there was no need to remain married if the conditions of divorce could be met.[40]

Such a decision was not easily made by women who lived in communities that generally did not approve of divorce as a means of resolving marital conflict. Though it was a rare choice, those who contemplated or filed for divorce are not difficult to locate. Mrs. Taylor, a Cass County farm woman, endured years of physical and mental abuse before she sued her husband for divorce. He had raped her, beaten her and their son, verbally abused her, and brought a woman home to share his bed. The court awarded Mrs. Taylor their quarter section of land, the house and its furnishings, four horses, two colts, two wagons, one cow, a harness, a harrow, a buggy, a drill, a fanning mill, a sulky rake, an anvil, and one hundred dollars a year in child support for their two surviving daughters. Mr. Taylor received only his bed and bedding and use of the farmland until after the next spring's planting.[41]

Although Ragnhild Raaen considered divorcing her alcoholic, abusive husband, she did not because she feared she would not be able to earn enough through domestic work in town to support herself and her disabled daughter. When her neighbor, Sennev Solem, consulted a lawyer about divorce, she was told that she did not have enough money to pay legal fees and that she should go home and "obey her husband." Raaen and Solem both believed that divorce would leave them destitute and that they had no choice but to remain married. Access to the law designed to protect them was hampered by their inability to speak English, by their fear of debt and poverty, by bad legal advice, and by their sense of marginalization as immigrant women.[42]

The experiences of these three women reflect the statistics of divorce (Table 4). Those whose parents were native born were more likely to be divorced than any other ethnic group; the foreign born were the least likely. Among all three groups of pioneer women, the divorce rate rose consistently between 1890 and 1930. American-born daughters of foreign-born women, trained to expect and withstand difficult relationships but raised in a society that allowed them to choose their partners and that granted them the freedom to stand up to an abusive husband, were better equipped to negotiate the trials of marriage.

Table 4: Divorced Women per Specific Populations in North Dakota		
Foreign Born	Native Born Native Parents	Native Born Foreign Parents
1890 .15%	.37%	.27%
1900 .28%	.60%	.23%
1910 .34%	.50%	.26%
1920 .42%	.56%	.30%
1930 .65%	.91%	.60%

Many foreign-born immigrants had a cultural or religious aversion to divorce. Black Sea German immigrant J. O. Meidinger stated that there was no divorce in his Lutheran community in South Russia. Some Norwegian immigrants thought divorce was an undesirable result of Americanization. One wrote that the American "spirit of getting something easy" caused young people to leave their farm homes and seek other work. Girls, he explained, wanted to be teachers, and this sort of work left them unprepared for housework when they married, leading to the many divorces he observed among Americans and his fellow immigrants. This argument reinforces Diede's reference to the new freedom immigrant women experienced in America. Whether they defended their position in a marriage or left an abusive partnership, a few pioneer women felt—and acted on—North Dakota's atmosphere of freedom and its residents' increasing interest in the rights of women.[43]

Table 5: Divorced Women Among Specific Urban and Rural Populations

	Urban Women			Rural Women		
	Foreign Born	Native Born Native Parents	Native Born Foreign Parents	Foreign Born	Native Born Native Parents	Native Born Foreign Parents
1910	.48%	.71%	.48%	.33%	.45%	.23%
1920	.74%	1.04%	.67%	.36%	.42%	.23%
1930	.80%	1.79%	1.36%	.60%	.60%	.42%

Note: Statistics drawn from decennial censuses. Separate statistics for the rural and urban populations were published beginning with the 1910 census. Statistics are calculated as percent of divorced women in the specific demographic group, i.e., divorced women among rural foreign-born women.

Divorce was rarely the solution to marital discord, but despite social disapproval, it occurred in all rural ethnic groups, most commonly among Yankee Americans (Table 5). Most notable is that there are any divorced women in the rural population at all. Statistics indicate that many farm women who divorced moved to towns and cities, particularly if they had marketable skills. Mathea Overly, who divorced her husband in 1891 after eleven years of marriage and three children, moved into town and worked as a dressmaker and milliner until she remarried. For other women, the decision to move to a town may have been less a choice for economic improvement and more a conclusion dictated by a farm encumbered with a mortgage on the land, livestock, and equipment; the lack of a partner to work the land; or many small children demanding supervision and limiting time for field work. However, foreign-born women and their native-born daughters were more likely to remain in the countryside than Yankee American women. With more experience in all aspects of farming and less appealing prospects for work in the cities, they were better prepared to continue farming if they could keep the land.[44]

Margaret Barr Roberts's story demonstrates that an energetic and enterprising woman could manage well on the land. She married J. L.

Roberts in Iowa in 1871, and they moved to western Dakota Territory in 1877. By 1883 they had bought a badlands ranch on which they raised livestock, but in 1886 J. L. Roberts left home and never returned. Margaret Roberts hired help to work the ranch. She fed herself and her five daughters on wild game, wild fruits, and garden vegetables. She produced butter, eggs, and meat and sold these items as well as surplus vegetables, wild fruit, and garden flowers. She sewed, knitted, and washed clothes for pay. She also had the help of the county commissioners, who did not tax her ranch one year. Utilizing available resources, she managed to keep the ranch and raise her family without her husband.[45]

On average, North Dakota's divorce rate was lower than that of neighboring states and the nation. During the 1920s, when North Dakota's divorce numbers rose sharply, it still remained at roughly half the national rate. In 1929, when South Dakota's divorce rate reached 1.13 per thousand, North Dakota's stood at .83 per thousand. This difference probably reflects the cultural patterns of North Dakota's population. Given the state's relatively small number of Yankee Americans and large number of foreign-born residents—both groups predominantly rural—the statistics demonstrate a cultural commitment to marriage, women's allegiance to a promise of obedience and to the care of their families, and an inadequate understanding of the divorce laws.[46]

A widowed woman often had more options available, depending on her age and the ages of her children (Table 6). She could sell the farm and move to town; rent the land and outbuildings and use the income to stay on the farm; continue to manage or operate the farm on her own; or turn the farm over to her children (usually sons) and live with them. Widows who had faced financial difficulties while farming with their husbands or who were quite elderly at the time of their husband's death often migrated to towns and cities. Personal circumstances and an ability to manage with the available resources contributed to each individual's decision. Widowed with young children at age thirty-six, Anna Simonson wanted to stay on the farm, but after struggling through five years of poor crops, she gave up and moved into Williston. Clara Peterson faced better circumstances when she was widowed. She stayed on her "good ranch" for ten years after her husband's death and at age sixty turned it over to her son and moved to Washburn.[47]

Widows who chose to stay on the farm could manage the work with skills they had acquired as farm partners, and, if crops were good, they often prospered. In many cases, this positive choice demonstrated a woman's ability and judgment in farm management. Margaret Nordgaard Brunsdale had seven children and a homestead when her husband died in 1899. She moved to nearby Portland so her children could attend school, but she continued to manage her farm, increasing its size and becoming "a farm manager and business woman of rare ability," according to the interviewer who took down her story. But the records indicate that many other widows were also successful farm managers. Marie Sund Thompson had eight children, the youngest aged two, when her husband died in 1907. She kept her farm near Finley for a few years, then sold it, moved west to Ray, and rented a farm. By 1916 she owned a half section and had built an eight-room house. Isabelle Sinclair Cusator farmed with her husband but bore most of the responsibilities because he worked as a sailor on Lake Michigan during the summer. His death on the lake in 1896 left her with five children and another on the way. She continued to farm, schooling the children at home, until the youngest was seventeen. Then, at age fifty-five, she moved to Jamestown.[48]

Table 6: Rural and Urban Widows in Specific Populations in North Dakota					
Foreign Born		Native Born Native Parents		Native Born Foreign Parents	
rural	urban	rural	urban	rural	urban
1910	3.2%	10.8%	1.0%	6.4%	.6%	3.3%
1920	11.5%	16.7%	4.5%	7.4%	2.7%	5.0%
1930	16.4%	21.8%	4.1%	6.0%	3.3%	5.6%

Note: Statistics drawn from the 1910, 1920, and 1930 censuses.

Some widows chose to homestead in North Dakota, believing that a farm offered financial advantages they could not find elsewhere. Deeby Zine immigrated from Syria after her husband's death and eventually made a claim in Williams County, hoping to earn enough from the farm and from her other work as a traveling salesperson to bring her children to the United States. Though she had a "sad and lonely life on the homestead," by 1914 she was able to mortgage her farm to pay for her daughter's passage. Mrs. Andrew Severson of Iowa, widowed in 1899 with two young children, worked as a hotel maid for a time but decided to farm in North Dakota, moving there in 1904. Though friends tried to discourage her, she insisted on going, explaining, "I knew quite a bit about farming and I wanted a place of our own. ... My mind was made up to get a piece of land and have a home for myself and [my] children." By 1912 she was farming 120 acres and had made substantial improvements on the farm, the management of which she turned over to her eighteen-year-old son, though she continued to live there.[49]

North Dakota's farm widows fit a pattern noted in a 1900 federal study of working women. Though only 6.4 percent of all "female breadwinners over sixteen years" claimed the occupation of "farmer," the position ranked sixth nationally in the number of women employed, behind categories for servants/waitresses, agricultural laborers, dressmakers, laundresses, and teachers. More than twice as many white women were farmers than farm laborers, but African American women laboring on farms neither they nor their husbands could ever own tipped the balance, making agricultural labor a larger job category for all working women. Farming, the analysts noted, is "pre-eminently an occupation for women over forty." Of the women claiming "farmer" as their occupation, 66.4 percent were over the age of forty-four and most (73.4 percent) were widows who continued farming after their husband's death. Farming was among the most important means of making a living for widows and was particularly important in the north-central states for foreign-born white women. Indeed, when the figures were broken down by state, "farmer" became the third-ranking job category (behind "servant" and "teacher") for North Dakota's women and the second-ranking category for its foreign-born women.

The study also indicated that women of Norwegian birth or descent were more likely to be farmers than women of other European origins. Though the available figures do not reveal whether Norwegian women were also more likely to continue farming when widowed, the anecdotal evidence from North Dakota hints at a strong correlation with this national trend. This study suggests that farm women who protected the family's investment in the land also provided themselves with security in the event of their spouse's death. Costs to the family were balanced by the income and security a good farm offered.[50]

A second marriage was also a possibility for widows. In fact, an im-balance in the sex ratio favored women who wanted to marry again. Widowers with small children, men like John Geizler, often remarried quickly and began a second round of parenting with their new wives. But widows often chose to remain single. Of this study's twenty-six widows whose stories are fairly complete, only three remarried. Each of those women had young children.

The quality of a pioneer couple's emotional relationship is difficult to determine. While anecdotes offer a means of peering into the pio-neer home, gossips rarely took an interest in happy or contented cou-ples. In her study of French peasant families, Martine Segalen cautions that it is impossible to evaluate happiness as a quality of marriage in a past society. However, this study would fall short if it did not seek to understand the nature of marriage as the settlers experienced it. Most pioneer unions appear to have been primarily economic relationships in which women held (at least nominally) a subordinate position. Some marriages were bad matches, and beginning family life in an overcrowded sod house on the northern plains could not have brought comfort to distressed couples. But some marriages were graced by con-tentment, love, and passion—emotions that occasionally emerge from the typically unemotional historical documents about family life.[51]

Transplanted in the United States, the tradition of arranged mar-riage became a raw wound in the cultures that had practiced it. Daugh-ters like Pauline Neher Diede regretted their mothers' "miserable ex-perience" as a "wife . . . the subject to her husband . . . married to a man she hardly knew." Diede's remarks are confirmed by J. O. Meidinger in comments on his early years in North Dakota: "We thought more of horses in those days than we did of women."[52]

Women's subordination was established by custom and religion. Rosina Riedlinger stated that "we women were told right at the [wed-ding] ceremony that it was our duty as a wife to stick with our men through thick and thin and that it was a sin to leave the husband or not let him be the ruler of the house." When her spouse decided to immi-grate to the United States, she accepted her future although she did not want to leave her home, recalling, "My husband wished it otherwise and so his word was law." According to E. M. Sondreal, a Norwegian woman's subordination was symbolized by the custom of serving the husband first at mealtime. Custom, however, does not ensure practice. Women did not accept complete subordination, and when they chose not to obey, their husbands often stepped aside. Luke Perekrestinko related that when his wife, Daisy, "refused" to leave the baby crib behind in Ukraine, they struggled over the decision and she prevailed. And Guri Sondreal contradicted her husband's statement that men were served first in Norwegian homes, testifying that "no one was served first in particular" in their home.[53]

Women and men who approached marriage as an economic partnership sometimes came to feel respect and growing affection for each other. Few pioneers recounted the joy of a loving marriage, but two women, Rachel Calof and Elizabeth Solem, offer insight into the affection they felt for their husbands. Calof wrote about a day during the very difficult early years of her marriage when, pregnant with their first child, she prepared a special meal for her husband and they shared a pleasant evening without the company of his extended family: "It was evident that we liked one another because . . . we were happy to be together." Solem summarized her married life by saying, "I'd probably get married same as I did. Marriage is a lottery, but I have good children and have enjoyed life. . . . I was very happy 'til my husband died, we never had much money and always worked hard, but we were happy just the same."[54]

Others hinted at the quality of their marriages by relating specific incidents in which affection was apparent but not named. When Mary Ann Nelson Barclay suffered a miscarriage during her first pregnancy, her husband promised that if she recovered he would build a house in town and she would never have to spend another winter on the farm. He kept that promise, and they moved to town every fall. Johanna Swenson Anderson remembered one autumn when she cried because she was pregnant, winter was coming, and she had not yet spun the yarn with which to knit mittens and stockings for her children. Her husband, Jens, sold a load of grain and bought stockings, mittens, and underwear for the family and a wringer to make the onerous task of washing a bit easier. Amanda Norell's husband, Ernest, brushed her hair one hundred strokes every night.[55]

These pioneers sought two things in marriage: to bring into being a new generation of the family and to secure a piece of land that would maintain the family through generations. Within this framework, married women pivoted on the contradictions between subordination and independence, obedience and partnership. Love made life better, but women did not despair its absence. How well a woman negotiated her marriage and how successfully she raised her family depended on her ability to marshal her resources in the face of the changing realities of pioneer life on the northern plains. The slip of fate that might leave any woman widowed or abandoned in any season or time of her life—or her children motherless—challenged every woman who dismissed the complexities of marriage as a simple matter of yielding to her husband's wishes.

3

"By the Hand of Woman"
Women's Work in House, Barnyard, and Fields

I started farming with five horses, a hand plow and a wife.
AUGUST BAUER

Available land and the riches promised to those who cultivated "splendid fields of wheat—No. 1 Hard" brought immigrants to Dakota. Acquiring the riches, if indeed any were to be had, required labor and cash, both of which had to be secured from the resources of the pioneering family and the surrounding community. To make a northern plains farm produce, families developed an integrated system of productive and reproductive labor that extracted a huge physical and emotional toll from women, men, and children. In this system, the assignment of tasks according to gender operated under rules that were both flexible and subtle. They had to be, given the daunting and numerous tasks required to build a northern plains farm.[1]

August Bauer's simple, single-sentence history of his pioneer experience indicates that women's labor was significant in the settlement process. However, it is unclear whether Lena Bauer worked under her own authority or under that of her husband. Were women—who provided necessary income, children, farm and household labor, and community social services—subordinate to their husbands, as Bauer's arrangement of farming elements might imply? Or did women draw power and authority from their income-producing work, their management skills, and their labor, subverting the assumption of subordination and placing themselves in positions roughly equal to those of their husbands within the marriage, if not in society?

In interviews and memoirs, women's work is often obscured by habits of language. Women spoke of "helping out" in the fields; men frequently used the first-person singular when describing farm work.

Carolyn Sachs has labeled farm women the "invisible farmers" because women's work on farms is rarely recognized. But the work of pioneer women was conspicuous to their contemporaries. So hard did they work, and so often in communal settings, that it is impossible not to notice the presence and significance of women when reading pioneer memoirs and interviews.[2]

In part, the work women did in establishing and maintaining farms grew from a simple need for survival and a desire for family continuity. They did what had to be done, and if they could not physically manage the tasks themselves, they found ways to get someone else to do them. Their decisions about their work were shaped by a complex of behaviors and attitudes drawn from training, pride, opportunity, desire, and economic change that motivated women to marry farmers, develop northern plains farms, and provide a start in farming for their children. The kinds of work women did varied with circumstances related to their age; the number, age, and sex of their children; their ethnic customs; the season of the year; their marital status; and the nature of their marriage relationship. General patterns of pioneer women's work can be determined, but whether a woman worked in the house or the fields does not change the fact that her work was one of the threads—along with those of kin, marriage, religion, and education—that connected her to a larger community. For it was the work of women in the house, barnyard, and fields that fed their children and husbands, kept neighbors and family in their debt, built their homes, schools, and churches, and often paid the mortgage and taxes.

Settlement in Dakota Territory took place at a time when the economic role of U.S. women was shifting from producer to consumer. Sociologists, newspaper editors, professional agriculturists, and home economists who turned their attention to farm women wrote in a confusion of dismay and admiration. On the one hand, farm women lacked the conveniences of urban homes and were "rather poorly trained buyer[s]." On the other, their productivity and skills were admired by many social commentators, who found rural women to be better examples of American womanhood than "some of the gossamer embodiments of an effete civilization." Dakota farm women were not disturbed by these contradictory images. They used their productive skills to their personal and their families' advantage while resisting urbanization and its degradation. For settlement women with poor or no English language skills, urban life—working in a factory or in domestic service for very low pay—held little appeal. Land ownership afforded them financial security in case of a husband's death or disability. Americans and Europeans came to Dakota to get rich, but they also came with a firm belief in the financial security of land, security that would allow them to keep their family intact. The work required to turn 160 acres of grassland into a productive farm held rewards for women as well as for men.[3]

The work began immediately. Most families migrated together to this farming frontier, and the labor of nearly every member contributed in some way to the family's success in establishing a farm. Upon arrival in Dakota, they chose the location of land to claim or purchase. They had to arrange for shelter, food, and water for themselves and the livestock immediately, but most important was the matter of putting in a crop. These activities, required of those who filed a homestead claim, were essential for those who intended to live on the land they purchased.

Nearly as important as the crop was a source of cash income. Even pioneers who took homestead claims—so-called "free" land—required a good deal of cash to succeed in "proving up." The fourteen-dollar filing fee for a 160-acre homestead claim was just the beginning. Gilbert Fite has estimated that a family would need eight hundred to one thousand dollars to purchase necessary supplies and equipment after claiming a homestead. Farming demanded at the very least draft livestock, a plow, and seed. Though shelters were often constructed of locally available, free materials, luxuries like board or shingled roofs, board floors, windows, and doors required cash or good credit. Settlers also needed food supplies to last several months.[4]

A family arriving reasonably early in the spring would break sod and plant flax or wheat and, for household consumption, a large garden plot of potatoes. Breaking sod and planting a first crop generally involved the efforts of two people. An older boy might work with his father, but frequently women joined men in the fields for this difficult task. The division of labor varied with circumstances, but women seldom handled the plow while breaking. Anna Carlson, who settled with her husband near the Canadian border, remembered, "I had to drive the oxen while my husband plowed the land and we sowed it with our hands." Oxen, inclined to follow their slow-witted will, needed constant goading from a driver while someone else guided the breaking plow through the tangled, centuries-old grass roots. Once the breaking was done, however, women maneuvered all kinds of horse-drawn equipment, especially at harvest. Anna Kuhlsbraaten Berg drove a binder and a hayrake "for several seasons," and Isabella Roberts and her fifteen-year-old daughter, Mae, mowed and raked hay.[5]

The poorest immigrants had to do all of the farming with few implements during the first years. They might borrow a breaking plow or exchange work for the breaking, but the seeding and harvesting had to be done with primitive tools or none at all. At first, many families sowed seed by hand and harvested grain with scythes. These methods were familiar to European immigrants who had farmed perhaps as few as five acres in their home country, but they were inadequate on a 160-acre farm. It might take three or more years to complete the breaking, but eventually homesteaders would have to acquire implements for extensive farming, either through trade, by cash purchase, or on credit.

Use of even the simplest tools was governed by a hierarchy based on gender. Men usually operated the more advanced tools while women worked with primitive tools or none at all. Ukrainian immigrant Luke Perekrestinko remembered that men harvested the grain with scythes while women and children shocked and tied the bundles by hand. This arrangement was probably carried over from the sexual division of labor practiced in Ukraine. However difficult it was to swing a scythe all day long, it was easier than working solely with one's hands. Writing of her parents' settlement experience, Pauline Neher Diede recalls the pitchfork her father, Ludwig, purchased on credit. It was the only implement anyone in the family had for that first harvest, and only Ludwig used it.

> Every time Ludwig picked up the pitchfork that he had bought on time at his last visit to Hebron, he thought of how fortunate he was to be able to use something that handy, and how lucky he was that the lumberman trusted him until fall. Christina had to use her open arms and ten forked fingers to grasp armsfull of ripened wheat and carry them to the gumbo floor. Then to rest herself she led Bay round and round to stamp out as much of the wheat as possible.[6]

Primitive or not, a tool in a man's hands signified power over those with no tools. If the tool had to be sharpened or repaired, if the oxen needed rest or water, the work halted. Those toiling with their hands had no such external and compelling means of pacing the work of everyone in the field. This hierarchy should not be understood to mean that women were "just helping out" but rather that the authority over field work and field labor remained a masculine privilege. No matter how important women's labor or skills were to completing the work, unless they had sole responsibility for the farm they rarely had equal access to implements. Though women occasionally worked with horse-drawn equipment—usually while alone in the fields—the exchange of labor was uneven, for men did not perform stoop labor while women operated equipment.

It is difficult to determine from the available records if field work was more common for women of certain ethnic groups or if these work patterns applied generally to all settlers. Yankee American pioneering traditions leave the impression that field work was a man's job and that women labored in the fields only when there were no other men or boys to help. Americans took pride in stating that white American

Woman driving four oxen pulling a binder.
Women worked in the fields when necessary or if they preferred.

women, unlike European farm women, did not have to work in the fields. European agriculture was more labor intensive than that practiced in North America, so men, women, and children customarily shared in the work of a small farm. However, during the Dakota settlement period, women of all European and European American cultures took on farm tasks widely considered to be men's work. Yankee American women seem to have understood more clearly that field work defied social expectations for their sex, but they were just as willing to cross gender boundaries as were their European counterparts. Because of North Dakota's high percentage of European immigrants, the overall impression tends to be that women who worked in the fields were European, but Yankee American women also did such work, by need or by choice.[7]

This pattern seems to have been a departure from trends noted by historians. John Mack Faragher reports that, before the Civil War, native-born, midwestern women rarely labored in the fields. Deborah Fink finds that women who engaged in field work in eastern Nebraska after 1880 tended to live in "more marginal households" than women who did no field work. Women's labor in the fields was apparently more necessary as agriculture spread into the drier climate of the plains and as improved machinery allowed for more extensive farming. But even on the plains, where women farmers were more visible, if a family could afford the luxury of hired help, women could refuse to do field work. One of these privileged few, Gertrude Enger, was the subject of some comment among neighbors because she insisted on working only in the house, caring for her eight sons and one daughter, cooking for field hands, and supervising two hired girls.[8]

In addition to field work, women performed tasks that both supported and decreased the time necessary to complete the work of plowing and harvesting. A Traill County woman drove the oxen one-half mile to the river for water while her husband ate his noon meal and rested. While her husband took a break at midday, Helga Aasen Thompson walked four miles to have the scythe sharpened by a neighbor who owned the area's only grindstone. In western North Dakota, where plowing turned over endless numbers of rocks, it was often women who removed them from the fields, transporting them on sturdy and useful stoneboats, while men continued plowing.[9]

Men and women also shared the work of building a house, which

could be constructed of various materials, each affecting comfort, security, and cleanliness. On the northern plains, there were four basic
house-building materials: log, sod, board, and clay brick. Log houses
were usually available only to those who lived near a river. Fairly comfortable if properly chinked, they often lacked board floors, windows,
and doors. Helga Aasen and Paul Thompson built a log house, and
Helga plastered it inside and out with clay. They constructed a good
roof of bark covered with sod, but the floor was packed dirt and a blanket covered the doorway. Paul Thompson remarked, "Helga was a
proud woman when later a door was made."[10]

Mary Hagan Lee built a sod house with her husband, John. It was
large as sod houses went, sixteen by twelve feet, and had a plank floor
and a board roof supported by wooden beams. The house was divided
by a wall that gave half the space to the livestock. Though houses
shared with livestock smelled like barns, the warmth of the animals
and the extra insulation of the attached shelter kept human occupants
comfortable in winter. The Lees added a board lean-to for a kitchen.
The sod walls were two feet thick, and Mary remembered with subtle
humor that in the summer they turned green with vegetation. The
Lee's house was a substantial and elegant prairie home, and the board
floor made it the favored location for neighborhood dances. Sod walls
meant a solid house: warm in the winter, cool in the summer, impervi-
ous to prairie fire. If plastered with clay and whitewashed, the walls
were reasonably easy to keep clean. But the roof and the floor made the
difference in comfort. Ukrainian and Black Sea German women sometimes made thatched roofs, which shed water more effectively than
sod. For all its notoriety, the sod house offered comforts in Dakota Territory that uninsulated board houses could not, even under the com-
mand of the most conscientious housekeeper.[11]

Though women were seldom responsible for the construction of
frame or tarpaper shacks, they often applied both labor and ingenuity
to making these tiny, thin-walled boxes comfortable for winter and
summer. Mrs. Thomas MacPherson, a Scottish immigrant to Canada
before she moved to Dakota Territory, nailed her fine Brussels carpet
to her homestead claim shack to keep out the rain; the moisture, of
course, ruined the rug. Rachel Calof gathered, mixed, and applied clay
to her board shack to insulate and smooth the walls.[12]

The most comfortable and enduring houses were made by Black Sea

Germans, who had learned to cope with the treeless steppes of South Russia. They combined clay with straw and water, formed this mixture into blocks, and dried them in the sun. They built the house and a large oven from the bricks, plastering them with a clay mixture inside and out. This type of shelter took longer to build than did sod houses or board shacks but was intended to be permanent. Christina Hillius estimated that she laid four thousand bricks to build her McIntosh County home. Though neighbors of other nationalities rarely adopted the clay-brick house, among Black Sea Germans some men and women traded their house-building skills for food or labor.[13]

With the family's shelter provided and perhaps enough sod broken to cultivate a small crop, men frequently left home for a job that would bring cash, food, or livestock in trade. In their husbands' absence, women looked after the household, the livestock, and the season's field work, pursuing the duties of commercial agriculture. While her husband hired out, a Ukrainian immigrant woman planted two acres of flax so they would have a crop to sell in addition to what he could earn. Sarah Gray Braddock, born and raised in Pennsylvania, "found it necessary to do a man's work since Mr. Braddock was away from home

Sod house interior lit by two large windows.
The wooden roof and floor made for a comfortable home.

most of the time." She completed many tasks in the evening after returning home from her teaching job.[14]

Women's presence on the claim while men "worked out" had a second and very important benefit. One requirement of the homestead
law was residence for six months each year: if the family did not stay
on the farm during the period of minimum residence, neighbors or
claim jumpers could contest the claim. Although women were sometimes physically attacked by claim jumpers and often frightened by
cowboys who tried to drive settlers away from land previously used for
cattle grazing, their presence was sufficient to establish a legal claim.[15]

Women remaining on the farm also performed a variety of daily
chores in the house, barnyard, and garden to provide food and clothing
for the family. Milking cows, gathering eggs, harvesting garden produce, maintaining all of these food sources, and preserving foodstuffs
for the winter occupied a large part of a woman's day. The task of
preparing or gathering fuel was generally performed two or three
times a year, but several times each day the fuel had to be brought into
the house to fire the stove for cooking and washing. Water had to be
drawn from a well or hauled from a slough or creek. In addition, most
women had children to feed, clothe, bathe, train, and protect. Between
and after chores, women participated in religious organizations or
services, embroidered and crocheted fancywork, and engaged in community welfare projects such as caring for sick neighbors or orphaned
children. Women rarely spoke of their daily chores in memoirs or interviews. They assumed that everyone did them; thus, these everyday
tasks did not merit much comment. The necessary quality of women's
daily work does not reflect the reality: her chores were set aside or reorganized during harvest, planting, and other periods of peak farm activity, her workday extended to accommodate all of her responsibilities. It was difficult to replace a woman's labor in the house and
barnyard, for hired girls were scarce and unreliable and older children
often went to work in the fields, too.

The amount of field work women did depended on the age and sex
of their children. If there were boys old enough to work effectively in
the fields, women and girls seldom had to do heavy work, except perhaps during harvest. When Kristen Fahlgren began her homesteading
experience, her sons were well grown, and she never worked in the

fields. However, when Amelia Neveu Chartrand and her husband, Peter, emigrated from Ontario to Dakota Territory, their only son was an infant. While Peter worked out to earn money, Amelia and her nearly grown daughters did the field work as well as the barnyard and household chores. Though women proved themselves capable field workers, boys were preferred for their strength and because they freed women to complete the house- and barnwork on time. Pauline Neher Diede contrasted the situation of her family—only daughters—with that of her uncle, Fred Martin—his family including several half-grown sons when they arrived at the Knife River. Despite the fact that Ludwig Neher put his older daughters, Matilda and teen-aged Otillia, to work in the harvest fields, Diede wrote, "Dadee faced these critical tasks . . . practically alone. . . . Everything depended on one man's decisions and doings. Boys' help was missing." Though Ludwig Neher was able to complete the field work with Matilda's and Otillia's help, it troubled him to have daughters toiling at what he considered to be men's work.[16]

As Julie Roy Jeffrey has noted, the common hardships of settlement in the West allowed the rules of gendered activity to be bent, regardless of what the various ethnic traditions viewed as proper. Dakota farm women generally accepted field work as important to the farm's success, and few looking back on their pioneering experience expressed shame or dismay at the work they did. Many continued to work in the fields until their children became old enough to take their place or until the family became wealthy enough to purchase equipment and to hire labor. Some continued to do field work all their life, either by choice or by custom, as did Caroline Erickson, who hired her housework done because she had always worked in the fields as a young girl and had never acquired homemaking skills. Many felt that as long as they obeyed their husbands and contributed to the family's survival, the work they did was worthy and respectable. They did not concern themselves with anyone else's concepts of sex roles.[17]

Work in the fields and barnyard usually prevented women from caring for their children as they might have under different circumstances, but most found some way to keep their sons and daughters safe while they worked outside the home. If more than one woman lived in a household, childcare responsibilities were generally shared.

In Olga Zarodney's crowded three-family claim shack, two women stayed in the house to cook and care for the small children while one went into the fields to clear rocks with the men.[18]

Women alone on a homestead had to devise ways to complete their work while providing adequate supervision or restraint for infants and toddlers. Karen Bjorlie brought along her infant daughter when she walked a mile to the pasture twice daily to milk the cow. If the child was sleeping, Bjorlie left her outside the fence; if awake, she tied the baby to her back while she milked. Hannah Bell wanted to shoot a deer that had approached her house, but she did not dare leave her toddler alone for fear he would wander into the tall grass. In later years she wrote about that day as an example of problems facing women on isolated homesteads:

> I tied him to a bed post with a rope while I shot and brought home the deer. This is just one little incident among many that needed thought and precaution as so many little dangers seemed to be around us, especially to the children.

Thinking that isolation meant security, Emily Carlson left her sleeping baby on the bed while she ran an errand to a neighbor's house one and one-half miles away. Upon her return, she was terrified to find two land seekers eating a meal at her table while they played with the baby. In time, the two men became good neighbors, but Carlson remained deeply aware of the danger of leaving a child alone.[19]

Young children were often assigned to watch babies and toddlers. Catherine Geizler was just five years old when she was left in charge of the house and the babies so her mother could work in the field. Matilda Lushenko recalled that leaving a six-year-old in charge of two or three younger siblings was a typical arrangement for Ukrainian farm families. However, the responsibility of long hours of childcare weighed heavily on young girls. Returning from the harvest fields one day, Helga Thompson asked teen-aged Caroline Thingelstad how she had gotten along with the baby. Caroline replied, "We have both cried today." Pauline Neher's schooling was delayed so she could care for the babies while her mother attended other chores. In addition to this task, Pauline was also expected to carry fresh water out to harvesters in the fields, leaving the younger children unattended in the house. Though still a child she faced the multiple and conflicting responsibilities of an adult woman.[20]

Childhood was short on Dakota homesteads. Women trained or supervised their children in adult tasks, and youngsters worked as hard as their age and size permitted, on their own or alongside their parents. Herding cattle was a common assignment for children as young as eight: with little fencing in the early years, someone had to keep the livestock from trampling and grazing on the wheat fields. Cattle that strayed onto a neighbor's field could incur damages their owner was responsible to pay.[21]

Other children worked in the fields. When Ingaborg Homme harvested a neighbor's potatoes in exchange for half the crop, she and her daughter walked five miles to the field and back over the course of several days until they had finished the task and brought home their share. The Kindsvogel children gathered buffalo bones to sell and carried rocks from the fields. The work young children accomplished was enormous and wearying. Lydia Metzger Kungel recalled,

> I learned to work from childhood on and as a young girl one of the jobs was to aim a gang-plow along the furrows all day and then milk cows by hand late in the evening. Or when a midwife brought a new baby into the neighbor's home, I was hired out to do the back-breaking washboard washing. I'll never forget how tired and worn out I often was.[22]

Some girls found it empowering to do a full share of work on the farm. When her older sister married and her older brothers died, Julia Sackman became the oldest child and the most important field worker on her parents' farm: "I did love to work[.] I thought I was big when I could do all that. . . . The more I could do alone . . . the more important I felt." Sophie Trupin, working alongside her older brother in the hayfield, noted that, "[after] a long day I would have blisters on my palms and aching muscles, and yet such a feeling of accomplishment and camaraderie."[23]

The work of barnyard and field proceeded according to need and season, without regard to the needs and seasons of a woman's life. When the fields demanded attention, other work was set aside. Christina Link explained the hierarchy on a homestead: "When the husband needed help, it was the wife that left everything lay and went and did it, whether it was gathering stones off of a field, or doing the hay-stack setting." A short growing season and unreliable weather patterns meant that every possible hand was needed to complete field work before frost, hail, prairie fire, or any other routine threat destroyed the crop.[24]

Dakota farm women were strong and capable, but their bodies suffered from the strain of overwork. Pregnancy and childbirth did not guarantee rest during a harvest or permit dependence on someone else to do the heaviest household chores. Indeed, pregnancy increased the danger of the work. Thersia Bosch fell from a load of hay while pregnant. There was no doctor in the area, and she died three days later of complications identified as "blood poisoning." Kari Stavens became an invalid following the birth of her third child: she attributed the illness to carrying heavy pails of water up a steep hill from the Goose River to the house and to fighting a prairie fire during her pregnancy. Ragnhild Raaen suffered a fallen uterus after the birth of her sixth child. Though she continued to do field and barnyard work until the final three years of her long life, she had to wrap her belly for support when she performed heavy tasks.[25]

Women generally did less field work as they aged. Grown sons and sons-in-law replaced them in the fields, or labor was hired as farms prospered and expanded. But some women continued to work out of necessity; others did by choice. The subordination of housework to field work sometimes meant that women, no matter their age or condition, had to work in the fields in exchange for male labor in and around the house. Elderly Annie Johnson had grown sons to do the field work, but she joined them in the hayfield so they could complete the work more quickly. After the crop was in, Johnson's sons were to help her build a frame house to replace their sod structure. The tradeoff resulted in her death when she fell from the hay wagon and broke her neck.[26]

Housework and field work were intricately linked during harvest and threshing, particularly when it came to feeding the threshing crew. The demands of this chore varied according to circumstances. In the early years of settlement, crops were harvested from just a few acres and wheat was threshed at home with simple methods or transported to a neighboring farm's threshing machine. In some communities, farmers set up a cooperative association called a "threshing ring," with members traveling from one farm to another until threshing was complete. The woman hosting the threshers usually had to fix only a noon meal and morning and afternoon "lunches" for the men, and other women associated with the ring often helped with the work. Isabella and Albert Roberts finished the first harvest on their farm in two and one-half days. Four days later, on a neighboring farm, Albert helped with the threshing and Isabella assisted with meal preparation. Shared work lightened the load; the threshers were all neighbors and friends.[27]

As their wheat acreage increased, the Roberts hired a custom threshing crew. Some crews brought their own cooks and cook cars, but farmers could save on threshing costs if they—utilizing the labor of wives and daughters—provided meals. In such cases, the farm woman, helped by her daughters or a hired girl, prepared three main meals and two lunches for the crew. In 1887, the Roberts housed and fed twenty-three threshers, including five Native Americans, for one week. When the weather turned cold, threshing ceased, but the crew still had to be fed. The work was exhausting, lasting from four in the morning until eleven at night and requiring labor that included hauling water and fuel as well as kneading bread dough and performing other cooking chores. This work so entangled a woman's labor and skills with the farm economy that any imagined division between household and farm was effectively eliminated.[28]

The harvest brought into farm homes men who would not become neighbors, who were of questionable character, or whose ethnicity made them unwelcome, as was the case with the Indians who worked for the Roberts. Women often feared that threshers would endanger the family or adversely influence their children. Thomas Isern, in his history of threshing, notes women's dislike of threshers, while David Schob, writing about an earlier period, states that crimes committed by threshers, particularly sexual crimes against children, were rarely reported but common enough to warrant a cautionary comment in *American Agriculturist*. Women who housed and fed transient workers with obviously falsified names, such as Hobo Chicago, must have known that many were trying to conceal their pasts. Their presence in a farm woman's home very likely made her uncomfortable, adding to her burden of work and threatening her children's safety.[29]

Among the most important and often the most difficult tasks pioneer women faced was procuring, preparing, and distributing food for family members, guests, and neighbors. For many families, food was scarce in the first year or two of settlement. Well-prepared settlers arrived with provisions and food-producing livestock. However, most who came from Europe had little in the way of supplies with them and had to work for or purchase food. Many endured hunger while every available resource was invested in the farm.

Knute and Barbo Pladson were among the early Norwegian immigrant settlers of Newburgh Township in Steele County. They came, as many of their neighbors had, from a farm in Iowa; thus, they were able to bring milk cows and two barrels of cured beef and pork, food enough for the first year. Others expected to buy livestock upon arrival in Dakota, but milk cows and chickens were hard to find in pioneer communities. The Harris family purchased a cow soon after arriving in Jamestown; though it slowed the journey out to their claim, they were glad to have it. They had to turn to relatives in Iowa to secure chickens and pigs, which were shipped by train several months later. Within a

A threshing crew enjoys lunch brought to the field by a woman cook.

year, the pigs and chickens were producing food for the family and a surplus for sale.[30]

Many other families were not so well prepared. Berit and Erich Erstad, Norwegian immigrants to Steele County, had to labor at field work and housework on other people's farms to earn meat and milk to feed themselves and their child. A year passed before they could buy a bred heifer and some hens so they would have milk, butter, and eggs.[31]

In Dakota Territory, as in so many other places, food was symbolic of wealth, hospitality, and spirituality. Many women secured high standing in the community if they were able to provide food to those in need. However, the food supply in pioneer households was often unreliable. Women's first obligation in securing and preparing food was to their children, but social responsibilities to feed needy neighbors and travelers put extra demands on their often scanty provisions and on their labor.

Many European immigrants—particularly those who left their home country to escape poverty or lack of opportunity—suffered from hunger. The land's implicit promise to produce wheat and wealth became an ugly lie to those whose children went hungry. For three summers, Icelandic immigrant Maria Sveinsdottir Benson left her husband and children to work as a domestic in Winnipeg, Manitoba, to earn money to buy food. When asked how she could leave her children for months at a time, she replied that she had to work out because she had heard her children cry in hunger. Pauline Neher Diede recalled that hunger drove her to taste wild rose hips, which eased the pangs. Her cousin, John Martin, had to be cautioned against eating the green stems of wheat growing in the field. Though the children were hungry, every spear had to be saved for harvest.[32]

Rachel Calof sought prairie foods—wild garlic and mushrooms—to supplement meager supplies, but few settlers depended on wild plants. Instead, they put in gardens of potatoes and other vegetables as soon as they could acquire seeds. Within a few years of arrival, women's gardens reliably produced plenty for their families' needs. Some managed to grow a surplus, which they could sell to newcomers or to merchants in a nearby town.[33]

In addition to feeding their own families, women often had uninvited visitors who expected or demanded a meal. Sometimes these guests were newly arrived families, but often they were traveling men seeking land or work. Men were more mobile and could "ride the grub line"—that is, show up at a prosperous home at mealtime—or buy or trade for food where they found it. Newly arrived women who lacked adequate provisions generally depended on their own resources or on others coming to them with food. Frau Jaeger, midwife of the Knife River neighborhood, shared her abundant garden produce with Christina Neher while she recovered from the birth of her second child, but Christina's husband, Ludwig, had to travel about, begging food, showing up at mealtime, gauging who was most likely to be sympathetic. After Christina returned to the Nehers' new homestead claim and sod house, Ludwig still had access to these other sources, while she had to feed herself and two small children from scant supplies and with neighbors' gifts of food. Ludwig's opportune absence allowed the family's food supply to stretch farther, but the quality remained poor.[34]

Though "wheat was everything" in North Dakota, household reserves of this basic foodstuff were often depleted. August Bauer described the difficulty of finding surplus food on homesteads while, as a young unmarried man, he, along with his brothers, built clay-brick houses for other family members on distant claims. When they ran out of food and set out with cash to buy supplies from homesteaders, they encountered women reluctant to share or even sell bread because flour was so hard to come by. At one soddy they were given three hard biscuits; at another house a woman refused to sell a loaf of bread until Bauer offered her the astounding sum of one dollar for it. Elsewhere a woman refused to feed them, but at the next house the woman fixed them a meal of coffee, bread, potatoes, and some unidentifiable food that Bauer could not eat. Though Bauer thought the meal inadequate for the two dollars they paid, the woman no doubt provided for the strangers the same meal she prepared for her own family—using up precious supplies to do so.[35]

Traveling men expecting to be offered high-quality food when they stopped at a farmhouse at mealtime were often disappointed. With short supplies in the poorest homes and demanding responsibilities to family and farm, women could hardly be expected to share limited rations with strangers or to fix a fine meal in the midst of other chores.

As producers, women exerted control over the food supply, and of course their families came first. In plains settlements, no artificial standards encouraged women to impress guests at the expense of their own families. Traveling men, especially Yankee Americans, often seemed unable to adapt to local customs. When Irving Gardner stopped at a Steele County soddy for a meal, he expected to find a hostess whose circumstances and manners matched those of women he had known in Maine. The woman he met did not speak English but offered him a cup of milk. "She wasn't very tidily dressed," he recalled, "and as I looked into the one room sod hovel, and noted the pig and cow occupied the adjoining quarters with her, I lost my appetite, gave back the milk, and started again for [the town of] Hope."[36]

The year of settlement helped determine accessibility to foodstuffs. Late arrivals often benefited from established families willing to share supplies or a store located within a reasonable distance from the homestead. But in a year of drought, grasshopper invasions, or early frost, even well-established families might suffer from lack of food. The late 1880s were a period of intense drought. Though the new state was reluctant to admit that many residents were impoverished—tarnishing the carefully polished image of a land of bounty—in the winter of 1890 the legislature finally appropriated $2,500 for relief. Neighboring states sent trainloads of food, fuel, and clothing, and the railroads shipped supplies free of charge from Minneapolis. In 1891, prairie fire—a frequent companion to drought—left forty families destitute in Emmons County, and, again, the state provided modest relief. Public relief efforts moved slowly and were very limited, however; direct neighbor-to-neighbor assistance—dependent mostly on the accumulated surplus from women's garden and barnyard work—rescued many families from starvation.[37]

In addition to the challenges of procuring food, pioneer women also faced a variety of problems as they sought safe, reliable sources of water for both people and livestock. At a time when women in New York, Chicago, and even Fargo were drawing water from a kitchen tap, their rural Dakota counterparts were securing it through primitive methods in use for thousands of years. After hauling the water, women made it safe to drink by straining out visible animal life, usually referred to as "wigglers," and boiling it to kill parasites and pathogens. Those unaware of the dangers of contaminated water often became ill; small children were particularly at risk.

North Dakota rivers carry a reliable quantity of thick brown water that in the early years of settlement was frequently contaminated with typhoid-causing bacteria. Immigrants from rural Norway, accustomed to clear water streaming down from mountain snow packs, felt dismay when they saw the murky, sluggish water of Dakota rivers. One woman, out to get water a few days after arriving at her brother's homestead, looked at Antelope Creek but did not see any clean water, so she returned to the house with an empty pail. Her brother told her she could no longer be "particular" about water: unappealing as it was, the creek was their only source of water for drinking, bathing, cooking, and washing.[38]

Central North Dakota sloughs hold water during wet years, but as they also serve as watering holes for domestic and wild animals, the water was often unpalatable and contaminated. The Dronan family of Steele County used slough water for five years, but most settlers drank slough water for only a few months before digging a shallow well. Jennie Pratt Codding dug a well at the edge of the slough to keep the family's water supply separate from that of the livestock. The Fays made a similar well but continued to boil and strain the water before drinking.[39]

Those not located near a slough or a creek had to haul water some distance until they dug a well. For Bertha Hanvold Olson, that distance was one and one-half miles. Marian Kramer used a stoneboat with a hitch of oxen to transport barrels of water from her brother's farm, one-half mile away. Owners of good wells sometimes took advantage of the situation to earn much-needed cash: Fred Daniels of Barnes County sold water for one dollar per barrel.[40]

Well digging was usually men's work, but some families considered anything related to water (with the exception of dam building) to be women's responsibility. Christina Bossart dug a fourteen-foot well about three hundred yards from her house, climbing a ladder to remove dirt by the pailful. However, she unknowingly dug the well on the section line, designated to become a road, and the "road boss" filed suit against her husband, Frederick Bossart. The case was dismissed because, though required to do the work of digging a well, women were not expected to "know anything about [land] rights in those days."[41]

The Dunn family found good water in an artesian well and piped it into the barn for the livestock. Though the water pressure and quality were good, the water line was never extended to the house. The men on the Dunn farm, as on most others, viewed farm matters as more important than household work. Although Lizzie Dunn kept house for her brothers all of her life, she was never able to assert enough power within the family to demand that they improve her working conditions inside the house.[42]

For many settlers, the lack of good and abundant water presented a major obstacle. Particularly in the western part of the state, water supply remained uncertain. As late as 1925, some families were still hauling water in barrels or catching rain in cisterns. Creeks, rivers, and sloughs were dangerous sources of water for human consumption, and during a drought even good wells might run dry. Many women were shocked by the poor water quality in their new home; they had to learn alternative ways of dealing with water in order to protect their families and complete routine chores such as cooking and washing. For some, water problems would represent the single black mark against a

Family standing near claim shack.
The water barrel rests on a stoneboat.

comfortable life in North Dakota. Gunhild Oiehus Grimsrud spent her adult life in the state and established a successful farm with her husband and six children, yet she continued into her old age to speak longingly of the good water and rivers of her native Norway.[43]

Beyond a reliable water supply, cash was an essential component of successful living and farming in North Dakota. Many pioneers arrived with far less than the eight hundred dollars Gilbert Fite estimated as necessary to establish a homestead. The shortfall usually affected family and household needs rather than being extracted from the farm. Pioneers gave priority to buying livestock, equipment, and seed, for without these there would be no reason to stay in Dakota. Men's earnings from working out almost always returned to the farm, and for many years all farm income was used to support the farm rather than the household. Women's earnings went to both the farm and the household, first meeting the family's food and clothing needs. The absence of complaints about this financial arrangement gives one pause, suggesting the subordination of not only women and all their interests but of the entire family to the land and crops. Women rarely protested this distribution of money as long as the family remained needy. Instead, they looked to the future and to the advantages their children would have because of their parents' sacrifices.

The routine return of farm income to land, crops, livestock, and outbuildings increases the significance of women's cash or credit income because farm income often did not provide for the family's needs. In addition, women's income resources take on greater importance when considered in light of the agricultural fragility of the northern plains. Irregular rainfall, early frost, prairie fire, or damaging hail wiped out crops without warning, sometimes annually over a long period. Poor market prices attended the most productive years; the Great Dakota Boom proved particularly disheartening in this regard. Ben Overby's parents immigrated to Griggs County in 1886, bringing with them a walking plow, four horses, forty chickens, three pigs, and a few cows. Though they arrived with enough farm equipment and livestock to make a good start, they harvested almost nothing during the first five years because of drought, which unfortunately coincided with decreasing market prices. Their sixth crop grew well with good rains, but hail destroyed most of it before harvest.[44]

Drought was the most common form of disaster, but excessive rain, especially during threshing, could be equally devastating. Andrew Johnson also took a claim during the dry years of the Dakota Boom. In 1891 he finally realized a good crop, but autumn rains and a shortage of threshing crews forced him to store it for threshing in the spring. By then, the grain had been ruined. Johnson sold some for fifteen cents a bushel, gave away the rest, and spent the remainder of 1892 working to pay for the threshing of his "good" 1891 crop.[45]

Sometimes crops grew well but events interfered to prevent the family from realizing a profit on the year's work. Ole and Mary Bolkan struggled for five years in the drought and frosts of the 1880s, and just when they began to think that the crop would be good, one of the draft horses died. With wheat selling for less than fifty cents per bushel, replacing a good draft horse at seventy-five to one hundred dollars commanded a large portion of that year's income.[46]

Because of the irregularity of crops and prices, women sought to develop stable sources of income. Some arrived on the northern plains with specialized skills that found a market even in cash-poor communities. Trained as a seamstress in her native Sweden, Elna Erickson made baptismal gowns that were over a yard in length, "with rows and rows of pin tucking, and yards of lace embroidery insertion, shirring and ruffling, some with tiny buttons and button holes the entire length of the back." Karna Monson Hanson graduated from medical school in Sweden and practiced there until she immigrated to the United States late in life. Though she never obtained a medical license in North Dakota, she continued to attend women in childbirth and to perform minor surgery until the age of seventy. Many other women with no training—but with plenty of experience—practiced midwifery. Their pay was more likely to be vegetables than cash, but their work was necessary, and some realized a small income from it.[47]

A variety of jobs occupied women beyond their usual farm and household chores. A few arranged to become neighborhood postmasters, a job with benefits beyond the small paycheck. The indoor work suited a woman with small children to watch, and neighbors stopping by for their mail provided social relief. Several women wove rag rugs on ancient and well-traveled looms, including Julia Abbott, whose loom had been sent from Iowa so she could fashion carpets to sell during the dry years, while her husband worked in Wisconsin.[48]

Most women, however, earned money or merchandise from the sale of surplus butter and eggs. Barnyard chores were so closely linked to household needs and so carefully integrated into a farm woman's other daily tasks that it might be useful to consider the barn and barnyard as extensions of the house. Though the barn was neither exclusively a woman's work arena nor a space over which her authority was absolute, it was the site of much of her daily labor and most of her income-producing work. Some chores could be completed by small children: certainly by age ten many had learned to feed and milk the cows and to feed the chickens and gather eggs. Women with no children or with very young children, of course, performed all of these chores themselves, fitting them into their workday, balancing them with their family's needs and/or seasonal farm work.[49]

Keeping cows and chickens regulated household chores. Cows had to be milked twice a day, ten months of the year, and they had to be fed and taken to water or have water drawn for them. After the milk was strained and set aside to allow the cream to rise (few farms had mechanical separators before 1900), a portion of the skimmed milk was fed to the calves. Chickens usually had free range of the yard to gather most of their food, but they had to be herded into the chicken house at night, both for protection and to force them to lay eggs where they could be easily found and collected. Eggs were gathered daily in the spring, though some hens had to be encouraged to set—to keep the eggs warm until they hatched—to increase the flock's size. If chicks arrived by train in the spring, they needed careful attention for a few weeks until they were big enough to be on their own.

Basic barnyard chores could be performed by nearly anyone (if the cows were reasonably well behaved), but the processing, preserving, and marketing of butter and eggs was skilled work that women either did themselves or closely supervised. During peak milking season, women churned cream two or three times a week. When weak winter daylight and late gestation ended bovine lactation, women had a rest from milking and butter making. Chickens also produced seasonally, responding to springtime's longer daylight hours by laying more eggs.

Pioneers had a hard time finding chickens to buy during the early years of settlement, but eventually women purchased eggs or chicks locally or had them shipped by train. Once the flock was established, women vigorously pursued poultry production. Between 1880 and 1900, the average number of chickens per farm nearly doubled from 15.9 to 31.1, a far greater increase than that of dairy cattle.[50]

In rural counties, the expansion of poultry production was more apparent. McIntosh County began to attract settlers around 1884, and by 1890 there were 675 farms with 10,694 chickens, an average of 15.8 per farm. Though by 1900 the number of farms had increased only slightly to 744 (1.1 times), the number of barnyard fowl had increased 2.3 times to 25,620, doubling the per-farm average to 34.4 birds. These figures reflect women's dependence on barnyard fowl to produce food for their families and a surplus for sale or trade.[51]

Dairy cattle were also scarce during the earliest years of settlement. August Bentz and his young wife homesteaded near Richardton in 1905. After their second child was born Mrs. Bentz walked "several miles" to get fresh milk for her children while August used their only horse for work. The following year, they both worked the harvest, earning enough to buy a second horse and a milk cow. By 1910, Dunn County farms averaged nearly two dairy cows each.[52]

Milking and butter making were considered women's work in North Dakota, as elsewhere, until commercial dairies were established around 1910. Raising chickens remained primarily women's work throughout the settlement period and into the twentieth century. No noticeable distinctions can be based on ethnic origins, though individual preferences for the work varied considerably. Swedish immigrant Elizabeth Solem, who settled with her photographer husband in McKenzie County in 1909, milked the cows and did all the work of caring for them. With spirit most pioneer women hid from interviewers, Solem exclaimed, "Talk about work! I pumped water and pumped water for that stock until I thought my back would break." But Norwegian immigrant Bertha Wahl enjoyed barnyard chores on her McLean County farm, describing them as a "restful change from household tasks and the care of babies."[53]

Contrary to the popular conception that butter and eggs earned women a small amount of discretionary income or "pin money," these products provided reliable income and necessities for the family, even in hard times. The stability of barnyard income and its significance to the family's well-being impressed many farmers. Gottlieb Breitling, a Black Sea German, acknowledged not only that women performed barnyard chores but that the work provided an important source of revenue for the farm family: "My wife always made enough from the chickens and geese to take care of all grocery bills and clothing for all of us." Perhaps Breitling stated more clearly what August Bauer meant when he said that he "started farming with five horses, a hand plow and a wife." Women's work—producing a small but reliable income from farm resources—complemented men's work in the fields of beguiling but unreliable wheat.[54]

When considering women's heavy, endless tasks and long hours combined with distance between homes, periodic separation from husbands, and concerns over childcare, the physical and emotional burden of homesteading seems staggering. Yet homesteading Dakota women rarely complained that their work was drudgery or demeaning. While their lives were difficult and most were overburdened, to label their work "drudgery" suggests that homesteading women were exploited laborers in an enterprise over which they exerted no authority and from which they expected no returns. The words "drudgery" and "drudge" refer to servile labor and the person who performs it. Whether applied to a man or a woman, the term disparages the worker as a servant, as one who does the lowest forms of labor at the bidding of some authority. Though used in a kindly way, intending to show sympathy for the woman who appears to be overburdened with work and family, the word "drudge" suggests that farm women had no control over their work and no management role on their farms.

In objective usage, "drudgery" creates or enhances class and ethnic distinctions and can be used to deprive women of pride in productive work. As Julie Roy Jeffrey has noted, western women usually could identify someone who appeared to be less fortunate than they were, allowing them to define "drudge" as someone other than themselves. Jeffrey's example is Indian women, but in North Dakota, where most settlers had little contact with Native Americans, women of other European ethnic origins often served as the representative drudge.[55]

While Dakota women were getting settled on their claims, their counterparts on established eastern farms complained of drudgery. Grangers, recognizing that "mindless, repetitive, exhausting drudgery was farm women's most basic problem," offered conventional solutions: shorter hours, an occasional vacation, household help from other members of the family. Grangers did not associate drudgery with the absence of authority over work, nor did they develop the idea that women who did not control their work and the products of their labor, who did not find any satisfaction in work, and who could not see their work in the larger context of farm and family experienced that work as drudgery. Though Dakota farm women saw periodic or seasonal subordination of their work, complaints of drudgery are noticeably absent from their descriptions, suggesting that they did not view their role as drudgery or as just "helping out" but as a partnership. Along with their husbands, Dakota women made an enormous emotional, financial, and physical investment in risking everything on a dry land farm.[56]

Mary Dodge Woodward worked as hard as any homesteading woman on the small bonanza farm her son managed, but she did not work in the fields. She believed field work was unfeminine, writing in her diary about two young German sisters who seeded wheat in windy fields and hauled wheat and wood while reining four-horse teams: "How they can work like men is beyond my comprehension." Nina Farley Wishek responded similarly when she saw Black Sea German women doing field work:

> To me, one of the strangest ways of the foreigner was the custom of women working in the field. As I had never seen it in my old home state, I rather resented it as an insult to my sex.

Wishek, unlike Woodward, eventually changed her mind about women's field work. It was not drudgery, but productive work that some women enjoyed:

> In later years I became accustomed to [women working in the fields] and even came to realize that the girls and women enjoyed the freedom of outdoor life. Many girls preferred working outside.[57]

These comments clearly indicate that in Woodward's and, initially, Wishek's view, the women were doing demeaning work that was too physically taxing. But their comments also imply that when an observer declares work to be drudgery, the term does not simply refer to a quality of the work but involves a complex of factors that include valuations of gender, class, and ethnicity. The observer feels comfortably superior in her assessment of gender relations in other households or cultures as demonstrated by women's work. Wishek adjusted her estimation of Black Sea German women and their work after she came to know and respect them. Woodward, however, socialized little outside her family and never learned to value the work of women in the fields.

Iowa agriculturist Henry Wallace had both political and economic motives to declare women's dairy work to be drudgery while he and others sought to establish commercial creameries. Arguing that enlarged dairy herds supplying commercial creameries could produce a profit from high-priced land, he noted that dairying had been women's work but insisted that they had "toiled and drudged at the churn" for inadequate returns. Though appreciative that women had proved a calf could be raised successfully on skimmed milk, he believed that "the bondage of the wife to the churn must be broken" and that commercial creameries would take "away half the drudgery of the farmer's wife." By declaring the productive work of farm women to be drudgery, Wallace neatly and without guilt severed from them an important source of income while reconfiguring dairying as men's work.[58]

Assuming that life on a plains farm meant numbing drudgery for wives and mothers, historians and writers have linked women's role in homesteading to insanity. According to these writers, the overwhelming workload, life's uncertainties, and environmental hardships combined to deprive women of emotional equilibrium. The fictional homesteading woman can barely be distinguished from some historical treatments—a sad victim of isolation, wind, dust, fear, and overwork. However, a closer reading of the historical record reveals a more complex pattern that breaks the link between work on a plains farm and insanity in women.[59]

Some settlement-era women did suffer from depression and despair: every community had stories of women who lost emotional stability. No doubt some were true, but as the stories were repeated and enhanced they emerged as folkloric warnings about the plains' power to rob women of their sanity. The tales warned that the hard work and isolation of a settlement farm could cause insanity in women, but they also served to deny women credit for their constructive role in the homesteading process and to assign blame for some families' failures. As Seth Humphrey futilely tried to collect on mortgages from settlers who had left the country, he assumed that the exodus was caused by "both the women who stayed until the prairie broke them and the many more who fled from the terror of it." Like Walter Prescott Webb, Humphrey viewed the plains as a place that empowered men and—based on his understanding of dichotomous gendered spheres—must therefore destroy women.[60]

The statistical record of the North Dakota Hospital for the Insane does not support the widespread assumption that settlement on dry land farms drove a disproportionate number of women insane. Between 1885, when the hospital was established at Jamestown, and 1928, the admission rate for women was generally lower than their proportion in the state population (Table 7). Among state hospital patients, the ratio of men to women was quite irregular but tended to rise during the same period. This difference is even more pronounced when the patient's age is considered: many were confined because of problems related to old age, including that of having no one to care for them. However, among patients over the age of sixty in the years for which statistics are available, the male-to-female ratio is 2.07.[61]

Though historian Walter Prescott Webb and others assumed that isolation was a significant factor in women's homesteading experience, North Dakota state hospital records indicate that women did not suffer disproportionately from loneliness. In fact, available documents reveal that men were far more likely to be confined for symptoms that might be attributed to isolation. In reports inventorying causes of insanity, sixty-five men are listed as suffering mental disorders due to "Lonesomeness" or "Living Alone" while only nine women appear in that category.[62]

Gender differences are also visible when considering the category of overwork as a cause of mental disorder, affecting women to a greater extent than men—nearly twice as many (32 to 18) in the nine reports examined. While this category suggests that "drudgery" may in fact describe the nature of Dakota farm women's work, it is important to note that overwork was not a major cause of mental disease. Compared to loneliness or overwork, worry was a more significant basis for hospitalization for both men and women, with men more likely to be confined for this reason (112 to 83). The cause of insanity most frequently noted for women was heredity (150 patients), followed by a complex of physiological factors listed as menopause, menstrual difficulties, and childbirth that accounted for twenty more patients (103) than worry. Given the great changes psychiatry has undergone since the early twentieth century, few of these diagnoses would stand today, but in the understanding of their own times, farm women who succumbed to mental illness seldom identified overwork as the cause.[63]

Table 7: Ratio of Men to Women		
Year	State Ratio	Hospital Ratio
1886	1.40	1.60
1892	1.25	1.37
1900	1.25	1.12
1910	1.22	1.77
1920	1.12	1.78
1928	1.12	1.55

Note: State populations for 1892 and 1928 are taken from the nearest federal census data, 1890 and 1930.

Though hospital physicians did not list "immigration" as a cause of mental illness, it seems to have been the most important factor among the various causes for confinement (Table 8). In every year for which data is available, foreign-born persons were represented by numbers far higher than their proportion in the state population. Immigration encompasses a complex of stressors related to mental disorders, including the distress of cultural isolation and separation from family and, for some North Dakota settlers, disappointment in the promise of "free land." Another possibility is that some individuals inclined toward mental instability may have been more likely to emigrate in the first place. Within this population, however, numbers for women and men in most years closely approximate their representation statewide (Table 9). Gender does not appear to have been a consistent factor in the number of cases of recognized mental disorders among European immigrants to North Dakota.[64]

Some writers have claimed that women suffering mental distress remained at home as long as they could contribute to the family labor pool. About the condition of women pioneers in Idaho, Annie Pike

Greenwood wrote, "So long as a woman can work, no matter how her mind may fail, she is still kept on the farm, a cog in the machine, growing crazier and crazier, until she dies of it, or until she suddenly kills her children and herself." But the figures comparing immigrant and native-born patients of the North Dakota Hospital for the Insane indicate that this assessment is probably not true. At least it is not the case that, among immigrants with mental disorders, women were more likely to remain at home than men. The only remaining, statistically sound conclusion is that women, especially native-born women—participating in the well-established American tradition of setting up homes and farms in a distant place—adapted physically and mentally to the work and conditions of northern plains life, and immigrant men and women—experiencing the stresses of relocation and cultural dissonance, coupled with intense feelings of cultural isolation and loss—displayed greater incidences of mental illness.[65]

In their memoirs and interviews, pioneer women never made light of the quantity and difficulty of the work required of them, appearing to have expected and accepted it as the cost of obtaining a farm. When asked late in life about the hardships of the settlement period, Ella Mae Ruland responded laconically, "Our homestead days was a struggle," and Bertha Marie Walley simply said, "There were no hardships. Just life." Women accepted the burdens of their work with grace and equa-

Table 8: Comparison of Foreign-Born Population in North Dakota and in Hospital for the Insane		
Year	State Foreign-Born Population	Foreign-Born Patients
1892	44.5%	60.0%
1900	35.4%	63.4%
1910	27.0%	58.0%
1920	20.3%	46.1%
1928	15.4%	33.3%

Table 9: Comparison of Male-to-Female Ratio Among Foreign-Born and Native-Born in North Dakota with Male-to-Female Ratio Among Foreign-Born and Native-Born Patients				
Year	Foreign-Born Population	Foreign-Born Patients	Native-Born Population	Native-Born Patients
1892	1.36	1.76	1.17	.96
1900	1.42	1.39	1.16	1.37
1910	1.45	1.46	1.15	2.14
1920	1.34	1.33	1.07	1.72
1928	1.35	2.16	1.08	1.74

nimity, but they seldom revealed why they chose such a life and what it meant to them.[66]

Several scholars have developed theories about the nature of women's work, attempting to explain why certain tasks are assigned to women and why women generally accept these designations. Judith Brown presents the idea that women's work in any society is that which can be completed regardless of family concerns, at any stage of life. Patricia Branca's theory poses that women moved slowly into industrial pursuits in an economy that still offered them productive agricultural roles; they sought work that suited them, especially that which allowed them to work within the family setting. Charlotte Perkins Gilman, an economist and contemporary of the women in this study, criticized the American industrial society in which men dominated the economy and provided "sustenance" to non-productive women. Emphasizing the link between women as producers and women in family roles, these theories help us understand why women agreed to farm the northern plains with their husbands—or agreed to marry farmers in the first place. They worked in a family setting, not only with their husbands and children, but often with parents, in-laws, and siblings, and they had help with heavy seasonal labor, with childcare, and in times of extraordinary need. Family ties were strong, and women's economic and social roles were the heart of the community.[67]

Those who settled on the northern plains viewed urban life and industrial work as threats to their treasured values. The deepening divide between the urban/industrial and the rural/agrarian economies was most visible in women's roles. As the industrial economy began to replace the agrarian economy, middle-class reformers and trade unionists argued that women were too delicate for long hours of hard factory labor, that such work led to the deterioration of families and of women's health. As women became more closely associated with household matters and child rearing, their productive role weakened and the importance of their social role increased. But those who farmed during this transition continued to view women as workers who made an important economic contribution to the family. Land ownership and the independence of farming provided financial security and family continuity in a stable community. Farm folk believed that urban factory or domestic work could not support these values, and their views

were often confirmed by negative reports about factory conditions for
women and children.[68]

One additional factor, perhaps more significant because it was important to pioneer women and their contemporaries, is the value of productive work. Charlotte Perkins Gilman believed that women should
have equal opportunity for economic independence, that they should
not have to rely on men's generosity for their basic material needs. Herbert Quick, writing about farm women for *Good Housekeeping* magazine in 1913, adopted Gilman's theory when he contrasted the productivity of urban women to that of their rural counterparts:

> Women of the cities complain that they have lost their economic use-
> fulness in the household and demand a share in the productive work of
> the world. No such wail ever arises from the women of the farm. Their
> hands are full of necessary and productive work from morning till
> night.

Farm women were not only workers but also producers. They made
products to hold in their hands, to trade, to sell, to display, to admire.
They felt the pride of accomplishment and the satisfaction of supporting themselves and their families even when the field crops failed.
They were not "gossamer embodiments" of womanhood. Though
there was some conflict between the concepts of women as productive
and as exploited workers, the productivity of farm women earned them
the respect of their families, their neighbors, and many observers.[69]

Married couples brought to farming the proper complement of labor and skills, as August Bauer perhaps intended to indicate when he
listed his wife along with his horses and plow. Lena Bauer worked beside her husband in the fields, prepared meals, cared for livestock, and
bore six sons and three daughters. By 1930, the Bauers owned 800
acres and sixty head of horses and cattle. The work Lena Bauer and
other women did on pioneer farms was essential to the business of establishing commercial agriculture on the northern plains. It meant that
families would stay in North Dakota and that attendant and necessary
growth would take place.[70]

4

"Many Dear Friends" & "Notorious Horse Thieves"
Creating Community

I heard a rooster crow this morning. We have a neighbor.
KATIE ULMER ROTH

As Katie Ulmer Roth described her parents' first months on their homestead claim, she told of difficulties facing three families: a couple with their two grown sons and daughters-in-law living for four months in holes dug under overturned wagons, where two of the women gave birth. They lived seventy-five miles from the nearest trading town. Though there were six adults related by blood and marriage, they craved a broader community. It is easy to understand Roth's "mother being most elated, gleefully remarking" on the single sign—the crowing of a rooster—that a community would grow around them.[1]

Neither the Homestead Act and other federal land laws nor the territorial and state governments offered settlers assistance in establishing communities on the plains. Land laws encouraged independence by allowing homesteaders to acquire quickly and cheaply up to three quarter sections, or 480 acres. Indeed, by 1900 the average size of a North Dakota farm was 349 acres. Many homesteaders acquired more land through purchase, and by 1930 the average North Dakota farm covered 496 acres. A farm might easily be twenty miles from the nearest town and as distant as sixty or seventy miles from a market town where grain could be sold. A polyglot population also isolated some settlers. Despite these realities, North Dakota was not a frontier of rugged individuals: community building began immediately upon arrival. No matter the official government position on the qualities of yeomanry, Dakota settlers shaped communities that reflected their needs and values.[2]

Rural communities were not necessarily focused on towns: town people and rural people had little in common beyond trade. "Community" in settlement-era rural North Dakota was a self-defined association of friends and neighbors (some related by blood or marriage) who shared an interest in the agricultural economy and in the establishment of schools and churches as well as a commitment to common social and political events and a concern for each other's welfare. The geographical boundaries of these communities did not always coincide with townships, school districts, or other legal delineations.

Pioneer-created communities differed according to geography, population density, and members' cultures and perceptions. Factors defining a community included institutions such as churches and schools, events such as harvest and Fourth of July picnics, and personal encounters such as midwifery and the sheltering of strangers. Creating community was like weaving cloth: each thread depended on the others for strength, but certain kinds of thread were more durable or more visible than others. The fabric's weave might be plain, with all threads the same size and color, or varied, with an occasional thread of a different weight or hue that did not change the fabric's substance but added something to its appearance or function. Communities had to be flexible in accommodating members who did not match the other threads but who needed to belong or offered some essential quality. However, even the most heterogeneous community had boundaries; members knew who fit in and who did not, even if the determining factor was only a vague sense of physical or social distance.[3]

In discussing rural communities, some historians have found membership and participation to be distinctly gendered, with men's contributions to community based on their economic and political roles and women's developed through social connections. In her study of New York's Nanticoke Valley, Nancy Grey Osterud finds that men formed community associations through their common interests as "citizens, taxpayers and economic agents." Women, on the other hand, entered the community through kinship associations, which, Osterud suggests, allowed them to interact informally with men. Studying a northern plains community, Seena B. Kohl found a similar separation: in southern Saskatchewan, community developed through men's work exchanges and through women's social relationships involving kin and neighbors.[4]

In North Dakota, settlers built communities through a variety of activities, many of them gendered but occurring in a context reflective of the intricately interlocked farm work of men and women. Men shaped political and religious institutions, acted as land agents and locators, and exchanged labor and equipment. Seldom responsible for the care of small children, they moved easily about the neighborhood, the township, and the county. In town, they mingled with other men at the grain elevator, livery, and saloon. In rural townships, they sat on church and school boards. These activities created bonds that tended to stabilize communities in the face of shifting fortunes endured during early settlement years. But such connections, while essential to community development, were not exclusively men's domain. Women created and sustained community through exchanges of labor and equipment; through neighborhood social, educational, and religious activities; through care of the sick; through participation in woman-centered societies; and through personal and communal relationships with women and men. Women's activities occurred simultaneously with men's community-building work or provided a foundation for their political, religious, social, and economic pursuits. It is impossible to ignore the significance of women's roles in the settlement community or to separate them from those of men. Some institutions or events were labeled "male" or "female," but a closer examination reveals the intertwining of sex roles in establishing and maintaining community.

Women settling Dakota homesteads established community through a complex of activities that included sheltering newcomers; boarding teachers and itinerant preachers; sharing equipment and neighborhood responsibilities; caring for women in childbirth as well as for orphaned children and the sick; contributing to school and church activities; hosting or attending social gatherings; and participating in formal and informal organizations. Some of these activities centered on women and their work; others involved a mix of neighborhood men and women. Even the so-called male-dominated arenas of church and politics depended on close cooperation with women's organizations. In settlers' communities, only the saloon remained an all-male province, and even it yielded on at least one occasion to women's demands.

Community builders' first task was to establish contact with neighbors who could offer support as they built houses and broke fields for planting. To hear a rooster crow, even before laying eyes on new neighbors, was heart-lifting. Distances between farms and to even the smallest of towns were daunting for some pioneers, who had to adjust to entirely new concepts of community compared to what they had known in their homelands. In Norway, the community was often contiguous with the valley in which the farm families lived. In South Russia, the village was the foundation of community. Though delighted with the opportunity to claim land in Dakota, Black Sea Germans and Ukrainians were not pleased with the social circumstances of homesteading. Sometimes four families located their houses at the point where four quarter sections met, but this arrangement did not yield a village. More often, selection of the quarter section and the house site were determined by the landscape rather than by the proximity of family and friends. Houses could not be built in a slough or on the best piece of arable land, for example.[5]

In fact, so scattered were prairie houses and towns that when Black Sea German immigrant Magdalena Job got off the train at Medina in 1914, she was shocked by what she saw. "There was nothing," she em-

Family gathered by house. The neighboring farm at the far right horizon indicates distance between homes.

phatically stated seventy-six years later. The little town, the railroad, even her sister's home did not possess the qualities she associated with community. In South Russia, the village supported family life and provided extra labor when needed, clerics established and enforced standards of behavior, and elderly men and women shared their wisdom and skills. All of these activities took place within the confines of the village. When Fred Marzolf arrived in McLean County in 1911, he thought the settlement pattern could not sustain life, much less community. "When I first came here," he said, "I could not see how it was possible to live[,] the farms were so far apart."[6]

To lessen their isolation, homesteaders encouraged newcomers to settle nearby. Often families stayed at an established farm while one of the group continued on to find a suitable piece of land to claim. Most travelers were welcomed into a settler's house no matter how crowded their additional numbers made it. A warm place to sleep and a good meal in a friendly household went a long way toward convincing prospective settlers to locate in the vicinity. Mrs. Frank Davison remembered,

> [the] Land Company located my mother, a widow, on a claim half way between Richardton and Mott in 1904 before the main rush of people into Adams County in order that they might have a place to stop with land seekers for dinners and night lodging.

In this mutually advantageous situation, Mrs. Davison's mother received a home with land and the land company had a place to make newcomers feel comfortable.[7]

Feeding new arrivals was a social obligation as well as a means of building community, so most women happily opened their simple homes to travelers, offering whatever comforts they could in the hope that some would choose to become neighbors. Betsy Lekvold Bakke found that the appearance of newcomers broke the "monotony of the prairies and the humdrum everyday tasks." By all accounts, women did the work of sheltering prospective homesteaders. They made the beds and prepared the meals, drawing on the part of the farm economy they controlled—their own labor and the produce of garden and barnyard. Some homes became known as friendly stopping places. The Esler ranch in Stutsman County offered shelter for homestead seekers for weeks at a time and was often full of travelers. Elizabeth Warner Bechtel, a Canadian immigrant to Pembina County, opened her home to Icelanders arriving in large numbers from their failed settlement in Gimli, Manitoba. She provided meals and lodging to fifty-six people during the migration and sent them on their way with a supply of food. Most of the Icelanders chose to remain in Pembina County.[8]

Providing for the needs of these new neighbors until they could move onto their claims could prove overwhelming. Charlotta Lundquist Leidholm arrived in McLean County in 1887 with her husband and three other families of relatives and friends, fourteen people altogether. This crowd took shelter with the Meyer family for two days while a blizzard prevented them from traveling and stayed with two more families before arriving at their own claims several days later.[9]

Some of these encounters led not just to new neighbors but to enduring friendships. Alice Ransier Barrington walked "miles" across the prairie with a baby in her arms to welcome the Blair family; she and Mrs. Blair remained lifelong friends. Other interactions were simply acts of human decency, expected of all homesteaders but posing social problems few were prepared to resolve. An overnight stay did little to change anyone's mind about intercultural relations, for example. Annie Julia Schwalier Reuter welcomed all travelers into her house, even "notorious horse thieves," but not Indians, to whom she would only pass food through the window. Christian Klaudt, a Black Sea German of the Lutheran faith, stopped for a rest with Catholic Black Sea Germans in McIntosh County; they told him of other Protestants located to the southeast. The encounter was polite, but both families were inclined to settle with people who shared not only their language and heritage but also their faith.[10]

The presence of so many people who were foreign in language, religion, dress, and custom—and who often considered those of other nationalities to be inferior—enhanced the sense of isolation that settlers sought to correct by creating communities. Some located in neighborhoods that were ethnically pure, but for others "community" was not the same as "neighborhood"—proximity alone did not create community. Jennie Pratt Codding, who moved to Barnes County from Michigan in 1883, wrote much later of her community, explaining it in terms of neighbors, though not all of them lived in her neighborhood:

It did seem as though I could not stay here and I do not think I could if I had not had such good neighbors. Of course, some of them were a good distance away, but were neighbors just the same. And nearly all came from southern Michigan same as we did.

The Coddings included as "neighbors" some who lived twenty-five miles away, but their nearest neighbors in proximity were Mr. and Mrs. Adoph Nelson from Sweden. While the children of the two families became friends in school, Codding noted that she and Mrs. Nelson did not because of differences in language. When Mrs. Codding passed the graves of two small Nelson children who had died on the homestead, she regretted that she had been unable to comfort Mrs. Nelson in her loss.[11]

In some areas of the territory, especially during the Great Dakota Boom, community development was stalled by a constant turnover of settlers. Bertha Daniels Brown could count on few permanent neighbors when she and her husband claimed a homestead in Ramsey County in 1884. Settlers moved in, stayed a few months, borrowed money, and left—a pattern that demonstrates the homestead system's vulnerability to speculation. Loan agent Seth Humphrey noted this tendency in South Dakota when he tried to locate farmers who had borrowed from his company, often finding only the remains of a sod house slowly returning to the prairie. European immigrants established more stable communities, however: being interested in land ownership rather than in short-term profits, they were more likely to stay during both the boom and the lean years that followed. Indeed, many European immigrants spent all of their money to get to Dakota Territory and could not afford to return even if they found prospects for success on the plains to be sorely disappointing.[12]

Once settlers had established their claims and moved into some sort of shelter, they set about organizing the community and overseeing basic requirements for its security and stability. Women participated fully in these activities, sometimes dealing only with neighboring women, sometimes functioning as part of the larger whole. A woman known only as "Eittah" wrote to the *McLean County Mail* in 1887 to suggest that women use the newspaper as a forum for the "exchange of ideas" and offered a recipe for Frontier Cake, made with ingredients easily available to North Dakota pioneers. She encouraged women struggling with settlement to write to the newspaper: "In this way we [will] be able to help each other out of some of the difficulties that beset us so thickly in this new country of ours." Eittah's approach to the challenge of creating community reflects her experience in American middle-class women's associations, which typically utilized collective efforts to educate and support as well as to foster social change. But as the community of Steele County's Newburgh Township faced a more immediate problem, women's roles were not any different from those of men. During the fire season, all neighbors—women included—took turns staying up to watch for prairie fire. On Brita Berg's watch, fire first approached the community. Berg roused her family and the neighbors, and women and men fought the blaze together until nine o'clock the next morning.[13]

Neighborhood exchanges of labor and equipment were fundamental to creating community. Women's interactions were somewhat different from men's but equally important in establishing bonds. Mrs. Abraham Nelson remembered how, despite the distance between farms, "we women used to cooperate with each other and would work together and often on different problems." Cooking for threshing crews was women's most common cooperative activity. Every September, Isabella Roberts helped her nearest neighbor prepare food for the threshers and then fed them in her own home. During her first year on the claim, when crops were small, she spent only a day or two working in someone else's home, but by 1887, her fourth harvest in Ramsey County, Roberts cooked for threshers on her own farm and on the Van Dusen farm almost every day from September 27 to October 27.[14]

In some communities, cooperation brought women together more frequently. For example, throughout the summer of 1888 in McIntosh County, six families baked bread in an outdoor clay-brick oven, the only one in the neighborhood. The women carried bread dough to the Kroll farm, where they spent the day baking. Community use of the Kroll oven maintained the food supply so that time and labor could be turned instead to breaking sod, planting crops, and building houses and barns on those six farms.[15]

Exchanging farm equipment was a common form of interaction between men, but most of the tools of women's work did not travel easily. Women cooked on primitive stoves and milked by hand. Though cream separators were available, impoverished settlers seldom saw the advantage of buying the machine when cream in a shallow pan would rise of its own accord. As farms matured and cash became more abundant, women began to acquire technologically advanced stoves—kitchen ranges that stayed in the house and were never lent. Sewing machines, however, could travel about the neighborhood, linking women and establishing community boundaries and hierarchies. Gunhild Grimsrud's sewing machine, brought from Norway in 1888, had "many stone boat rides because it was the only one around." Sewing machines were lent without charge because they were so useful in completing a basic chore, and, unlike stoves, butter churns, and some other household equipment, they could be shared because they were not in daily use. If a woman had both a machine and the time to sew for others, she could charge a fee for her work: her skilled labor had a value exceeding that of the machine. Ingeborg Larson willingly lent her machine, but if she sewed for neighbors she took their labor in exchange. For helping neighbors with their sewing, Mrs. Abraham Nelson once received a heifer calf, a profitable trade because "it would in time mean another cow." Karen Oien Bjorlie and Jane Fulton Burnett sewed for cash income: Bjorlie bought seed and livestock feed for the farm, while Burnett, a widow, used this income to commute her homestead. Sewing machines were generally considered important investments: having the only one in the area enhanced a woman's social status. These intricately woven exchanges of equipment and labor among women as well as men—carefully balanced between economic necessity and advantage while drawing in the threads of social order—created the fabric of community.[16]

Visiting and sharing supplies and equipment laid the foundation for further community organization. Simple acts of neighborliness helped to cement community relations and to define boundaries. Mary Baxter Cannell brought the first houseplants to her Benson County neighborhood and distributed cuttings from the plants, later noting that they "gained many dear friends for us." Susannah Preece Bonde sent for rhubarb plants and gave some away to her Foster County neighbors. Isabella Roberts visited weekly with neighbors and often had overnight guests.[17]

Birth and death and the rituals attached to them often created bonds among pioneers who did not yet know their neighbors or how their communities would develop. Death, especially if unexpected, broke down cultural barriers that might otherwise have been viewed as insurmountable. When a new settler, a Yankee named Williams, died before his family's shelter was complete, Swedish homesteaders named Christianson paid for Williams's funeral and provided food and shelter for his family until Mr. Christianson finished their dugout. In McLean County, the recently arrived Mrs. Eschenko sought neighbors' assistance with her baby's burial because her husband was working away from the claim and she wanted someone to construct a coffin. She walked to the nearest neighbor, but there, too, the woman was alone and had nothing to offer. Mrs. Eschenko then walked four miles farther to another homestead, where the owner agreed to build a coffin if she had boards and nails. She offered a board off the roof of her dugout but

Marie Gjevre and Kari Erickson sew while Ole Gjevre plays guitar. Sewing machines were important economic and social assets for pioneering women.

had no nails, so the neighbor set out for the Eschenko home while she walked another mile to ask for nails. The neighbors thus involved constructed the coffin, prepared the child's body, and dug the grave. The new community, as in so many others spread out across the prairie, began its life with the burial of one of its members.[18]

However, some pioneers let their fear of strangers interfere with ordinary acts of kindness that would begin the process of community building. When Mary Elizabeth Madden Collins's sister died, Jerry Collins went to their only neighbors in search of a woman to help prepare the body for burial. Fearing that the stranger had died of a contagious disease, the neighbors refused to help. Collins had to travel seven miles to the nearest town to find "a couple of women to go out to us."[19]

Birth, like death, brought strangers together, creating bonds that strengthened communities. Attending women in childbirth—almost exclusively the work of women—created an "impressive network" that was "renewed each time a woman went into labor." Bertha Daniels Brown, who gave birth to five children on her homestead, was fortunate to have as her only neighbor for some time "Grandma" Fogarty, a competent midwife. The presence of other women during birth was important to those who discounted the help of their husbands and even that of trained medical doctors. Minnie Witkop Barr did not see a woman for nine months after she and her husband took land in Barnes County, and when the first of her eleven children was born, "no woman was there to help—just the doctor and her husband." Minnie Barr's idea of community included women who could attend her in childbirth.[20]

Some immigrant women had been trained as midwives in Europe. Those with good reputations were likely to be called to attend all varieties of illness and injury. Norwegian immigrant Dorotheo Jensen Christofferson "cured ailments of the mind and body, even homesickness," a skill likely to be in great demand among homesteaders trying to adapt to new circumstances. Gudrun Jonsdottir, who had trained with a doctor in her native Iceland, skillfully set broken bones and treated infected wounds and internal injuries with a small pharmacy. Angeline Peranto Carter cared for sick neighbors with little more than compassion and the pail of soup she carried to every home that called upon her services.[21]

Women with medical skills often extended community boundaries to include people marginalized by race or by culture. Mrs. Ole Stokka served as midwife in Griggs County, and while many of her patients were, like her, Norwegian, she was often called to Yankee homes, where she fulfilled her duties though she could not understand English nor her patients *Norsk*. Similarly, when Mrs. J. C. Fay, a Yankee American pioneer, received a Norwegian woman who brought a piece of beef to pay for medicine, the visitor explained "through much pantomime . . . that some one had a fever so [Fay] produced the belladonna, and aconite" needed for treatment. Gudrun Jonsdottir attended patients of varied nationalities in her community using only the "language of sympathy and the understanding of human need." A woman of unusually flexible social standards, she showed no reluctance to treat Métis patients, explaining to her curious daughter that even the dark skinned were "God's children."[22]

Moving beyond economic or social interests, electoral politics formed a secondary community, one defined by political boundaries. As communities began to organize politically, men elected township and county officials and legislators. After 1883, both sexes participated in school district politics. Documentation indicates that women did vote on school issues, though their rate of participation suggests some reluctance, perhaps in part due to particular communities' resistance to woman suffrage. The Greendale Township School District (Griggs County) record for the June 19, 1894, school election lists 87 women voters out of a total 273. At a ratio of three to one, this figure probably does not represent all of the district's possible women voters. There is, however, no indication that women of certain ethnic groups did not vote or were prevented from voting: names on the list represent people of Swedish, Norwegian, German, Irish, and English heritage. In one McLean County community of Black Sea Germans, however, cultural traditions apparently held sway over women's political activities. One community member recalled that women did not participate in school-board activities: "No women was suppose[d] to come [to school meetings] and they didn't. That was all for men."[23]

School suffrage gave women access to public office. In 1887, the *McLean County Mail* listed thirteen women acting as county superintendents of schools in Dakota Territory. Four were located in the northern part of the territory; of those, three were married. Women also held seats on school boards. The perspective of one of these women, Anna Esby, suggests that she viewed such service as a family responsibility, an extension of a woman's role. Upon her husband's death, Esby was appointed to his position on a rural Barnes County school board. A few years later, when her son was ready to assume that position in society, she yielded her seat to him. Though she served for several years and presumably performed adequately enough to be re-elected, her position on the board functioned to secure her family's place in community politics rather than to promote her own political interests.[24]

In North Dakota, full woman suffrage did not enjoy sustained interest or the support of vital organizations until 1912. The Woman's Christian Temperance Union (WCTU), led for many years by Elizabeth Preston Anderson, maintained an interest in woman suffrage as part of its vigilance over the constitutional prohibition of alcohol. But the WCTU snubbed immigrant women and never tried to organize rural women, assuming that they lacked interest and were too isolated to be effectively assembled. Anti-rural sentiment, typified by one city dweller's reference to "the little 'Mother' in the sod shanties out on the prairies," prevented urban women from seeing their rural counterparts as allies, as intelligent women with strong credentials in community organization, as the source of change in rural communities.[25]

Votes for Women clubs formed in Grand Forks and Fargo in 1912, holding annual conventions and blaming the German vote for the failure of periodic suffrage bills. Their campaign received a big boost from the Nonpartisan League (NPL), which essentially took over state government in 1916 and as part of its platform promised a woman suffrage bill. The Votes for Women clubs arranged to have most of the state's newspapers print a special suffrage edition in 1917. These papers would have reached a fair number of rural women, but there is no evidence of a rural woman suffrage movement. In fact, as noted by an editor of the *Grand Forks Herald*, "the great mass of the people of North Dakota, men and women, were impassive." The 1917 bill passed by the legislature granted women the right to vote for presidential electors, county surveyors, county constables, and most officers of cities, towns, and villages.[26]

The NPL held contradictory views as to women's public role, however. Before 1917, women could be league members only if married to a leaguer. In 1919, their role was formally distinguished by the creation of a woman's auxiliary, in effect removing them from the NPL's more public activities. The league saw women's votes as a means of countering those of urban women, who were likely to be hostile toward the NPL. Members of the women's auxiliary used concepts similar to those of urban suffragists as they encouraged rural women to vote, saying that voters would raise better children more devoted to their mothers and that voters would be more attractive and interesting companions to their husbands. The "impassive" response noted by the *Herald* editor suggests that the NPL and its women's auxiliary were no closer to identifying rural women's interests than were the urban Votes for Women clubs. Rural women voted their interests but also valued direct political action through community associations.[27]

Though rural women did not demonstrate an interest in electoral politics beyond school matters, and though they found themselves generally excluded from formal organizations devoted to political activity, they did draw on neighborhood associations—formed through kinship, midwifery, and agricultural economies—to promote or protect their interests. The events of a single afternoon demonstrate that rural immigrant women were not ignorant of their collective power to influence the political and economic order of their communities.

On January 10, 1890, a group of farm women attacked the saloons of Hatton in western Traill County using axes, hammers, and long sticks. They broke whiskey bottles and smashed kegs and kept at it until "their shoes and long skirts were wet" with liquor. The saloons did not close, however: they remained open until July, when the state's prohibition law mandated their closure. But the women had made their point. The saloons threatened the rural community by encouraging farmers to spend their money on alcohol. If they then lost their farms, their families faced poverty, and if they were forced to move away, the solidly Norwegian community would be weakened. The cultural loss for both the community and the family would be tragic to first-generation immigrants. The women had a clear understanding of the relationship between their personal situations and public activity, between the financial stability of their farms and the continuity of their culturally homogeneous community.[28]

The ties binding these women had been forged in the realities of their homesteading experiences. Most of the women were near neighbors; some attended the same church; some were related by blood or marriage. They comforted each other in grief and despair; they sheltered one another when necessary. Their children had worked for pay in neighbors' homes and fields, and their daughters had, as a matter of course, kept house for women who had recently given birth. These sisters, friends, and neighbors organized informally to shape the community in ways that suited them, but they did not intend to reorder society along egalitarian lines. The saloons stayed open and the women remained married to men who drank too much, but the town of Hatton acknowledged their actions with approval and accepted their right to curb the saloons' excesses.[29]

The saloon smashing in Hatton was extraordinary. There is no evidence of other North Dakota pioneer women taking such extreme action to shape the nature of their communities. These women came together with a common purpose that was clearly identified as both social and economic, and they acted communally to achieve their goals, both personal and communal. The farm women of rural Hatton attacked the saloons because they had identified them as places where underhanded deals were made, as places of lawlessness that threatened their homes, their financial security, and their community. Through informal alliance they shaped the community to their requirements, and through collective action they imposed those requirements on a town they recognized as an extension of their rural community.

Interlocking with these informal networks was one highly significant organization that gave women a stronger voice in community affairs and allowed them to expand their interests and influence beyond the boundaries of their rural communities. This organization was the Ladies' Aid Society. Norwegian Lutheran women's organizations were generally called by that name, Methodists termed them the Women's Home Mission Society, and Catholic women joined the Christian Mother Society or the Altar (or Altar and Rosary) Society, but they were all commonly referred to as Ladies' Aid. Though officially based in a local Christian congregation, Ladies' Aid also functioned as a community organization. Ann Firor Scott has written that voluntary associations gave nineteenth-century American women a public role through which they exercised social power and challenged social norms. On the rural northern plains, Ladies' Aid Societies followed that pattern, demonstrating that women controlled their time, labor, money, and collective power to promote a subtle form of gender equity in their communities. Ladies' Aid activities strengthened the church, extended its influence into the entire community, established a system of social control, and placed women-centered, women-controlled events at the heart of public life.[30]

Many Protestant congregations got their start in pioneers' homes, with members organizing and incorporating their churches before calling for a minister. Except for Catholic congregations—their formation directed by the Fargo or Bismarck dioceses—and a few Baptist and Presbyterian missionary efforts, rural churches grew out of the needs and traditions of their members. Women's organizations evolved with the same sense of participation and ownership. Sometimes women formed Ladies' Aid Societies weeks before the congregation organized, thereby serving, in a sense, as midwives to their local church.

Ladies' Aids usually organized as soon as several families established claims in a neighborhood. Members were usually of the same nationality and religious affiliation, though there were some exceptions. Ladies' Aids often formed earlier among rural women than among their counterparts in town, and sometimes town dwellers traveled to rural homes for meetings. Women enjoyed the social aspects of these gatherings, which provided an important break in the work and isolation of homestead life. Ladies' Aids also allowed women to participate actively in church decision making through fund raising and to assert influence over community activities and politics through sponsored events.[31]

Aids of all faiths typically met monthly—all day during the winter, in the evenings during the summer—to sew and knit "aprons, men's shirts, underwear and children's clothing" and sometimes quilts to be sold at public auction. Members usually paid dues ranging from five to twenty-five cents or paid a small fee for their lunch. While the treasury grew with these steady additions, auctions yielded significant income. Even in a cash-poor society that reeled at times from drought and low commodity prices, Ladies' Aids could generate impressive amounts of money. The Froen Aid estimated that its members raised more than $10,000 in small increments through persistent efforts over a period of forty-six years. In 1889, a bedspread knitted by six women of the Bruflat Ladies' Aid sold at auction for five dollars—a small amount, but during one of the worst years for North Dakota farmers, that five dollars came from one person's pocket.[32]

Democratic practices prevailed in Ladies' Aid Societies. Members elected a president who, according to the historian of the Bruflat Ladies' Aid, was responsible for arranging meetings, keeping order, upholding the constitution, purchasing and distributing material, and storing finished pieces. Through these tasks women gained experience in handling money, in organizing community resources, and in American political practices. Presidents and treasurers managed the money and distributed supplies so that every member, no matter her personal financial status, had projects to work on for the annual auction. In one example of leadership, when the Froen Aid, organized in 1881, did not have a source of funds to launch its first projects, the president, Mrs. Didrick Pederson, went to Fargo and, using the good name of the Ladies' Aid Society, bought twenty dollars worth of fabric—several bolts—on credit. After the first auction, Pederson paid off the account and bought more fabric for the next round of sewing.[33]

Women's intentions to shape their communities through Ladies' Aid were evident in the events they designed to raise money for their churches. Almost every Aid sponsored an annual picnic and a fall supper, usually timed to coincide with other community celebrations such as the Fourth of July. Welcomed at these events were the entire community and visitors from other neighborhoods, not just families of the congregation, though in many places the congregation and the community were nearly identical. The historian of the Froen Ladies' Aid recalled that "people from nearby communities came here to celebrate the Fourth [of July] and meet old friends and make new ones," and she described a celebration that included pastor-led devotions, choir and community singing, patriotic speeches, ball games, supper, and a fund-raising auction. Mrs. Maurer, a founding member of the Altar Society of Starkweather's Assumption of Mary Church, hosted in her home a supper open to all friends and neighbors, Catholic and Protestant; her Altar Society compatriots donated food and then turned over the money to the church. These public events unified a community scattered over miles and across township lines. Picnics and autumn harvest suppers also provided a forum for local politicians to campaign for election.[34]

Societies tailored their fund-raising events to the community. One Aid served lunch to voters on election day in 1888, raising money for the church while also suggesting that those who enjoyed the meal might vote in favor of the prohibition issue on the ballot. More subtle was women's political role in the picnic and harvest supper, celebrations at which women took a service position. Through picnics and auctions, church women gained control of some of the community's expendable money and directed it to support institutions they preferred. This money would not be spent at saloons or on other profligate activities; instead it would primarily support local congregations and parochial schools and their attendant social functions.[35]

While raising money for the church was the central activity of Ladies' Aid Societies, they also performed a secondary but important function. At church picnics and suppers, settlers celebrated their ethnic traditions by singing familiar songs and by reciting stories and poems of their homeland. They shared letters from relatives who had not emigrated and met newcomers who infused a fresh dose of Old Country culture into the community, helping defer the trend toward Americanization. Traditional holiday food was served: Norwegians prepared *lutefisk, lefse,* and *rømmegrot;* Black Sea Germans, *borscht* and *kuchen.* Though the festive celebrations and church services were open to settlers who did not share the congregation's ethnicity, no effort was made to accommodate them culturally. Thus, Ladies' Aid events established the dominant culture of the community.[36]

Historians have suggested that maintenance of cultural characteristics in the church helped ease the transition to American life. In worship services and at social events, settlers spoke the language of their homelands, which in America became the "language of the heart." Seeking to retain cultural heritage in their younger members, most immigrant churches provided at least three months of parochial school for religious education, at the same time offering students an opportunity to practice the language they were beginning to forget as they progressed through public schools. Robert C. Ostergren has pointed out that the immigrant church was the institution that preserved cultural identity in rural communities. As culturally homogeneous congregations celebrated immigrant cultures, they also established one of the exclusionary boundaries of rural communities.[37]

In Jewish and Islamic communities, the religious cultural center was far more challenging to establish. Because rabbis and practitioners of rites such as the *shochet* and *mohel* were rarely available in rural areas, Jewish religious services took place in homes and many traditions were difficult to maintain. Lacking a *shochet* to perform the ritual kosher slaughter, Jewish settlers sometimes ate no meat for years. Gittel Turnoy's husband built a *mikvah* for her use, but these were rare in North Dakota rural communities. While Jewish settlers lacked the sustaining embrace of a larger community of believers, Islamic Syrians were even more isolated in their religious practices. The small Islamic community—its members living mostly in or near Williams County—was fractured by frequent moves and by people leaving the area to earn a living as peddlers. Construction of a mosque was begun but never completed. If the absence of a close-knit community weighed heavily on women who settled in North Dakota, the burden was much greater for Jewish and Islamic women. They could maintain their personal faith and endeavor to raise their children in the precepts of their religion, but they could not create a community of faith where so few people shared their culture.[38]

Regardless of denomination or cultural origin, the church was a male-dominated institution. Men were ministers and council members. Women had no say in church affairs other than through their husbands; thus, the voices of single women, widows, and those whose husbands did not attend church were necessarily excluded. Women were not represented at state Methodist Episcopal Conferences, where committees composed of ministers supervised funds raised by the Ladies' Aids. These same Ladies' Aids did not have an official voice in church business or on theological matters. However, women found they could make demands through their control of a major source of pioneer church funding—the Ladies' Aid treasury. Women asked that social rooms be added to the church and secured the council's consent by donating Ladies' Aid funds for construction. Sometimes Ladies' Aids promoted the use of English in immigrant churches through the purchase of English-language hymnals. In 1888, the Beaver Creek Ladies' Aid used the power of the purse to influence a major decision, specifying that the church must join the new synod, the United Norwegian Lutheran Church of America, or the aid would withdraw its financial support from the congregation. The question of union among the Lutheran synods was very divisive—some congregations or their members refused to accept the new arrangement—but members of the Beaver Creek Ladies' Aid forced the congregation to accept their position through their control of a significant portion of the church's funds.[39]

Male leaders of the congregations responded to the Ladies' Aids' assertions in various ways. When the Ostervold Lutheran Church constructed a basement for the church building and the congregations' two Ladies' Aid Societies decided to unite, the "men graciously allowed" the new, larger society to use the basement, half the cost of which had been provided by the women's fund-raising activities. The council of New Salem's German Evangelical Church used similar rhetorical tricks in an effort to limit the perceived power of the women's group. In 1899, the council noted that "the offer of the Women's Society to buy a pipe organ for the church was accepted"; a few years later, council minutes recorded that its members had "given permission [to the Women's Society] to furnish a furnace for the church."[40]

Collectively, using the power of the money they raised, women were able to make demands on the church. Individually, women drew on this power to assert their right to participate in Ladies' Aid. Most men recognized the importance of Ladies' Aid Societies for the support of the local congregation and community, but individually some demonstrated hostility. The Trondenes Aid's historian quietly stated that "not all men favored women's activities." Meetings took women away from house- and field work; supper on meeting night might consist solely of cold potatoes. Aurdal Church's historian wrote that although men disapproved of women's meetings, they supported the goal of raising money for the church. Wielding control in the church when their authority at home was threatened enabled men to maintain fictive dominance of both church and home when women walked off to meetings.[41]

In his study of Norwegians who immigrated from Balestrand to Wisconsin, Jon Gjerde states that women in Wisconsin organized and worked for Ladies' Aid Societies in their leisure time and created a new public role for themselves in the process. Gjerde concludes, however, that the impact of this role was diminished by the fact that women gathered in the name of the church to do traditional textile handwork. The situation was a little different in settlement-era North Dakota, where women rarely knew leisure time and could only manage to attend Aid meetings if they rose early to finish their regular chores beforehand. Sewing and cooking may have been traditional women's work, but the results earned women not only a public role but also a position from which they could shape the nature of gender roles and relations in their new communities.[42]

Distance was only a fact, not an obstacle, for pioneer women determined to attend Ladies' Aid meetings. Some traveled by buggy as many as eighteen miles. If a man was thoughtless in not providing transportation, or purposefully denied any means of travel, or was using all the horses and oxen in the field, women found alternative ways to get to meetings. A rural Aneta woman took a hayrake drawn by a pair of oxen to the Norway Church Ladies' Aid meeting. Mrs. Heskin rode a wild colt—the only option left to her—to an 1888 meeting; since she carried a satchel containing the yard goods for the day's work, her presence was worth the risk of mounting an untrained horse. In 1896, Mrs. Ole Gronlie walked one and one-half miles to a meeting, carrying her youngest child and a bag of fabric while two other children toddled behind. Women did not allow travel time to be spent idly if their hands were free: many knitted as they walked, perhaps to justify the time taken from housework. One woman said, "The faster I walk, the faster I knit."[43]

Some Ladies' Aid meetings included men who may have participated in the devotions, but usually men's informal gatherings were separate from women's formal meetings and work sessions. In her study of colonial women, Laurel Thatcher Ulrich described women who took their husbands' place in business or family matters as "deputy husbands." In an interesting turnabout, the significance of the Ladies' Aid Society in pioneer communities is heightened by the Aneta Norway Aid's decision in 1896 that if a woman had to miss a meeting for a valid reason, her husband had to attend and act in her place.[44]

Ladies' Aids were usually successful in maintaining autonomy and in leading the congregation on some matters, but a woman's direct

Women, men, and children attended Ladies' Aid Society meetings such as this one at Schollsmade.

challenge to male authority in religious activities or to accepted community gender roles was not well tolerated. In the Norwegian Lutheran communities of Steele and Traill Counties, a young itinerant preacher, Lena Myrold, raised the question of a woman's right to speak in church. Myrold appeared from time to time, singing and preaching a simple message of love, but she was not allowed to preach in the churches. She conducted revivals in schools and homes that filled to overflowing with worshippers curious about a woman preacher. Her services drew people from miles around who bought her songbooks and repeated her phrase, "Have you found peace?" In 1898, while she was preaching in the Northwood area, men began to condemn Myrold for taking a public role, telling her, "You ought to be at home attending to your housework!" Her presence divided the community and contributed to discord within one congregation.[45]

Lena Myrold's revivals brought into focus the communal and religious constraints that allowed Ladies' Aids to take a leadership role in church and community while remaining at least nominally under the control of men. The problem Myrold posed in this gender arrangement was clearly understood by those who told her to tend her housework. She was outside the control of the only two institutions that had any social power in a settlement community—the home and the church. Neither married nor ordained, she followed only her heart and her spirit. Ladies' Aids organized within the church, supposedly under the direction of the pastor or the council, and were assumed to be operating within society's norms. Women linked to an Aid Society could be visible and active in community and church affairs without posing a direct challenge to male authority because they were burdened with household, family, and farm responsibilities and because they accepted the official leadership of men in the church. Myrold probably would not have proposed any different social arrangements, but her personal status and her vocation gave many men cause to fear social disorder resulting from her revivals.

The relationship of Ladies' Aid Societies with bachelors illustrates the extent of church women's influence in establishing social order in settlement communities. Bachelors as a generic group or as individuals show up regularly in Ladies' Aid histories or in members' memoirs. Interactions between bachelors and Aid Societies illuminate members' power to assert some control over community resources and social events. Society members targeted bachelors for their auction sales, knowing these men needed a supply of shirts, underwear, and socks and did not have women to produce such goods for them. Bachelors were often present at society meetings and sometimes provided entertainment. When McKenzie County bachelor Sivert Botnen invited the Aid to his shack, he made coffee, prepared a place for babies to sleep, and arranged a space where the women could sit and work. Bennie Berntson invited the Aid to use his house for a winter meeting. He had traveled to Ray shortly before the gathering, and "Grandma" Gilbertson was not sure that his place would be ready, so she arrived early to check its condition. She found a clean house, freshly baked bread, roasted meat on the stove, coffee, and "store" cookies arranged for the meeting.[46]

Bachelors' interest in Ladies' Aids may have been a reflection of their relationships with neighboring married women. Entertaining the local Aid and supporting sales may have been a means of repaying women for their help with daily or seasonal chores. The amount of work married women did for bachelors was in some cases prodigious. Gustapha Granstrom often worked for her African American bachelor neighbor, Philip Whamsley, cooking for his threshing crew, making his clothes, preparing his meals, and sending food home with him. She and her two small children once spent the night in Whamsley's barn caring for his sick cow. Other women performed similar work in order to maintain the community's integrity and to keep bachelors within the bounds of social and moral standards.[47]

When attended by entire families, Aid meetings were the heart of a community's regular social activity. Men exchanged important information, talking about crops, prices, land, and, undoubtedly, the weather. Bachelors could establish themselves as responsible, permanent community members by attending and hosting Ladies' Aid meetings. Women asserted some control over bachelors' households by accepting their invitations and making it clear, as "Grandma" Gilbertson did, that the men and their houses had to meet community standards of cleanliness, social graciousness, and moral behavior.

Ladies' Aids supported women in their roles as wife, homemaker, and mother, but through group activities members became leaders in community organization. Ladies' Aid Societies of every denomination created a fragile gender balance in rural communities that, though complicated by the fiction of public male leadership, contested men's power and ensured that women would be visible and influential in community activities.

Churches were one of the most important and visible rural institutions representing the formation of culturally homogeneous communities. Many settlers sought land near people who shared their language and traditions, one solution to the problem of cultural isolation that resulted in communities defined by culture or native origin. Rural folk sought to maintain the integrity of their homeland's language, religion, and values and to raise their children within that cultural context. Most of all, they feared being swallowed up by Yankee American culture. Similarly, Yankee Americans wanted to live in communities where their language and traditions dominated.

Fear of losing one's culture to English-language and American customs or to other European immigrants motivated settlers to build communities with cultural boundaries. Such boundaries were often flexible enough to accommodate people of other races or backgrounds, especially if their numbers were few: Philip Whamsley's story is a good example of this sort of limited inclusiveness. However, most North Dakota communities excluded American Indians. Though northern plains tribes had been assigned to reservations by the time of agricultural settlement and there was little hostile contact between settlers and natives, immigrants brought with them from Europe a fear of Indians that had sifted into local legends about America. Some, especially Norwegians and Germans, were familiar with the 1862 war between the Dakota and settlers in Minnesota. Others had a blurry sense that their destination was the American frontier and that its history was marked by warfare with Indians. Fear impaired settlers' abilities to create inclusive communities.[48]

Meetings between settlers and native peoples were usually brief, involving trade or a social visit. Sometimes pioneers let their fear interfere with common prairie courtesies. Mary Madden's imagination got the best of her one day when an Indian man came by her house and asked for a match. She refused his request, and when he left she ran the half-mile to a neighbor's to get help. She returned expecting to find the entire household dead but instead discovered her sister-in-law enjoying refreshments on the porch with the Indian and two white men. What Mary Madden had imagined would become a massacre was simply an ordinary visit. Gust and Mary Burg's fear of Indians likewise led them to overreact to news of the Ghost Dance taking place on the Standing Rock Reservation, more than one hundred miles from their homestead. They mortgaged their farm, left the area, and did not return until news of Sitting Bull's death reached them in Minneapolis.[49]

For those who received Indians as occasional travelers or as neighbors, the encounters were far more pleasant and routine. Indians often journeyed from one reservation to another for festivals or to visit relatives, and their needs were the same as any other traveler—a place to rest, feed for their horses, sometimes food for themselves and their children. Some settlers learned through these ordinary visits that Indians were willing to trade. Jennie Robinson, who ran a store in Coal Harbor, not far from the Fort Berthold Reservation, remembered Indians as her best customers. John Koehn noted that Indians traded for the things they needed, giving beadwork or buckskins in exchange for cooking utensils or salt. Occasionally settlers let go of irrational fears when experience showed that Indians intended no harm. Mrs. August Borner overcame her suspicions when she found that Indians were fond of her children and enjoyed playing with them during visits.[50]

Only a few people, such as storekeepers Jennie and George Robinson, engaged in substantial communication with the same Indians over an extended period of time—in other words, became friends. A story told by Mrs. Alf Eastgate indicates that even pleasant and recurrent encounters did not necessarily result in a sustained friendship. Mrs. Eastgate lived near a trail the Dakota used when they traveled from Fort Totten. When she met a Dakota woman with a sick infant, Mrs. Eastgate took the woman to her home for the night and helped care for the baby boy. The woman traveled on with her company the next day, and Mrs. Eastgate did not expect to see her again. A year later, however, a man delivered a pair of beaded moccasins, a gift from the woman whom Mrs. Eastgate had sheltered. Had this interaction taken place between two homesteading women, they might have become lifelong friends, but Mrs. Eastgate never saw the woman or her child again.[51]

Opportunities to incorporate Indians into fledgling communities were rare and generally neglected by settlers. An example is provided by the story of Bridget Burke Cranley and her husband, who lived with an Indian woman when they first came to Pembina County. Her generosity allowed them to spend the summer in the fields and to put off building their own house until fall. Cranley taught the woman to "braid her hair, [to] discard the blanket in favor of a dress . . . to make butter and to keep house in general." The Indian woman looked after the Cranley baby while Bridget worked in the garden and shared vegetables from her root cellar while they waited for the crops to mature. She showed the Cranleys how to make a footbridge of willow shrubs so they could easily cross the small stream on their claim. Despite the time they spent together and the exchange of labor, food, shelter, and culture, Bridget Cranley did not name the woman or her tribal affiliation in her memoirs. Writing for European American readers, she maintained a proper distance, focusing on how she encouraged the woman to adopt new styles of housekeeping and dress. Friendship can be inferred from the acts described, but it was not claimed by Mrs. Cranley. Though the Cranleys shared a great deal with this generous woman, and though Mrs. Cranley was grateful and retained a fondness for her, the community they became attached to did not include her or other Indians.[52]

Many pioneer women shared spare food with traveling Indians as was customary, but others responded in ways that would have been considered extremely rude among their European American neighbors. One woman gave Indians crackers when they asked for bread, and although most people would not consider crackers to be an adequate substitute, she was offended when they threw them on the ground. Another woman ignored Indians who asked for some potatoes as she was harvesting her crop; the next day, she reported, half the crop had disappeared and "there was no difficulty in solving that robbery." Sharing food is such an important element in building community that the refusal to offer food to visitors or those in need must be seen as a means of delineating community boundaries.[53]

Only rarely could settlers understand the consequences of such attitudes. In one instance, Sarah Braddock encountered race prejudice precipitated by gender expectations. Hauling grain by ox-drawn wagon to the railroad terminal forty miles distant, she sought shelter at a home one night and was turned away because the owners feared she was an Indian. After all, a white woman would not likely be hauling grain over such a distance and certainly would not be traveling unescorted at night. Braddock reported the incident as a curiosity of her life, but she did not indicate whether the experience expanded her consciousness of either race relations or the nature of rural communities.[54]

The few African Americans who settled on Dakota farms were either excluded from European and Yankee American communities or included only on the margins. Between 1880 and 1920, homesteads were claimed by sixty-five black men and five black women, most arriving after 1900. Although black men appear in photographs of work crews on farms and ranches and although Era Bell Thompson reported that her African American family worked alongside Norwegian and German immigrants in such communal activities as threshing and fire fighting, the place of African Americans in rural North Dakota communities was conflicted. In 1862, the legislature considered a bill to prevent "persons of color" from settling Dakota Territory. The bill passed only one house, but others restricting the rights of African

Americans did become law: jury service and voting privileges were limited to "free white males," public schools were open only to "white children," and marriage was permitted only between persons of the same race. All of these laws except the one governing miscegenation were repealed in 1868, but these legislative changes did not mean that North Dakota settlers welcomed African American neighbors. In her exhaustive history of African Americans in North Dakota, Stephanie Abbot Roper states that blacks remained "ephemeral members of the northern Dakota Territory community."[55]

In any North Dakota community, the number of African Americans was small. In 1885 only thirteen African American men farmed in ten counties in the territory's northern tier; by 1910 the number had risen to forty-six mostly single men working on farms they owned or rented. The invisibility of African American women supports Roper's statement that blacks were marginal members of the community. Era Bell Thompson's mother seldom went to town and never socialized with neighboring women. When she prepared meals for the threshing crew, neighbors did not come to her aid or send their daughters and dishes. She met with two other black families some distance away or with her white sister-in-law for rare social activities. And when she died, only her frightened young daughter attended her. In another example of community exclusiveness, while Bob Cody, a black farmer in Benson County, tolerated his neighbors' racism, his wife refused to, returning instead to New York. Men's work relationships provided a connection to the community that, though fragile, was sufficient to sustain their sense of belonging, but women's communal relations were more intimate, existing inside the home as they exchanged work, social visits, or midwifery. Without interracial, woman-centered activities, African Americans remained outsiders in the white communities of rural Dakota.[56]

Immigrants from Europe, some of whom had never seen a dark-skinned person, brought with them ideas about race that were largely based on ignorance, their misconceptions compounded by vague stories repeated without regard to fact. Thomas Yecovanko, who followed his sister and her family to McLean County, had heard in his Ukrainian village that all babies were born black in America. Upon arrival at his sister's house, he brushed past her and ran to the crib to look at her new baby's skin, relieved to see that it was white. The inability to communicate also bred fear. Swedish immigrant Hannah Anderson tried to escape the house with her children when a black man, out on the prairie collecting buffalo bones, approached to ask for food. She did not understand what he wanted, but when he pointed to an egg she let him take it. She was relieved when he left. Very likely he was, too.[57]

To some extent, community building depended on excluding those who did not fit—people of other races, backgrounds, or religions. Indeed, all northern plains communities utilized categories to separate individuals by social and economic class, by sex, and by culture. The federal government encouraged limited communities by offering large, individually owned farms without provision for social organization and, further, by separating settlers from Native Americans through the reservation system. As settlers created communities, they looked for people with whom they shared many qualities, the most fundamental being the practice of agriculture, but language, religion, race, and social customs were also important. Women were among those able, under some circumstances, to transcend boundaries, to weave interesting threads into the community's fabric. But women also actively transferred to the northern plains cultures that tended to define community by degree of sameness and that exaggerated the differences between those who were members of the community and those who were not.

By the 1920s, as the pioneer generation grew old, the state and counties and even townships began to recognize the earliest settlers with a celebration of whiteness that took the form of honoring "the first white woman" of the area to do something—usually to give birth. So important was this designation that Mrs. Abraham Nelson proudly declared to a Writers' Project interviewer her status as "the first white woman to have a sewing machine" in her neighborhood.[58]

While the European American women who settled North Dakota are considered by modern scholars to be "white," that elite categorization was not so apparent to their contemporaries. European American women whose families had been in the United States for generations— "Yankee Americans"—had earned the label "white," but foreign-born women of the fairest hair, eyes, and skin were not considered white unless compared directly to dark-skinned women of color. The narrow distinctions were relative, but they became more rigid as immigrants experienced cultural transition and class division to lay claim to the status of "white" Americans. As European immigrants proudly claimed "white womanhood," their communities became less flexible regarding people of color.[59]

The concept of "first white womanhood" is based on several assumptions. The first is that there were other people occupying the area before white settlement, a significant departure from the "empty land" comments made by many settlers. The second is that the presence of women in a settlement made a difference, signifying permanence and leading to the establishment of continuous communities that grew within European traditions and were generally ethnically homogeneous. The third assumption—particularly pertinent if the statement is associated with childbirth—is that giving birth was exceptionally dangerous in a newly settled area, even though for centuries women had been bearing children on the northern plains under conditions no more primitive than those elsewhere. The fourth is of racial or cultural superiority, a sense that battles (literal or figurative) had been fought and won and obstacles overcome—and that white settlers had emerged victorious because of their physical and moral fitness. Claiming to be the "first white woman to . . ." was part of the process of bounding European and Yankee communities. Though numerous boundaries limited these communities, those of race were more clearly and firmly drawn than those delineating one European culture from another.

Helga Aasen Thompson was celebrated as the first white woman to give birth in Steele County. She was honored in 1924—fifty years after arriving in Dakota Territory in a covered wagon with her husband and a group of friends and relatives—and again upon her death in 1929. Letters from President Coolidge in 1924 and Governor Shafer in 1929 attested to the importance of her status as a pioneer mother. Thompson made many personal sacrifices but rarely saw anyone of a race or nationality other than Norwegian. Her experience in giving birth did not differ significantly from that of women who lived there earlier or who settled there later, but the first white birth signaled the foundation of a particular community. Her presence in Steele County, and the fact that she and her husband, Paul, built a farm and raised a family there, established with finality what military action alone could not: the northern plains were to be the province of white farm folk.[60]

North Dakota's pioneer women accepted what they had first seen as "nothing," made it into something they recognized, and claimed it as their own. Rural women relied on formal and informal neighborhood, cultural, and kinship associations not only to break the isolation of homesteading but also to create close-knit communities of people with whom they shared many cultural characteristics. Despite social limitations, these communities were functional and discreetly gender balanced. "Community" meant a place where women could celebrate their successes and rely on each other for help in harvest or childbirth despite the distances between farms. While they shared the task of community building with men, they did not yield to male control of the community and its institutions. Women enjoyed full membership in settlement communities because the survival of the community required the skill and labor of every member and because women asserted their right to build and belong.

5

The "Main Stay"
Managing Butter and Egg Production

The poorest farming is not having enough stock and poultry
and just relying on crops for all of the income.
ROSINA RIEDLINGER

King Wheat captured the imagination of Dakota settlers, but most recognized that wheat alone could not sustain farming families. At the advent of settlement—years that saw only a few acres of sod broken annually, low wheat prices, and uncertain yields—farmers needed reliable income to make improvements while they awaited high prices and big crops. They counted on good wheat crops to allow them to buy more equipment, land, and livestock; to build comfortable, permanent homes and large barns; and to afford a few luxuries, but they soon realized that such opportunities would not appear annually (Figure 1). As economist Scott Stradley has noted, the wheat market "brings prosperity to North Dakota like no other economic or political phenomena. Conversely, when the demand for wheat collapses, the prosperity turns to its opposite and recessions and depressions can last very long." Such uncertainty created a need for additional means of generating income. North Dakota farm income was generally derived from two major sources: the field crops, mostly wheat, and the dairy and poultry products of the barnyard. There were occasionally horses to sell or a small herd of beef cattle, but such income sources were not consistently available to most farm families.[1]

During the settlement era, butter making and egg production were women's work, as they had been elsewhere for generations. At the time, states such as Iowa, Minnesota, and Wisconsin were in the process of commercializing dairy production, and on many midwestern farms women were no longer in charge of the dairy. But the division of labor and land on a settlement-era Dakota wheat farm required that women and children perform barnyard work and that the dairy herd and poultry flock not draw too heavily on farm resources. This work was central both to maintaining the farm and to surviving the lean years. Dairy and poultry economies also contributed to the stability of plains towns—their future as uncertain as the farmers'—and of railroads, which needed not only freight to carry but also a source of local part-time labor. Not every farm woman raised chickens or kept cows, but most did, even those who earned money through other skills. The products of barnyard animals provided food for the family and a surplus in butter, eggs, meat, and calves to sell or trade.[2]

Professional agriculturists tended to overlook—or to obscure through selective data collection—the significance of farm women's productive work. In doing so, they not only exaggerated wheat farms' potential but also denied women appropriate credit for their work. One woman protested the lowering of this veil over farm women's work, resulting in one of the few public recognitions of the importance of barnyard income to the wheat farm. Writing to *The Dakota Farmer's* editor, who chose not to print the woman's name, a "lady reader from a sequestered locality in North Dakota" stated that

> there is no place where women work so hard and receive so little recognition as on the farm. . . . If the women entirely support the family with eggs and butter and cheese, it is all credited to the man.

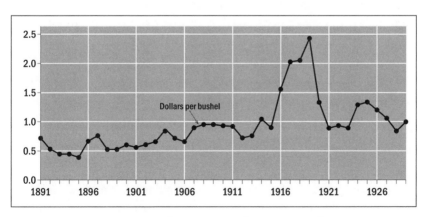

Figure 1: Average National Farm Price for Spring Wheat, 1891–1929

The editor, presumably W. F. T. Bushnell, tried to restore farm women to what he considered their proper place by giving them "due credit for their faithfulness," but he did admit that

> [the] steady, persistent influence of the mother who has marketed the eggs and made the butter has proven the main stay of the thousands of Dakota farm homes that would otherwise have been wrecked.

Grudging though it was—and contrary to the paper's consistent editorial position—Bushnell's statement acknowledged that northern plains farms operated within a fragile economy that depended on women's productive work for survival.[3]

Dairy and poultry operations utilized minimal farm resources. Women pastured and fed cows and chickens on marginal or unbroken land and in the area around the house and barn. Cows were staked out in the prairie grass for feed and led to water once or twice a day. Under these conditions, the investment in barnyard livestock was negligible: the expense of keeping a milk cow and a flock of laying hens amounted to the price paid for the animals, a cost diminished by the sale or productivity of their offspring.

Men worked on hundreds of acres, planting and harvesting small grains and perhaps managing a beef cattle herd as well. The size of the investment in land and other resources reflects the well-known dominance of grain crops in northern plains farming and the legal and traditional assumption of patriarchal farm family relations.

Several factors governed this hierarchy of productive work. Settlement in North Dakota occurred during an era of intense industrialization that affected farms as well as cities. In this industrializing society, cash crops represented power—the ability to buy machinery, livestock, and household goods—and this power accrued to the person who managed and marketed the crop. Further, the scarcity of labor meant that women could not be relieved of field work. Some historians have argued that on extensive grain farms a woman's reproductive work in the house was more important than her labor in the fields, but on the northern plains the latter was often essential. As women frequently had to leave other tasks to participate in field work, their own productive work could not demand too much of her time during planting, harvest, or threshing. Finally, women of every ethnic group brought to their new farming communities a tradition of subordinating their interests to those of men.[4]

Who would control and distribute money was one of the most private decisions couples made, but it appears that the use of farm income was usually assigned to the person whose labor earned most of it. Expenditures thus conformed to the gendered division of labor. For example, when men hired out, their wages generally went to make improvements on the farm, which might include building the house. But sometimes, especially before much acreage was broken, off-farm work purchased food essentials like flour. Elizabeth Harris wrote to her sister that, while most groceries could be bought on credit, flour required a cash down payment. Since men's wages were paid in cash and women's income usually in kind or credit, a man's earnings would have to be used to buy flour. When farmers did not have access to a grain market, wheat itself could sometimes be traded for flour, a practice Johannes Otto engaged in before the railroad built a branch line to nearby Bowdon. Andrew Davidson also traded some of his wheat for flour at a nearby mill shortly after moving onto his preemption claim in 1887.[5]

As the early years of settlement passed, a fairly common pattern developed around the distribution of income. Johannes Otto noted the difference when he finally gained access to a wheat market: "[T]he railroad came in, then supplies came in. Machinery . . . plows, drills, discs, binders, and . . . steam powered threshing machines. . . . That [machinery] was bought from the produce you grew. . . . Wheat was the biggest crop." Luke Perekrestinko told the Writers' Project interviewer that every year he planted more land and bought more machinery. When grain prices were high and the crops good, he was able to buy another quarter section and more cows and build a new barn and house. Sometimes men used crop money to increase their holdings at the expense of their family's need for shelter. Laura Wheeler remembered her brother-in-law, Edward Hamilton, "building outbuildings, a smoke house, corn crib, pig barns." She noted, "He wasn't paying much attention to the house, but he sure was to the farm!"[6]

Women's income, generally derived from butter and egg production, was small but reliable, increasing steadily over the decades. Women controlled their earnings, which for the most part were used to feed and clothe the farm family. The division of income in Rosina Riedlinger's household closely matched the division of authority over farm work:

> The best way to farm is to let the men seed the grains, and the women have about 200 chickens, 100 turkeys and a few cattle. We had chickens and during the summer they supplied us with groceries, and during the winter the turkeys paid for fuel and clothes for the family. Cows and cream paid for the repairs and spending money we needed and the grain crop was money that could be laid aside, or invested in more land.

Riedlinger's economics subtly reveal that grain income was not reliable or perhaps not essential, that, instead, the sale or trade of butter and eggs was the farm's primary source of income. Since this income was usually in the form of credit at a local store, women had limited discretionary use of it. They could not, for instance, apply credit to a mail-order purchase or use it to open a bank account. Store credit was good for a range of household and personal supplies, however, including groceries, kerosene, clothing, shoes, tobacco, candy, fruit, yard goods, and sewing notions.[7]

The dollar amount generated by egg and dairy production—never large—steadily increased. According to federal agriculture census statistics, butter income in 1899 averaged $12.77 per farm. (Reliable figures for egg sales are not available.) In 1909, combined sales of butter and poultry products averaged $40.88 per farm. In 1919 and 1929, as farm sales of butter were declining, the combined figures for butter and poultry sales continued to rise, to $64.40 and $76.80, respectively. Wheat income reflected the instability of both crops and markets: the average per farm was $673.77 in 1899, $1,444.77 in 1909, $1,909.03 in 1919, and $1,188.93 in 1929. Dairy and poultry income generally ranged at between 2.5 and 3.5 percent of the wheat income, but in 1929, with wheat yields and prices low, dairy and poultry income amounted to 6.5 percent of the wheat income.[8]

Other sources suggest that barnyard income could have been far more substantial than official figures indicate. Mary Barrett Still noted in her diary that she sold butter worth $9.67 and eggs worth $3.03 during the month of December 1911, adding "not bad for December." Her figures show that some farm women's annual income exceeded averages for that period. Storekeepers' accounts, though extremely scarce, suggest that an individual farm's income from butter and eggs might have been significantly higher than that recorded by census statistics. H. M. Heen noted that in April 1895 Ragnhild Raaen twice traded butter against her bill at his store in Hatton: for one delivery (weight unknown) she received $5.25, and for the second, four days later, ninety cents. If Raaen earned $6.15 over four days, her butter credit very likely exceeded the $12.77 annual average calculated for 1899.[9]

In 1901, Mrs. Frances F. Fitzmaurice of Crystal wrote for the Farmers' Institute *Annual* an article about the dairy work she had been pursuing for several years. Using conservative figures, she calculated that a cow should produce seventy-two dollars worth of butter as well as a calf that could be sold for ten dollars, yielding a total annual income of eighty-two dollars per cow. The 1899 federal agriculture census indicates that farm women sold 39 percent of the butter they churned, a figure which if applied to Fitzmaurice's butter production calculates out to $28.08 in cash or credit per cow. Given that in 1899 the average number of cows per farm was three, a good dairy manager theoretically should have been able to earn $78.62 from her yearly butter sales. Were similar records available for egg and poultry sales, their income figures would likely rise as well. Settlement narratives attribute the purchase of most household supplies to credit or income earned from the butter and egg trade, suggesting that the higher figures may in fact be more accurate.[10]

Even if the income for an individual farm was small, dairy and poultry operations did not tax its resources. Quartered in sod or wooden barns or sheds, chickens and dairy cows required very little investment to produce more than enough for a family's needs. During the lean times of the settlement period and the years of poor crops or low prices that followed, this small income sustained families that might otherwise have had to abandon the farm. As Margaret Griffin Cohen noted in her study of Ontario, most farm families could wait out the tough years if they produced some of their own necessities and derived income from a source other than crops.[11]

The production of eggs and butter on Dakota farms followed very different courses between 1879 and 1929. The number of eggs, the size of poultry flocks, and the income derived from both rose steadily, if not

Chickens feed in front of a homestead shack in Cavalier County, 1896.

dramatically, during this period; egg production in particular grew at a faster pace after 1920. Home butter production increased until 1909 and then dropped off through 1920 as commercial creameries took over the manufacture of butter for market. The points of change coincide with a crash in market prices for all farm commodities, indicating that farm women managed their flocks and herds while keeping an eye on the markets and on family needs in order to determine the most profitable use of their time and energy.[12]

Study of poultry and egg production on settlement homesteads is complicated by a lack of attention to this area by federal and state entities. The 1880 federal census counted barnyard and "other" poultry but not the number of eggs sold or the value of the birds and their products. Egg production (not sales) figures were listed in 1890, but census officials discounted poultry's value to the entire farm enterprise. A decade later, the federal census reported that previous "estimates of the total value of livestock on farms" took into account "neat cattle, horses, sheep, mules, asses, [and] swine," noting the probability that "before 1900 this was all that was included." Poultry, far more important economically to northern plains farms than mules, asses, or swine, was not counted in the total value of farm livestock. Following the same pattern, the state agricultural commissioner ignored poultry and poultry products altogether in his first biennial report. Beginning in 1892, the commissioner reported on the total dollar value of poultry and eggs sold but neglected to note flock size or specific dollar values for each product. In a society that increasingly valued cash income, poultry—returning in trade as often as in cash—was not considered a valuable component of farm livestock by federal census officials or the state agricultural commissioner. Official disregard for the production of farm women is but one aspect of their invisibility. Nevertheless, the available data, supported by narrative evidence, indicate trends that can be used to assess the contribution of poultry products to the farm economy.[13]

Census and state agricultural officials did count cattle, but the distinction between dairy and beef cattle or even draft stock sometimes depended on the animals' use at the moment the census was taken. Most Dakota cows were "dual purpose" and not specifically bred for milking ability; few purebred dairy bulls were available in the state before 1910. A cow that was being milked or that was expected to calve and produce milk was a milk cow; others were "neat cattle" or draft stock. This crude distinction did not prevent a farmer from hitching a milk cow to the plow when draft stock were not available or butchering a milk cow when the family needed beef.[14]

The contrast between officials' and settlers' interests in poultry and dairy resources is unmistakable. Thirty or forty years after settling the prairies, many pioneers remembered the price they paid or received for eggs and butter. To interviewers more interested in stories about blizzards and grasshopper plagues, they offered details about their efforts to engage in the egg and butter trade. They remembered quite clearly the things that trade bought, stating, perhaps without sufficient emphasis to impress their listeners, "our cream and eggs supplied us with groceries and other necessities." Both women and men tended to credit women's productive work with providing the foundation for the farm family's survival and success.[15]

Household supplies such as coffee, sugar, and kerosene were almost always secured by barnyard surplus trade. In lean years, these goods became luxuries as egg and butter income was diverted to pay for essentials. Farm women could "make do" without trade items, but the hardship and labor of homestead life increased as a result. Like countless other settlers, Mrs. Hans Emmanuel Anderson made coffee from roasted barley when she could not get it by trading eggs. Many families burned a rag in a shallow dish of tallow to make light when they could not afford kerosene. Sugar simply disappeared from the menu.[16]

So significant were these surplus sales that distance was only an obstacle to be overcome, not a factor determining who engaged in the trade. Though homesteads were often located miles from the nearest trading center or town and perhaps even further from a railroad depot, women managed to find some way to get their products to a place where they could trade. In the early 1880s, Agnethe Jensen Borreson walked to Valley City carrying butter and eggs when the horses were occupied with field work. Thersia Sherman Bosch walked fourteen miles to Tower City to trade eggs for groceries. Pernella Bjerke Herred usually walked the nine miles to Washburn in McLean County with only a small pony to pull the stoneboat. One day the pony gave up on the heavy load one mile from town, so Herred picked up the two-gallon butter crock, walked the rest of the way, traded for her groceries, and hiked back to the worn-out animal. Charlotte Anderson Swanson sold her butter and eggs in the nearby town of Hancock until it withered at the end of the Great Dakota Boom, after which she walked ten miles to Coal Harbor and George Robinson's store. A few years later, she and her husband bought a wagon and a team of horses, making her trading trips easier.[17]

The nature of farm women's trade involved them in a web of social and economic ties, binding them to families, communities, travelers, newcomers, and distant markets. Selling farm produce at a nearby town obviously gave women opportunities to socialize, but such visits needed to be justified by the more practical purpose of trade. Isabella Roberts frequently walked or drove the two miles to Devils Lake to trade. Her daughter, Mae Roberts Jensen, looking back over her diary, commented with some concern that her mother's visits to town might be viewed as excessive socializing, noting in the margin, "it looks like we went to town a lot, but we took butter and eggs to the store to trade." The frequency of such trips depended on distance, transportation, and season, but they alleviated the isolation of the homestead for many women.[18]

A flock of laying hens, so important to a farm family's success, was a fairly common wedding gift. Chickens were among the important tools a young bride needed to begin her marriage as a productive partner. Josephine Jacobson received such a gift when she married Axel Ax-elson, and Tirsten Swenson received six hens and one rooster from her brother for her 1891 wedding. The following year Swenson raised sev-enty-five chicks, and within two years of her marriage she was buying the family's groceries with her egg money. She also sold broilers for twenty-five cents and laying hens for fifty cents each.[19]

The first woman to produce surplus butter or eggs in a newly set-tled area had a brief opportunity to make an enormous profit. Betsy Halstenson Broton sold eggs for fifty cents per dozen while there were few competitors in the local Nelson County market. Settling in Barnes County in 1881, Marian Koehn Kramer was able to sell butter at forty-five cents per pound while she had the neighborhood's only milk cow. When other homesteaders acquired their own cows, the price of butter dropped to a far more ordinary five or six cents per pound. It is likely that many of Kramer's first customers were bachelors or married men whose families had not yet arrived. Population figures indicate that the ratio of men to women was highest in the 1880s and then dropped as the state became settled. Those early arrivals, many working for oth-ers as well as on their own homesteads, purchased basic foodstuffs from neighboring farm women at high prices.[20]

Women who lived near a sizable town could count on a steady market, particularly if settlement in the area was increasing. At Wash-burn, the largest town in booming McLean County during the mid-1880s, travelers and newcomers formed a small but stable market for farm products. Gustapha Granstrom sold cheese directly to the Sat-terlund Hotel and traded butter and eggs in the stores; Mathilda Jones sold chickens, butter, and garden produce to Missouri River steamboat captains.[21]

Such markets were localized, profitable only to individuals prepared to take advantage of them. The situation was very different for Caro-line Radke Fregein, who lived in McIntosh County, far from the Mis-souri River, in an area not yet served by railroads. Like other counties settled primarily by German-speaking families from South Russia, McIntosh had few bachelors to form a local market for surplus barn-yard products. Fregein could usually trade her eggs, but she frequently found no market for the more perishable butter. In August 1889, she made the thirty-five-mile trip to Ellendale, where she was unable to sell the five pounds of butter she had brought. Returning home with melted and spoiled butter, she decided against trying to sell again in such an unstable market.[22]

Ubiquitous chicken flocks meant that a farm woman could quickly prepare a meal for travelers, their unannounced arrival a frequent and not always welcome event. A farmhouse could suddenly become a hotel sheltering any number of strangers with no more notice than a cloud of dust on the horizon. Traveling mortgage agent Seth Humphrey noted with some distaste and no gratitude that a "farmhouse supper" consisted of "the inevitable short biscuit, coffee, and ham and eggs." The flock not only provided food for the family and a surplus for trade; it also allowed a homesteading woman to meet her social obligations.[23]

Egg and butter markets fluctuated seasonally with supply. Warm weather and long days brought the greatest yield in chickens and cows. Egg production was highest in the spring but usually slowed in late summer, stopping entirely during the cold winter months. Milk production was highest during the first few months after calving, which usually coincided with the plentiful grass and water of spring and summer. Most cows, bred to calve in the spring, were milked for ten months. Farm women compensated for the seasonal loss of milk and eggs in various ways. Rosina Riedlinger's system for distributing farm income and purchases kept her family supplied with goods and cash throughout the year. When eggs were abundant, Gittel Turnoy put them in a crate and poured salt over them, making sure to cradle each egg in its own salt blanket. The crate was stored in the cellar, where the salt hardened, keeping air from the eggs. The labor involved in freeing each egg meant this method was best used for the family's supply; eggs for trade might be stored in straw in the cellar to await a later and more favorable market. An 1899 North Dakota experiment station bulletin described a method by which "poultrymen" could preserve eggs in water glass (silicate of soda) at the cost of one cent per dozen. Though economical, the new technique did not become popular because good quality water glass was not widely available. None of the pioneers interviewed through the Writers' Project mentioned water glass, but country storekeepers used it to store eggs until winter prices made shipping economically feasible.[24]

Methods of preserving and trading eggs changed little from 1880 to 1930. Anxious for business, rural storeowners took in crates of eggs packed in oats or straw. The eggs were often fertile, rarely candled, and likely to be covered with manure. Occasionally an overheated fertile egg might explode, making a mess in the storeroom. Storekeepers usually traded eggs for the same price they received when selling them, losing money on the labor and storage but aiming to retain farm women's business. If storekeepers did not accept the trade on a woman's terms, she could take her eggs, and the rest of her business, to a different store. Facing fierce competition, storekeepers might even offer the egg seller as much as five cents per dozen over what the market warranted. Under these economic circumstances—with farm women in control of the local market and prices the same for good- or poor-quality eggs—there was no advantage to investing time and money in producing large, uniform, clean eggs for trade.[25]

Farm women continued to market their eggs to country stores through the 1930s, an arrangement that proved advantageous to both the women and the storekeepers. While farm women and men alike acknowledged that eggs and butter helped them maintain their households during lean years, country stores also depended on the trade to sustain their business when the economy was weak. At least one storekeeper credited the farm produce trade with keeping his small string of country stores in operation during the Great Depression.[26]

Farm women managed their hen flocks for growth beyond household needs. While the average number of birds per farm grew continuously from 1879 to 1929, the sharpest increase came during the Great Dakota Boom, when flock sizes nearly doubled (Figure 2). Egg production per farm grew more rapidly during the boom than in any other decade until the 1920s. This growth was in part due to recently arrived homesteaders allowing eggs to hatch to increase flock size, but it was also in response to a burgeoning market, swelling with land seekers and new settlers willing to pay a high price for eggs. Isabella Roberts secured chicken eggs to start her own flock immediately after arriving on her Ramsey County claim. Hans Lindaas, a newcomer in 1883, paid dearly for eggs and complained about the price in letters home. During the 1890s, flock expansion tapered off, increasing by only 7 percent, but the quantity of eggs produced grew by over 27 percent. Growth in egg production that exceeds growth in flock size indicates that poultry managers were able to provide better feed and housing for laying hens, were allowing fewer eggs to hatch, and were able to take advantage of more distant markets as rail construction began to extend into small towns far from main lines.[27]

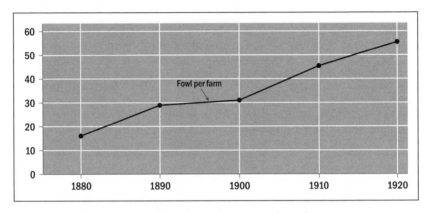

Figure 2: Number of Fowl per North Dakota Farm

Managing their flocks with an eye on the market, North Dakota farm women significantly expanded egg production after 1920 (Figure 3). The decade that followed saw a 20 percent increase in the average number of fowl per farm and a 29 percent increase in the average number of eggs per farm. The rise coincides with a sharp drop in the 1920 farm price index for eggs, poultry, grains, dairy products, and meat animals. Poultry, dairy, and egg prices did not fall nearly as far as did those of other farm products, however. Wheat prices had been good during World War I, but after 1920 a long period of low and unstable prices followed by several years of meager production due to severe drought meant farm families once again had to depend on poultry and eggs for many of their needs (Figure 4).[28]

Noticing a drop in prices, farm women increased their flock size and egg production accordingly. The necessary investment was small and the returns reliable. Nationally, farm women increased their flocks by 13.6 percent, but those in North Dakota responded more vigorously to the crisis, resulting in flock growth of 20 percent. In a report on farm poultry and egg production, North Dakota Agricultural College marketing expert Alva Benton noted that this increase was for the market: most farms had already met their own poultry and egg needs. As a result of these larger flocks, between 1921 and 1926 railroad freight tonnage of poultry increased four times and egg tonnage more than doubled. Because of poor quality, high production, and distance to market, North Dakota egg and poultry prices had been lower than the national average since 1915. Enlarging flocks tended to further force down market prices, but individual farm women made such decisions according to their own interests. They refused, for example, to invest more money or labor than necessary to maintain their flocks and to meet their own production plans. Experiment station and extension agents complained that chickens were not housed or fed for maximum production, nor were eggs properly prepared for market. The agriculturists' standards were high: most farm women could not afford the investment of time or money to build chicken houses according to published plans, to purchase hens that laid large white eggs, or to clean eggs thoroughly before marketing them. Farm women ignored the experts; they received the same price for eggs no matter their size, color, or condition.[29]

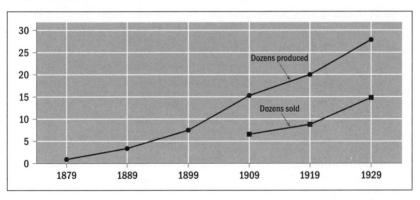

Figure 3: Egg Production and Sales from North Dakota Farms (in millions)

The continuous increase in poultry production through both good and bad wheat years indicates that farm women depended on the small income derived from egg and poultry sales and, perhaps, that they expected high yields and prices for wheat and other grains to be short-lived. Greater attention to poultry also refocused some of the labor women had previously expended in the farm dairy as, after 1910, butter production became increasingly commercialized.

During the early years of settlement, butter had much the same fi-

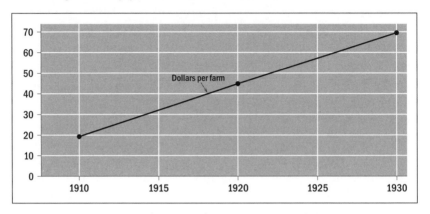

Figure 4: Egg and Poultry Income per North Dakota Farm

nancial importance to the homesteading family as chickens did, though farm women who made butter for home use may not have known how to meet seasonal and variable market demands for their product. When Norwegian immigrant Hannah Lovass Kjelland first brought her butter to Valley City, the storekeeper, Mr. Parkhouse, advised her to take it back home, "pack it [in crocks] with salt, put it down in the cellar and keep [it] until the price went up again." In order to meet local demands Kjelland would have to make her butter attractive to the buyer. Town women who purchased farm-produced butter demanded delicate taste and a pleasing appearance. The storekeeper set aside the finest specimens for local sales, allowing potential buyers to use a toothpick to taste them. The best butter brought a premium price, an advantage to both the producer and the storekeeper. Parkhouse taught Kjelland to use a mold to make her butter more visually appealing. Her success in producing a good-quality, fine-tasting, and attractive butter earned her a steady private market—including sales to Parkhouse for his own table as well as direct sales to other Valley City families—and a stable cash income.[30]

Women increased their dairy herds through hard work, determination, and luck (Figure 5). Most often they traded labor for a heifer calf, but some risked debt to enlarge their herds. Abigail Fuglestad increased her small herd by half one day. Spying a wagon with a cow tied onto it and a calf following behind, Fuglestad approached the driver and asked to buy the calf. The man agreed to sell it for five dollars, which Fuglestad arranged to borrow from a neighbor a half-mile distant. Though having a second calf increased her work somewhat, she knew that in time she would have two more milking cows and that the income from trading the surplus butter would satisfy her debt.[31]

Income from butter was so important to some families that they did not think of it in terms of subsistence and surplus. On these farms, butter was a commodity to be sold or traded but not consumed by the family. Joseph Falerius recalled that when he was a child his family rarely ate the butter his mother produced, instead saving sour skimmed milk for table use.[32]

While farm women were producing and marketing butter to support their families, the state agricultural commissioner was encouraging the establishment of commercial creameries. According to the various men who held the position, North Dakota agriculture needed to be diversified because a wheat economy was not reliable. But the commissioners did not set out to aid farm women in marketing a surplus homemade product. Their intent, as they addressed the state's "dairymen," was to increase and improve dairy herds in order to support commercial creameries where cream would be made into butter for both local and distant markets. From 1890 to approximately 1910, the agriculture commissioner and the dairy commissioner (who reported to the North Dakota Commissioner of Agriculture and Labor) alternately scolded and pleaded with farmers over the dairy issue. Cooperatives and privately owned creameries opened for business, but most closed within a year or two. Several factors—some gender related—inhibited their growth.[33]

Most creameries closed for lack of trade—often there were not enough cows in the vicinity to operate at a profit. Farmers declined to increase their dairy herds: the expense of investing in more cattle and providing feed and shelter was not appealing. Commercial dairying also meant morning and evening work every day for at least ten months of the year. Improving dairy herds would divert labor and money from wheat farming, and most North Dakota farmers were not yet ready to give up on the idea that wheat would make them rich. Creameries also failed for want of labor to tend larger herds. It was difficult for farmers to find men willing to milk cows. This meant that herds could not be expanded to a commercial size because the work would exceed the amount of time farm women and their children had available. A man (or, less likely, a woman) hired specifically to do this job could handle a commercial herd, but as long as milking was only one daily chore among the dozens a woman had to complete, the dairy herd had to remain small. In fact, some farmers indicated their preference for small herds that could be managed by women and children, thereby freeing adult males to labor during planting and harvest.[34]

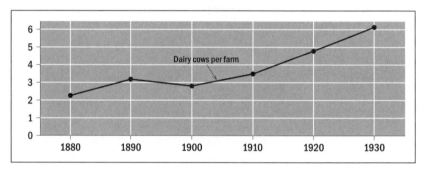

Figure 4: Average Number of Dairy Cows per North Dakota Farm

In 1894, the agriculture commissioner, seeking to assess the situation in economic terms, enlisted the advice and support of local and distant authorities. W. D. Hoard, a noted Wisconsin dairy expert and the publisher of *Hoard's Dairyman,* wrote to commissioner Nelson Williams that there had to be a sufficient number of cows within three or four miles of the creamery for safe and timely transport of milk. Assessing North Dakota's circumstances—the state sparsely settled, its farms scattered at some distance from each other and from town, its herds small and of poor quality—he expressed little confidence in its ability to become a dairy state. Other correspondents offered similar analyses, though most thought dairying could succeed if farmers put some money and effort into it. Their reluctance to do so was usually attributed to the ease and potential of wheat farming.[35]

But economic analysis alone—with no consideration of gender issues—could not explain the reluctance of North Dakota farmers to commercialize their dairy herds. However, experts rarely recognized the realities of farming's gendered division of labor, which farmers identified as a significant factor in the failure of commercial creameries. The veil hiding farm women's work from agricultural leaders simultaneously obscured the refusal of many men to take up that work. Had the experts recognized that men were reluctant to milk cows, they also would have had to acknowledge that women had been milking cows and producing butter for sale and trade. Commercial dairying's success in other states further muted the question of gender in North Dakota: if men milked cows in Wisconsin, why should they refuse to in North Dakota?

The dairy commissioner assumed that the economics of dairying had not yet been sufficiently explained, and he had no reply to farmers who pointed out the difficulties in getting men to take up the trade. J. H. Bosard, a farmer who had tried to start a creamery only to see it fail for want of cream, wrote to the commissioner, "Very many of our farmers think that it is cheaper and more economical to have their wives [make butter] for nothing than to pay the creamery for doing it." He also mentioned that it was difficult to get hired men to milk. Another correspondent, C. P. Smith, believed hired men did not like to milk because the twice-daily chore extended the workday. Smith did not comment on the length of a farm woman's day.[36]

There was also the question of propriety. Some men, especially bachelors, milked without questioning the social consequences. For example, Einar Brosten, an unmarried Norwegian immigrant, wrote home that he shared the milking of ten cows with his male companions. Neither Brosten nor his roommates separated or churned the cream because they sold whole milk to the Cooperstown creamery. His interest in dairying, and the enthusiasm with which he wrote about it to his brother, might be due to the work being done for profit, not for personal or family needs.[37]

In some communities, however, the distinction between men's work and women's work was quite firm, and milking was women's work. Rosina Riedlinger remembered that in her South Russia village men might herd cattle but they never milked cows: "It was the duty of girls to do the milking. A man never milked a cow as he felt it was a disgrace

Mrs. Emil Erhardt taking the cows to water

if he did." Scottish immigrant Christina Hills Caldwell recalled clearly her first winter on the homestead because the barn was not complete and she had to milk the cows outdoors, laconically explaining, "This work was done by the women."[38]

First-generation immigrants did not go against this early training in gender roles easily. Writing about his grandfather, Erling Sannes described Erick Sannes as a man who was "quick to disassociate himself from other Norwegian customs and traditions, [but who] never forgot that in old Norway men did not milk cows or perform household chores. Never in his entire life did he ever milk a cow." Some immigrant men first learned to milk when they sought work on Yankee-owned farms. When Swedish immigrant Otto Monson Lundstrom lost his job in a machine shop in 1896, he took a temporary position on a farm, an experience he remembered with some dismay: "A farmer ten miles out was sick and had fifteen cows to milk. I can milk cows, oh yeah, when [I] have to. Well, I done farm work and milked cows for two weeks. I went out fencing and hit my finger, lost a nail. No more cows."[39]

Men refused to perform labor that was considered to be women's work, and precisely because it was women's work, such labor was thought to have little or no value in relation to the farm's economy. So invisible and undervalued were women's work and the income derived from their labor—usually store credit rather than cash—that the idea of paying someone to do it—whether the milking or the butter making—seemed too large an expense for a poor wheat farm. Bosard stated that farm women were churning cream into butter for "nothing" because to him—and to other interested officials and farmers—women's labor was worthless. A few cents per pound for homemade butter compared poorly to the dollars earned from a good wheat crop; the stability of butter income was not noticeable enough to upset such deeply held notions of gendered division of labor.

As long as the work and the income of butter making were devalued as women's work, farmers refused to invest in the dairy. Even without addressing the question of who would do the milking, many farmers assumed that money put into improving the quality of the herd, the size or comfort of the barn, or the quantity or quality of feedstuffs would not provide a reasonable return. In other words, a dairy operation on a grain farm was considered to be a sideline, profitable only as long as it did not draw heavily on farm resources. Farmers doubted the value of dairy work, but it may be that, with women controlling the operation, few men really knew how much income dairy cows could produce. Unless she also controlled the grain income, a woman who milked three cows and used that money to buy groceries, clothing, and household supplies could rarely afford to put aside any reserves to buy another cow, invest in a good bull, or enlarge the barn—all of which required the cooperation of her farm partner.

Between 1890 and 1910, through agricultural publications and at public meetings, the agriculture and dairy commissioners pursued the goal of establishing commercial dairies. They were never able to shift North Dakota's agricultural foundation from small grains to dairy, but by 1910 there were seventy-three creameries around the state. The number of creameries fluctuated to some extent over the next few years but remained sufficient so that farmers who wanted to diversify their operations could invest confidently in dairy herds. Commercial creameries supplied local consumers with a consistent product and shipped a profitable surplus out of state. Satisfied with their success, by 1912 dairy commissioners focused more on feed and shelter for dairy animals and less on the gloomy prospects of making North Dakota into a dairy state.

Other indicators suggest that commercialization had finally taken hold. The federal agriculture census shows a decline in home butter production after 1910 while reports of the agriculture commissioner indicate that home production peaked in 1911. The decline in farm-produced butter was moderate, but the reduction in sales was dramatic, indicating a shift in butter's origins from the farm to the creamery. An analysis of these figures reveals a complex of human activities that signify the end of the settlement period, a gender shift in productive farm work, and the commercialization of butter production.[40]

From 1879 to 1909, on-farm butter production for the entire state increased, but during the 1890s average production per farm decreased, along with the average number of cows (Figure 6). The end of the Great Dakota Boom was a contributing factor. Disappointed in low prices, reduced wheat yields, and poor-quality, isolated farms, many would-be homesteaders packed up and left the state. They were quickly replaced by optimistic newcomers, causing continued growth in the state's population. New homesteaders frequently did not have many milk cows, and it is likely that some cattle belonging to earlier settlers were sold or handed over to mortgage companies. Thus, while the number of North Dakota farms increased 1.6 times, contributing to overall growth in the quantity of butter produced, the average amount of butter produced per farm actually decreased slightly.[41]

Following the decline of the nineties, farm butter production increased again until 1909, at a rate greater than that of the number of farms in the state. This growth coincides with a decline in the ratio of men to women in North Dakota. According to the 1880 census, this ratio was 1.56 (156 men per 100 women), representing an early stage of settlement, when many men without families came into the territory as soldiers, railroad laborers, and land seekers. By 1890 the ratio had dropped to 1.25; by 1910, to 1.22. As the number of farm women rose, so did the quantity of butter produced and sold from the farm. After 1910, however, changes in the gendered division of labor and a drop in the market for farm-produced butter resulted in the decline of such

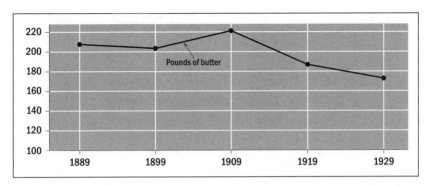

Figure 6: Average Butter Production per North Dakota Farm

production and sales even as the ratio of men to women continued to fall.[42]

Butter sales from the farm increased faster than butter production between 1899 and 1909 as women produced for the market while families consumed little at home. In 1899, farm women sold approximately 39 percent of the butter they churned at home; by 1909, sales had grown to 43 percent. Then butter production on farms declined by 12 percent between 1910 and 1920 and by another 7 percent during the decade that followed. The quantity of butter sold from the farm also decreased after 1909, but at a much faster rate: butter sales dropped to 20 percent of production in 1919 and to 11 percent in 1929. Creameries quickly cut into the market that farm women had once had to themselves, but the decline in butter sales exceeded the decline in production, meaning farm families were consuming more butter at home even though the farm population decreased slightly between 1920 and 1930. The only way to account for the remaining pounds of butter is to assume that between 1910 and 1939 farm home consumption increased by nearly 2.5 million pounds.[43]

Women recounting their lives on Dakota farms frequently mention the number of cows they milked and the price they received for butter, but they do not discuss a transition time during which the herd was enlarged, or they gave up milking, or the process was modernized with cream separators, cooling equipment, or a creamery truck to haul milk to the plant. An unexplained statistic, thus remains: women on 76 percent of the state's farms continued to make butter (225 pounds per farm in 1929), but they were selling less and less of it. In fact, of the farms where butter was churned, fewer than 12 percent sold butter. The gap between production and sales suggests that women were not anxious to give up butter churning and, therefore, considered it not drudgery but productive and valuable work. Some thought it a thrifty measure by which they could manufacture, rather than purchase, one household item, thereby conserving cash. As Bethel Herigstad noted, when crops or prices were poor, "only their early training in being frugal and economical saved them from giving up." Producing quality butter was also a source of pride, establishing the reputation of particularly skilled women, such as Hannah Kjelland, in their communities. The decline in farm butter production leveled off during the lean years of the 1920s, confirming that many women considered churning to be a means of conserving resources while maintaining a high-quality food supply for their families. For these women, resisting the trend toward consumerism and away from household production reflected their training for housewifery, sustained their roles and reputations as producers, and made good economic sense.[44]

Neither the census, nor the commissioner of agriculture reports, nor anecdotal evidence make clear whether women ceased to milk cows after 1910 or whether they lost control of dairying income as the labor and financial requirements rose. There are several indications, however, that after 1910 dairying became a stable form of cash income (rather than a subsistence/surplus product), encouraging some men to engage in and assume control of the work and the profits. In 1912, dairy commissioner R. F. Flint noted that bankers had found that (male) farmers who sold cream to creameries were more likely to pay their debts and that bankers would loan money for cattle even if they considered a loan for seed grain to be a bad risk—details suggesting that men controlled dairy income. In the same year, Flint received a letter from a writer who stated, "I have no difficulty in keeping men to milk because I have comfortable convenient barns for them to work in." Flint considered this statement to be "highly significant" because it supported his campaign to modernize dairying with proper barns and silos. It also suggests that, while women milked their cows in lean-tos, in sod barns, or even outside in the cold of winter, hired men balked at the task until they had a decent barn in which to work. Farmers who committed themselves to commercial dairying had fostered a shift in the gendered division of farm labor.[45]

Some women continued to milk, or supervised their daughters and sons in this chore. Evidence indicates, however, that, at least on some farms, men claimed both credit for the work and income from the sales of milk and cream. Timothy McNamara, an Irish immigrant from Canada, told a Writers' Project interviewer, "I have always kept a lot of cattle and milked about thirteen cows and the girls have always done the milking. I shipped twenty-three gallons of cream a week from Backoo." The ease with which McNamara moved from describing dairy work in the first person to his admission that his daughters actually did the milking suggests that, while dairying had become an acceptable means of making a living for a man, there were some who still would not milk a cow. Another was Mary Agnes McCann Farley's husband: Mary Agnes milked the cows and churned the butter, but her husband marketed the product to the State Hospital for the Insane at Jamestown.[46]

Farm women's productive work earned more than "pin money." Butter and egg sales, though small, stabilized the family farm economy, making it possible for families to stay on the farm when the wheat crop failed to live up to its promise. Women provided subsistence and a surplus for trade while maintaining residence to meet the legal requirements of homesteading. This arrangement freed men to work away from the farm on railroad crews or bonanza farms, in freighting or other endeavors important to the state's economic growth. Stable farm population and income also contributed to the success of the railroads, elevators, banks, and other major businesses that had an interest in North Dakota's farms. Butter and egg tonnage alone was not enough to keep railroads solvent, but the reliability of this portion of the farm economy encouraged companies to extend branch lines into remote towns, improving access to markets for wheat crops and other products. Between 1898 and 1915, while egg and butter production was climbing, while wheat yields bounced from one extreme to the other, and while wheat prices remained below one dollar per bushel, railroad companies doubled their lines to more than 5,200 miles of track. Though some areas remained unserved by rail, North Dakota contained three times as many miles of track per resident as any other state.[47]

As settlers remembered their early experiences on Dakota farms, they recognized the importance of the egg and butter trade but recalled the work and the products with little excitement. As with most quotidian enterprises, the dull but reliable chickens and cows rated small notice in memoirs and interviews, while King Wheat was always accorded a special place, for its beauty if not for its wealth-generating potential. The contrast is evident in the memoirs of Johanna Kildahl, who settled with her family in Ramsey County in 1883. "From the proceeds of our chickens and cows we set our table and bought most of our clothing," she wrote in the plainest language. But as she remembered the first wheat crop, harvested from just a few acres, her words expanded and became descriptive: "It was beautiful, golden, Scotch Fife, No. 1 Hard." The common chicken and the quiet milk cow tend to disappear in the golden haze through which settlers remembered their homestead experiences. No one forgot that wheat crops failed or that prices remained low for years after settlement, but neither did they forget the crops that were too large to be contained in the granary or the year the per-bushel price reached one dollar. It is difficult to maintain a clear perspective on the value of different kinds of work when blinded by bright hopes and the potential for success.[48]

Concurrent with changes that took place as women lost one part of their productive farm work and shifted their focus to another were state officials' efforts to engage (male) farmers in dairy work. Dairy and poultry production remained the "main stay" on many North Dakota farms through the 1920s, but agricultural officials ultimately made dairying and other livestock enterprises more appealing to men, who originally preferred the hard but seasonal work of the grain fields to labor that in many cultures was labeled women's work. Dairying began to generate enough cash income to increase its appeal to men; in order to bolster that potential, farmers invested in purebred dairy bulls, good barns, and more cows. If they did not themselves engage in milking, they hired someone who would or had their wives and daughters milk while they delivered the cream and claimed the check. By 1910, the gender shift in dairy work had begun in earnest, but women's control of poultry production remained unchallenged. State agricultural officials never took an interest in this enterprise nor tried to make it into men's work. The chicken coop was seen as an extension of the household, distinct from the barn and other parts of the farm.

The gender shift in dairy work was linked to a national trend to remove women from farm production, a development supported by the state's agricultural establishment. Women continued to engage in productive, on-farm work, but their contributions were undervalued and marginalized by agriculturists.

Women understood their work in different terms. To them, it was not marginal but central to the family farm economy, proven through years of labor that had not only supported the family and kept the farm functioning but also sustained country stores and, by extension, banks, elevators, and railroads. Nevertheless, by 1910, women were being encouraged to give up dairying's dirty and laborious work with the implied promise of leisure and the cultural concept (false though it was) that "American women stayed home and let their men do the work." After 1910, women's perspectives on their work and on farming in general were lost as agricultural officials sought to make gender relations on North Dakota farms more closely match those of urban, industrial America.[49]

6

"Devoted Wholly to Their Interests"
Farm Women and the Farmers' Institute

But she asked no pity for her broken arches, her aching back, her poor gnarled hands, or for the wistful memories of a fairer youth in sweeter lands. She gave America the great Northwest and was too proud to grumble at the cost of the stalwart sons to whom she willed it. She mothered MEN.

MARY A. BARNES WILLIAMS

Changes in the marketing of cream and milk did not necessarily mean that women would have to give up the productive work and income they had controlled since homesteading; they could have easily managed an enlarged dairy with the assistance of husband and children or hired help. But this economic change was accompanied by social reorganization that saw the primary emphasis of women's work relocated from the barn to the house. Renegotiation of the farm's gendered division of labor was promoted by agricultural leaders through the Farmers' Institute (and later the Cooperative Extension Service) according to principles outlined by leaders of the Country Life Movement.[1]

The Country Life Movement—highly influential among lawmakers and agricultural academics—was led by individuals who were generally urban, middle class, and associated with business and professional interests. Businessmen, supported by academics, wanted to improve the business of farming and to increase farm profits. Cash was becoming more important in America, and farmers would need plenty of it to buy the new equipment and consumer goods industry was producing. No longer would trading butter for coffee and yeast at the nearest store be sufficient to meet farm families' needs or fulfill industry's requirements for an expanding consumer base. Another line of thought, supported by urban social workers, ministers, and educators, understood farming as a way of life. These two philosophical approaches to the problems of rural residents displayed an inherent contradiction. While the Country Life Movement's leaders believed that farming provided a superior lifestyle and livelihood because of its relation to the land, they also believed that rural life had deteriorated and needed modification, primarily through education. But the movement's business and social wings agreed that agriculture and rural life had to be reorganized to better suit an industrializing nation dependent on supplies of cheap food and abundant labor.[2]

In 1908, President Theodore Roosevelt appointed a commission to study country life. The commission gathered information, held meetings in rural communities, and encouraged farm folk to write about their experiences. In January 1909 it reported that farmers and their families were among the underprivileged in the rapidly urbanizing nation. Rural people did not have the material advantages urban life had made available to an increasing percentage of the population: electricity, indoor water supply, paved roads, public transportation, and good schools.[3]

The report also addressed the special role of farm women. While mechanization had improved farm efficiency and decreased the amount of labor required to complete many tasks, the work farm women did and the tools they used had changed little during the nineteenth century. The report declared that farm women suffered from loneliness and isolation more so than men, who went to town regularly and had opportunities to discuss business and politics in public places. The Country Life Commission recommended that farm families share housework as well as field work so that women did not have to bear full responsibility for cleaning, cooking, and laundry. It also advised that farmhouses be modernized through the installation of telephones, running water, septic systems, and electrical plants. The report further suggested that farm women form clubs and civic organizations that would allow them to get away from housework and socialize regularly with neighbors.[4]

Liberty Hyde Bailey, the foremost proponent of the Country Life Movement, chaired the commission and wrote extensively on rural issues. Bailey devoted an entire chapter of his book *The Country Life Movement in the United States* to the role of farm women. He wrote

that farming required "co-partnership between a man and a woman";
however, he defined this partnership as between a man, the farmer, and
a woman, the housekeeper. He recognized, as have recent writers, that
there is an inseparable juncture between the household and the farm,
and that if the farm was to be reorganized along industrial lines, then
so, too, must the household. In his directives, however, he focused only
on women's reproductive labor—providing a moderate number of children to work the farm ("farm labor should be resident labor"), cooking simple but nutritious meals, and keeping a plain but clean home
with the help of "labor saving devices."[5]

Bailey believed farm women had already advanced because of the
development of creameries and the reassignment of dairy chores: "the
care of milk has been taken from great numbers of farm homes by the
neighborhood creamery, or at least by the building of a milk-house in
which the men by the use of machinery perform labor that was once
done by the housewife." But taking women out of the barn was only
part of the solution: they also had to have a modern home with running water as well as the opportunity to get out of the house at least
once a week for activities beyond household shopping trips. Further
suggestions included establishing cooperative laundries and encouraging schools and colleges to "recognize homemaking subjects" as a
means to educate women for scientific housekeeping.[6]

Bailey did not suggest that labor-saving equipment installed in the
barn would have made dairy chores far easier for women to manage,
nor did he recognize the irony of reducing dairy labor with machinery
only after it had become the work of men. It follows, then, that his purpose was not entirely to reduce women's labor but instead to remove
women from the barn. If the farm was to become an efficient business
operated on scientific principles, then the dairy, which utilized farm resources—land, water, feedstuffs, and barn—had to be integrated into
the cycle of seasonal and daily work. Dairying could not remain just
one of many chores that a housewife performed each day.

Though some nineteenth-century farm literature suggested that
men take over the care of fowl, in the reorganization of farm and
household under Bailey and the Country Life Movement, poultry raising was to remain women's work. The income from a large flock could
be significant, but fowl do not require as much in the way of farm re-

sources as cattle do. They are small, and handling them does not require great physical strength. Although some North Dakota agricultural publications referred to "poultrymen," there was no national or regional effort to wrest control of the barnyard flock from women's hands.[7]

In North Dakota, the strongest voice espousing the principles of the Country Life Movement was the Farmers' Institute, established in 1894 by the fledgling North Dakota Agricultural College (NDAC). Institutes had been held in other states since the 1840s. Though they shared a common name and purpose, each was organized separately. In theory, Farmers' Institutes could reach the "less progressive farmers and the women and youth of farmers' families" by carrying information about new agricultural practices directly from the U.S. Department of Agriculture to farmers. To that end, experts, including lecturers from NDAC and neighboring states' institutes, specialists on the staff of the North Dakota Agricultural Experiment Station (NDAES), and, occasionally, successful local farmers who adhered to NDAC principles toured the state, speaking in town halls and courthouses. Attendance varied according to the season, with audience members generally numbering between twenty-five and seventy-five per session. After 1900, copies of the institute's *Annual* were distributed to attendees.[8]

A national association formed around the various state institutes in 1896, among its goals the distribution of information through public lectures on "educated farming" and scientific agriculture, the promotion of self-respect among farmers, and the endorsement of state agricultural colleges and experiment stations. The American Association of Farmers' Institute Managers adopted most of the principles of the Country Life Movement without recognizing the contradiction between the movement's assessment of rural life and the institutes' reasons for existence:

> The institute lecturers are showing that agriculture today is the best and most profitable occupation that exists; that it provides more comforts for more people than any other, is less exacting in its requirements than any other, gives more leisure and purer joys than any other, and is the only occupation in which absolute and unqualified independence exists.

The association became the guide for institutes as they developed programs tailored to the agriculture and farming communities of their states.[9]

While the institutes and the association frankly focused on commercial agriculture and the education of "farmers' boys," North Dakota institute workers noted that women also attended the lectures. Their presence created something of a problem, for "most of the teaching was directed to the work of men." The decision to add a couple of women-centered lectures did not resolve the issue because "topics of peculiar value to women were not of special interest to men." The solution: develop an entirely separate Women's Institute, directed by women and "devoted wholly to their interests."[10]

In much the same way that women were removed from the farm dairy, they were to be excluded from public lectures on scientific agriculture. Superficially, the division was related to the need for an institute fully devoted to women's work; however, it is apparent that the primary concern was men's comfort. Though women had already demonstrated an interest in, or at least a tolerance for, agricultural topics, institute workers reasoned that men would not sit through lectures on family nutritional needs or scientific housekeeping. Women would be removed from the Farmers' Institute's agricultural lectures in order to protect men from presentations on home economics. Implicit in the separation was the concept that men's work could not be discussed properly in a mixed audience. The director of Minnesota's institute, O. C. Gregg, explained that, while women attended lectures on cooking, men had opportunity to take up "questions of breeding and other questions that could not be discussed in a common audience." Propriety and consideration of women's needs obscured the assumption, based on urban middle-class standards, that men's and women's interests diverged at the point at which, supposedly, their labor did.[11]

North Dakota institute workers persistently pursued the goal of educating farm folk in scientific agriculture. During the winter of 1901–2, the institute held twenty-seven meetings, drawing a total of 9,967 attendees. Between 1900 and 1916, the Farmers' Institute published the *Annual*, a collection of articles and speeches: in 1902, it printed ten thousand copies, available at meetings or by mail without cost. The *Annual* may have been the state's most widely distributed periodical during the years of peak institute activity.[12]

The *Annual* reflected many goals of the Country Life Movement. It carried articles on scientific crop and livestock agriculture as well as occasional pieces on small fruit growing, tree planting, and homemaking. Most of the articles were written by either NDAC or NDAES staff or professional Farmers' Institute speakers, but pieces were also submitted by other writers, among them farm women writing on agricultural topics about which experience and study had taught them a great deal.

The number of women who submitted pieces for the *Annual* was never large, and the fact that they wrote knowledgeably about livestock and crop agriculture is not surprising given their familiarity with those subjects, but the context of their articles is paradoxical. Even though during its early years the *Annual's* position suggested that the proper sphere of farm women was the home, the editor continued to include articles by women that indicated clearly the extension of their knowledge and interests beyond scientific housekeeping. Indeed, some writers developed a concept of integrated reproductive and productive roles that confounded the official prescription for separation of farm and farm home.[13]

The 1900 edition of the *Annual* contained an article by H. U. Thomas, the commissioner of agriculture and labor, entitled "The Institute and the Farmer." Thomas addressed farm youth and their need for a college education that would, "as far as possible, eliminate the element of chance from their labors and brighten and sweeten life with its triumphs." He assured readers that the NDAC "advocates the education of woman for her domestic as well as her social duties . . . that she may have respect for home life and its employments." The NDAC, Thomas said, offered a course for the "housekeeper and home maker."[14]

In 1901, two women wrote for the *Annual:* Frances Fitzmaurice of Crystal prepared a technical article on dairying, concluding with a careful analysis of the profit to be expected from each cow, and Mrs. G. I. C. discussed turkey raising in a piece reprinted from *Breeder's Gazette.* These articles, like most that followed, emphasized good management techniques to maximize profit. In 1904, Alice M. Sheppard of Judson wrote about raising calves and pigs on skimmed milk returned from the local creamery, a practice that reduced labor yet provided milk for livestock. She also wrote "A Modern Farm House Built at a Moderate Cost," in which she described a comfortable home with heated rooms and a bathroom. Sheppard demonstrated equal competence in barnyard and household topics.[15]

Two *Annual* articles written by women demonstrate the complex interconnections between the farm and the household; like their counterparts elsewhere, neither accepted Bailey's position on the separation of the two. The first of these was "Our Farm Life, How to Decrease Its Evils and Increase Its Blessings," by Mrs. E. T. Curtiss, who criticized northern plains farming and its large, widely dispersed farms that depended on seasonal and intensive family labor and the assistance of hired men of questionable moral quality. This arrangement was detrimental to the family, possibly dangerous to young children, and not particularly profitable. The solution: reduce farms' size and raise "the Three P's"—pigs, poultry, and potatoes. Smaller farms would allow neighboring children to play together frequently. Further, Curtiss argues, the "P" crops are more profitable than wheat and require year-round labor, which could be supplied by dependable men rather than by transients. She suggests that hired girls might be easier to keep if not endangered by transient laborers and that taxes could be lowered if the state did not have to jail so many of the latter for criminal activity. Curtiss also tells the story of a wheat farmer who believed himself too poor to build a barn and buy pigs or seed potatoes. A woman who successfully follows the rule of the "three P's" tells him to build a sod pig barn and henhouse and to give up tobacco for several months so he can afford to buy livestock. Throughout her article, Curtiss carefully intertwines the story of profitable farming with examples of a happy, safe, and satisfying family life. In addressing both farm and family needs, the woman farmer not only connects house and field but also resists the Country Life Movement's efforts to separate her work from that of her husband. Farming as a business could not be separated from farming as a way of life.[16]

The second of these articles is deceptively titled "Home Making." Rather than offering a prescription for scientific housekeeping, Mrs. V. K. Wilcox describes a farm home in which prosperity and happiness depend on contributions from all members of the family. She begins by discussing child rearing: boys should learn to farm, girls should be trained in homemaking, and these lessons should be supplemented with school courses. But Wilcox complicates this simple gender arrangement by stating that boys should also be trained to cook and sew and girls should learn to milk cows because they "may accidentally or otherwise have to step into that sphere."[17]

Wilcox concludes her piece with a poem that illustrates her understanding of a farm couple's complex relationship. "Carrying Half" is about Katie Lee and Willie Gray, childhood sweethearts who eventually marry and settle into their expected roles, Katie caring for the house and their many children, Willie looking after the farm. One day Willie tells Katie that the farm is not earning enough to pay the debt and suggests that a new cream separator would make her work more efficient. Katie, however, sees the problem differently: she refuses new equipment, focusing instead on applying principles of scientific agriculture to their farming practices. "She has studied well her part" and tells Willie to cull the herd, keep accurate records, adopt new methods of feeding and breeding, and look to the NDAC for techniques to improve the wheat crop. "Home Making" as described by Wilcox encompasses all facets of farm life: household, barn, and fields. Katie is a knowledgeable partner who is less interested in labor-saving devices for the house than in applying intelligent management principles to the entire farm.[18]

Collectively, the farm women who wrote for the *Annual* argued in favor of a much more expansive role for women and for a conceptual integration of the farm and household that more closely matched the reality of early twentieth-century farm life than the vision put forth by the Country Life Movement. None accepted Bailey's prescription for a farm wife whose role was almost entirely limited to domestic work, nor were they willing to give up productive work. They deeply respected the importance of caring for the family and the home, but rather than separate household (reproductive) labor from farm (productive) labor, they wanted to more completely integrate the two.

While women's arguments for modified farming fit the diversification model that professional agriculturists at the NDAC and the commissioner of agriculture's office had been promoting for years, their reasoning differed. Women contended that diversified farming—the "three P's" is one example—meant greater financial and personal security for the farm family. In their conception, the family, not the crops, would be the focus of the family farm.

Between 1900 and 1905, the *Annual* printed five articles by women on dairy, poultry, and general agriculture (Table 10). Three were on topics that could be called housekeeping, though at least one of these— Wilcox's—might be classified as general agriculture. Four of the five articles were written by farm women; the other, about NDAC domestic science courses, was by instructor Susan Ried. After 1905, there is a noticeable change in articles written by women for the *Annual:* the number by farm women decreased and the number by NDAC staff increased, their topics predictably shifting from agriculture, dairy, and poultry to domestic science. In the eleven years that followed, the *Annual* published nineteen pieces by women: two on poultry, the rest on domestic science, all but three of those written by NDAC faculty. The voices of farm women—writing from experience and study, viewing farm home and farm work as integrated functions—weakened and nearly disappeared from one of the state's most widely distributed farm publications.

In some ways, the message farm women presented was welcomed by the *Annual's* editor, particularly when they wrote about scientific farming, diversification, and improved dairy and poultry techniques or when they referred readers to the NDAC and the Farmers' Institute for expert advice. But in their concept of integrated productive and reproductive activities, they strayed far from the Country Life Movement's ideal farm woman. Their interest in production, not only of poultry but also in the dairy and the field, was out of step with the intent of the state commissioner of agriculture, the NDAC, the Farmers' Institute, and the Country Life Movement to remove women as managers and laborers in agricultural production. Although couched in terms of protecting them from drudgery and ascribing a false delicacy to women and an exaggerated importance to housework, separation of house and farm also served to enhance farming as a masculine activity.[19]

E. E. Kauffman, editor of the *Annual* until 1907, decided to limit farm women's voices in the journal after attending a few meetings of the American Association of Farmers' Institute Managers. There, the concept of Women's Institutes as a separate and carefully constructed feature of Farmers' Institutes was developed through the efforts of

Blanche Maddock, who first addressed the national convention in 1901. Perhaps the only woman present—certainly one of very few—she began by declaring the twentieth century to be "the woman's age" but moderated her zeal by saying that women's influence in a changing society had

> not been accomplished by any "declaration of rights" on the part of women, but by the courtesy of the gentlemen who have had these matters in charge. In some quarters we hear a great deal about the necessity of woman asserting her rights; this is not our aim.

	Dairy	Poultry	Agriculture	Domestic Science
1901	1	1		
1902			1	
1904	1	1		1
1905				2
1907				2
1909				1
1911		1		9
1915				1
1916		1		4
Totals	2	4	1	20

Table 10: Farmers' Institute Annual Articles by Women Authors

Maddock explained that women needed to be educated about "household economy," including sanitation, foods, clothing, and child-care, proposing that lectures on scientific housekeeping be added to Farmers' Institute programs. Her speech brought several positive responses from male participants, but their comments suggest they did not fully grasp her message: O. C. Gregg of Minnesota replied, in part, "There is something grand in the fact that a woman can prepare food for a hungry family."[20]

The discussion of establishing Women's Institutes continued among Maddock and other female institute workers at subsequent conventions. In 1904, attending his second meeting, Kauffman participated in the conversation, enthusiastically noting that a woman speaker had joined the North Dakota Farmers' Institute circuit. The response had been so positive that the organization, which could not afford to sponsor a separate meeting for women, would try to have a woman speak at every gathering in the coming year.[21]

Also at the 1904 convention, G. C. Creelman suggested that the discussion of Women's Institutes be turned over to the women delegates and that "the men retire so the ladies might hold a separate meeting to consider the subject." Apparently, such discussion could not hold the attention of men who would be organizing meetings at the state level. Creelman's statement, like Gregg's at an earlier convention, suggests that for all the rhetoric about the importance of farm women's role, men still refused to sit through what they thought would be just another cooking lesson. Maddock and her compatriots apparently agreed to this arrangement, and they continued to pursue their goal of a separate institute in which farm women could learn to apply scientific knowledge to housework and childcare. After all, the separation of their work from that of the men attending the national meeting reflected exactly what they intended to do in the state Farmers' Institutes and in the farm home.[22]

Now that separation was ideologically complete, through the *Annual* Kauffman could foster the identification of farm women's work with the house and children and eliminate articles suggestive of their competence in commercial agriculture. The 1905 *Annual* included only one article by a farm woman, Wilcox, and though the substance of the paper is—like women's farm work itself—hard to classify, the title was "Home Making." Kauffman's shift to academic authors reflects the ideology of the Country Life Movement and the national leadership of the Farmers' Institutes, which dictated the importance not only of developing scientific housekeeping as a farm woman's issue but of professionalizing the work through academic training. In subsequent editions, until the last one in 1916, most *Annual* articles by women were on domestic science topics, the authors primarily faculty of that department at the NDAC (Table 11).

The timing of farm women's issues being professionalized and domesticated coincides, not accidentally, with the advance of commercial creameries. As women lost one important aspect of their productive labor, they were encouraged to concentrate on the home as their "profession." Poultry remained part of their daily work but received little attention (compared with cooking, nutrition, and childcare) from the experts who favored Women's Institutes. These experts told women to modernize, to buy equipment and labor-saving machinery for the home; at the same time, women's access to income had diminished. Farm women were trapped between loss of earnings and productive work on one side and prescriptions they could not meet on the other. Nowhere was this state of affairs more evident than on the northern plains, where "settler" remained a useful word and settlement conditions prevailed in many townships.[23]

Table 11: Farmers' Institute Annual Articles by Farm Women and NDAC Domestic Science Faculty

	Farm Women	NDAC Faculty
1901	2	
1902	1	
1904	2	
1905	1	1
1907		2
1909		1
1911	1	9
1915		1
1916	4	1
Total	11	15

While the institute's staff sought to industrialize farm life with science, machinery, efficiency, and organization, much of its constituency was not ready to act on the message. When the Better Farming train and its exhibits on agriculture and domestic economy rolled out of Fargo in 1910, the Neher and Martin families were building sod houses, trying to borrow equipment and draft stock, and begging for food. They and their neighbors had little need for sewing demonstrations or lectures on "White Sauce and Its Uses." Yet, despite their pioneer circumstances, they would be caught up in the changes happening around them. Men like Ludwig Neher felt left behind by earlier arrivals who had equipment, draft stock, good barns, and large, fine houses, but he and other late settlers would eventually acquire material goods that would make farming easier, if not progressive.[24]

However, few farm women could keep house according to standards set by the Farmers' Institute. Trained in nineteenth-century farm women's roles and receiving little in the way of assistance or household improvements, they found themselves working harder to maintain the family in an industrial world that gave them theory and rhetoric but not much else. After 1905, farm women received minimal advice on how to improve their earning capacity or reduce their labor in the field and barnyard. No NDAC academic described how to attach a nonhuman power source to a churn or how to go about getting men and children to help in the house. Not until 1928 would NDAES researcher Alva Benton publish an article offering farm women information on poultry raising. Indeed, had the North Dakota Farmers' Institute managed to arrange separate sessions for men and women, men would not have been exposed to modern concepts of domestic science at all.[25]

Meanwhile, North Dakota farms underwent significant changes, their average size expanding from 342.9 acres in 1900 to 466.1 acres in 1920. Increasingly, the land was being farmed with improved equipment, but machinery required operators in the form of male farm hands, whose numbers grew from an average of .37 per farm in 1900 to .56 in 1917. The number of women hired to help rose during this period as well, but peak employment remained pitifully small at .16 per farm in 1917. So, while women's work expanded to feed the growing number of farm hands needed for swelling acreages, the assistance available to them in household labor did not increase accordingly. Their housework expanded while their income-producing work contracted.[26]

Daughters who might have helped their mothers were often lost to the family labor pool because—the demand for female labor being consistently high—they could earn cash "working out." Kjersti and Aagot Raaen worked at neighboring farms or took longer-term, better-paying jobs in town. Money came back to the farm, but in their absence Ragnhild Raaen had little help with the house or barnyard. At the same time, she increased her workload by taking in boarders to earn a little extra money. Children of farm families also left home to attend high school in town. Though their labor was missed, their parents, particularly their mothers, wanted to see them educated so that they could obtain jobs more highly valued by society. Many farm daughters, like Aagot Raaen and Mae Roberts Jensen, became teachers; others, like Bernice Berg, became nurses.[27]

The Country Life Movement's efforts to educate farm youth seemed to have backfired, preparing them for life in an industrial society but not serving to return them to the farm. In her speech to the Tri-State Grain Growers Convention in 1905, Mrs. Wilcox tried to put a positive spin on the flow of farm youth to the cities, noting that not all children would stay on the farm and that those who were "a little duller than others, do not seem just as brilliant and have not quite as much stamina" would not be happy on the farm, for "[t]hey will want to take up professions." In spite of her positive outlook, young people—more girls than boys—were leaving the farm for the city, an out-migration that caused the ratio of men to women on North Dakota farms to rise slightly from 1.18 in 1920 to 1.21 in 1930.[28]

For young women who left the farm, prospects were fairly good. In 1922 the commissioner of agriculture and labor set up employment offices in Fargo, Minot, Grand Forks, Bismarck, Devils Lake, and Oakes to take applications from both skilled and unskilled men and women. Unskilled labor for women was primarily domestic work; for men, farm work. There were very few manufacturing jobs in North Dakota at the time. In the two years covered by the commissioner's eighteenth biennial report, 79 percent of men applying for unskilled positions were successfully placed compared to only 30 percent of skilled male applicants (Table 12). Percentages for female applicants were noticeably higher: 82 percent of unskilled women and 51 percent of skilled women found work. While the number of women applying for unskilled work in both years was considerably smaller than that of men, similar numbers of men and women applied for skilled positions. Women with an adequate education could very likely find work, and those applying for unskilled positions were more likely to be placed than their male counterparts. The unskilled labor was similar to the work they would have performed in farm homes, but in urban settings they were likely to receive better pay and to enjoy conveniences such as electricity and indoor water that would make their tasks less rigorous. The female labor supply that farm women might have drawn on to help in an expanded dairy or to take over some of the household work was diverted toward skilled and unskilled urban positions.[29]

Despite advice from Farmers' Institute speakers, Dakota farm homes did not modernize very quickly. Bathrooms, electricity, telephones, and indoor water supply and drains remained rare. Some women remembered fondly their first modern stoves: Christina Link "cried for joy" when she got a Monarch kitchen stove. She recalled: "Fragrant soup in the kettle simmered on the back top end; water heated in the reservoir; cast irons for ironing could be so easily heated and ever-lasting yeast bread loaves raised higher and higher in the oven and I kept stuffing in dry cow chip blocks for fuel." Link's work was more easily completed with this efficient stove, but her circumstances—evidenced by the fuel she used—remained primitive compared to those of urban women. Her kitchen did not match those in which the NDAC's domestic science faculty was preparing its students to work.[30]

Table 12: Employment Office Figures, 1 July 1922–1 July 1924

Men	Registered	Placed	Percentage
Unskilled	24,160	19,240	79
Skilled	1,623	481	30

Women	Registered	Placed	Percentage
Unskilled	2,666	2,195	82
Skilled	830	420	51

As the North Dakota Farmers' Institute prepared public sessions and publications, it was responding to farm women's issues raised in a national forum. Circumstances on the northern plains were notably different from those in other parts of the country, however. In some regions of the United States, Women's Institutes and the Country Life Movement offered hope to women who felt trapped by farm life, but in late-settlement-era North Dakota, farm women were both losing their customary productive work and watching their important role in establishing new farms and communities pass into history. Their hard but respected and productive work was to be replaced with work no less difficult but far less respected, no matter how elevated the rhetoric. Narrowing the focus of farm women's work to the household served not only to impose incipient urban-middle-class standards but, more importantly for North Dakotans, as a symbol of the settlement era's passing. Women's labor in the fields and barns was acceptable when hardship was the only bond uniting disparate immigrant groups settling the northern plains: the challenges of survival had made women's early field work necessary and respectable. But by 1910, state agricultural leaders were anxious to put those days behind them. They wanted to believe—and to assure outsiders as well as the farm population—that North Dakota was as modern as older states. Part of this concept included retiring women from field and barnyard work.

In a brief essay entitled "The Farmer's Wife," the NDAC's W. C. Palmer, a regular on the institute circuit, wrote in 1911 of farm women's changing role:

> When the farm was started, and likely on the frontier, perhaps with but little to make the start, [the farmer's wife] helped her husband, she managed the home, cooked, sewed, mended for the family and at times for the hired men. In busy times she often helped with the milking, cared for the milk, made butter, raised chickens, managed the garden, often supplying the home with the necessary groceries and clothes with the egg and butter money. When hired men were scarce she even would take a hand in the field work. No work too hard, no trials too severe; when husband was discouraged, she furnished the hope, the cheer, the inspiration to go on. . . .
>
> By the hard work of husband, wife and children . . . the debts were paid, a big barn replaced the straw shed or perchance sod stable; then came a big house, and often with all the modern conveniences—more to care for but offset by hired help.

Palmer's essay demonstrates the distance between the institute's speakers and the state's farm folk. He associates the changing role of farm women with the end of the settlement era, but these were only words. In 1911, most farm women still lacked "modern conveniences," and farm help, especially for housework, was consistently scarce.[31]

Palmer was, however, correct in noting that emergence from pioneering poverty was marked by a new, large, well-built house. During the first decade of the twentieth century, many settlers, especially those who had arrived in the 1870s and 1880s, hired skilled carpenters to construct two-story, eight-room houses. Sometimes the lean-to and its various additions remained on the property, recycled as a barn or a storage shed or simply providing evidence of struggles they had faced. A new house symbolized success, triumph over multiple sources of adversity. Pictures of these structures appeared in county atlases and boomer literature, advertising the progressive nature of North Dakota agriculture. There were, however, few of these fine houses in most counties. Their presence indicated the increasing distance between wealthy farmers and those with just enough to get by. Farms with a large frame house were also identified by the NDAC and the Farmers' Institute as examples of progressive agriculture, as places where, they assumed, women's labor had settled into a "sphere" centered on house and children.[32]

Though both wealthy farm women and those of more modest circumstances still contended with enormous responsibilities, differences—centered primarily on field labor and, to a lesser extent, barnyard labor—were apparent. Regardless, both groups recognized that total separation of farm work and housework was impossible. For example, a farm woman, even one who did not milk or churn, could not start the laundry on the day the threshers came. How could a boundary between housework and farm work be defined when women's chores included feeding hired men as well as doing their laundry, mending, and cleaning? In suggesting that farm women's labor should be concentrated in the house, advocates did not actually diminish women's workload: their work remained oppressively heavy and tightly interwoven with the rest of the work of the farm.

As professionals promoted their concept of progressive agriculture and consequent social reorganization, they established artificial standards for farm women's activities. Women who worked in the fields and barnyards by necessity or by choice became marginalized or were labeled "backward." For immigrants that arrived late, settled on the poorest lands, and had less time to become established before hard times returned in 1920, women's labor helped stigmatize their groups as un-American or hard on women. Women of any ethnicity who continued to work in the fields became objects of pity rather than respected farm partners, willing and able to contribute labor and management skills to a family business. The theory promoted by the Country Life Movement left most Dakota farm women without the advantages it suggested, and without the respect and income they had earned.

The historical record offers two categories of farm women who might have matched the ideal conceived by the Country Life Movement and the Farmers' Institute. The first includes English-speaking women who wrote for the *Annual*, who had some education and enough extra time to prepare papers for presentation or publication. These women were most able to give up productive farm work and to concentrate on the house and family. Yet, rather than focus their energies exclusively on household matters, they maintained an interest in agriculture and spoke eloquently about the farm as an indivisible unit that could not afford to disregard the skills and labor of all its residents.

The other category consists of Yankee women who appeared, especially to immigrant children, to be idle, pampered, and privileged. The image, fantastical or exaggerated, both appealed and repelled. Aagot Raaen defined Yankees as those who "live on bread as white as snow and on cake, pie, pudding and jelly[.] They dress in such beautiful clothes that they can't work with their hands, they all have hired girls to do that." Sophie Trupin described the wife of the rancher she worked for as a child of twelve:

> She was small, round, and feminine, with blond wavy hair and creamy skin. She had obviously never worked out of doors. For that matter, she had not worked much indoors; she had hired help in the kitchen. She was wealthy, and her family had lived here in this country for generations. She was really at home. I remember being fascinated by her arms, which were round and puffy like a baby's, with a line like a rubberband at the wrist. Her hands were white, and looked smooth and delicate as I watched the small, agile fingers on the keyboard. I had never seen anyone quite like her; pink and white, dressed in something pale and fluffy, with an untroubled, childlike face.

This, then, might have been the model farm woman. Doubtless the rancher's wife was not as idle as she appeared, but to young Sophie Trupin, a child accustomed to field work and the respect it earned her, this woman seemed weak and immature. Though her material and social advantages were fascinating, her apparent infantile idleness was a state to which few farm women of any ethnic group aspired.[33]

In spite of Farmers' Institute efforts and domestic science professionals' intense interest and support, farm women could not afford to accept—or plainly rejected—the household as their sole and "proper sphere." Many continued doing the same work they had done since they began building farms and communities. Had the prosperous circumstances of the twentieth century's first two decades prevailed, more farm women might have experienced the narrowed focus on housework that Liberty Hyde Bailey and the Farmers' Institute offered. But the 1920 drop in farm prices and the depression and drought of the 1930s ensured that some North Dakota farm women would continue to labor in fields and barnyards as well as in the house. Looking back from the 1930s to his early years of marriage, George Tymchuk recalled,

> [Julia] worked out in the field with me. I gave her in the evening one hour to go home before I did. It was necessary to feed the chickens, ducks and we had pigeons and calves. So I let her go one hour earlier. She helped me in the field. Then I bought a Ford tractor and a truck and she retired.

To which Julia replied, "Oh no, I didn't retire. I continued to seed."[34]

The Country Life Movement and agencies that advocated similar principles sought to rationalize and industrialize the social relations of family and work on American farms by using a model based on the ideal of the urban middle-class family. Professional agriculturists' goals for farm women parallel changes in middle-class women's status as described by historian Jeanne Boydston. Society's concept of middle-class women's roles underwent a transformation in the early nineteenth century, from "worker" to "nurturer." Though this paradigm had little real effect on women's lives, particularly working-class women's lives, the standards were prescribed for all women no matter how their circumstances differed from those of the middle class. This shift in the ideal woman's role, from worker to mother, took place three generations later in North Dakota, but its effect on social concepts of farm women's roles was no less significant.[35]

As pioneer women aged, some were recognized in official proceedings, but not for churning the first pound of butter in a county or for bringing the first rhubarb plants to a township and sharing sprouts with their neighbors. Nor were they honored for having hauled rocks from the fields or for having built houses, barns, and churches. They were honored as the first white women (sometimes called the "first woman") in their township or county to give birth, something only women can do, something quite appropriate for a woman of any period or location. They were honored for contributing to population growth that supported the state's development. As Boydston points out, the cost of this new social identity to farm women was the respect and power they had earned as working partners on Dakota homesteads and farms.[36]

In 1932, Washburn storekeeper Mary Barnes Williams wrote a book in tribute to some of the women who had settled in McLean County. Though she recounted the lives of fifty women who spoke with pride about their contributions to their communities and about the work they had done in the fields and in the barns, Williams overlooked the significance of that labor in her analysis. Her language suggests a reduction of farm women's work to the biologically essential role of sexual reproduction:

> Dakota was a land that coaxed and wooed men. Its fertile prairies were man hungry. It called for men, must eventually have men. There were thousands of acres awaiting them. The woman who mated up with one of these adventurous wheat growers, seemed merely a bridesmaid to a wider sort of marriage—the union of worker with his land. These pioneer women, labored between their narrow walls merely that their husbands might labor out on their wide acres. And they in turn, must produce man children of their own and give them to the land, the land that receded and beckoned and receded again, like a willful mistress.

Their work disguised and devalued, members of North Dakota's first generation of farm women were not recognized as partners in settlement but as background figures lacking any title but "mother," who gave birth to sons that would fulfill the state's destiny.[37]

From pioneering partner to supporting mother, the recorded role of settlement-era North Dakota farm women changed during the lives of the first generation of European immigrant and Yankee American women. Many could not afford to accept the new role, and few aspired to the degree of idleness they perceived to be part of the prescription. They continued to labor as necessary on the farm, but they lost the agricultural establishment's support of their pursuit of productive activities, of their claim to a portion of farm income based on their contributions of labor and management skills, and of their argument that the labor of each family member is integrated into a farm's seasonal productivity. Sally McMurry dated the beginning of agriculture's "defeminization" to the 1850s; by 1920, many academic agriculturists judged the process complete. The farm and its work were deemed appropriate to men, and "farmer," more assuredly than ever before, became a term synonymous with men.[38]

Conclusion

*Give her a reward of her labors and let her works
praise her at the city gates.*
PROVERBS 31:31

When North Dakota pioneer women looked over the long, unbroken prairies they had claimed with their husbands, they saw land for their children and their children's children. They did not look backward to see the Chippewa, Dakota, Lakota, Mandan, Arikara, and Hidatsa displaced and confined, their former ways of life taken from them by politicians, soldiers, and settlers with different economic and social systems. European American women looked forward, remembering from deep within their own pasts that a future secure for generations could only be based on land ownership and the ability to farm. But by the time these women retired from farming, the security offered by land ownership was becoming less certain. The 1920s depression in commodity markets followed by the Great Depression and drought of the 1930s meant that many pioneers would lose their land to mortgages or that their children would have to find jobs in cities and towns. For those who held on through the difficult years, there were good times to come, a period during which farmers dared hope the land would serve their children well.

Today, their vision is troubled again by unstable markets, as well as by a long spell of unfavorable climate and by dependence on uncertain government support programs that are subject to political wrangling and a tendency to engulf farmers in whirlwinds of paperwork. The state's population has fallen since 1930, when pioneers and their children numbered more than 680,000 residents, to a present figure of fewer than 640,000. A high percentage of the population lives in four major cities. Small towns that serve farm families are dying; some have unincorporated. Rural churches and schools are closing; some school

163

districts claim no children under the age of five. Distance is once again a factor in the lives of farm families: they may be thirty miles from a school, seventy-five from a doctor and dentist.[1]

The legacy of pioneer farm women—family, community, and work—still frames farm women's lives today. A recent study of rural North Dakota women reveals that they continue to occupy the heart of farm, family, and community. On many farms, labor performed by pioneer women is still being performed by their modern counterparts. Contrary to the plans of early twentieth-century agricultural experts, women have not been replaced by tractors or by hired help. Listening to contemporary women's voices, one hears a clear echo of pioneer women's lives. They wonder at their strength and skill and express dismay at their lengthy list of tasks and long days followed by more long days. "I do . . . all the cooking. . . . the ranch books. . . . a lot of riding. . . . I do fencing. I drive the tractors. I feed cattle," said one woman, trying to sort through all of her responsibilities. Another commented, "We do have to be very versatile out here, and . . . work like a hired man really . . . without the paycheck." Women work on the farm as partners to their husbands, and when they work off the farm, as many do, they worry about how the farm work will get done without them. Off-farm jobs provide health insurance, retirement benefits, and a reliable paycheck: the partnership now extends beyond the barnyard to an external system of economic support that sustains the family.[2]

Many women generate income from farm resources, too. Butter and eggs are no longer likely to find ready markets, but other, innovative means allow women to be at home to work on the farm when needed, to raise their children, or to avoid driving thirty miles to a low-paying job. Patti Patrie established a raspberry patch on her Bowdon farm to help her children raise money for college. Today she runs a six-acre "u-pick" raspberry farm with a gift shop and an Internet site for marketing her jams and other raspberry products.[3]

Family concerns still motivate many women to remain on the farm and work long hours. They prefer to be home when their children are, and they believe the farm is the best place to raise a family. One woman said, "I love the fact that the kids and Will and I are together all the time. . . . It's really good for the family. We work together. We play together." Childcare still presents a problem for those who do not have

family nearby to help. One farm woman, when asked how she managed to drive a tractor while caring for small children, reported on a
system remarkably similar to that of the pioneers: her children would
"sit in a corner of the field, [with] a bunch of toys [and] stand up and
wave every round [she would] make."[4]

Though neighborly activities and gatherings have changed,
women's efforts remain central to the vitality of rural communities.
Today's women seek to maintain the connections pioneer women built.
Medical care is an urgent need requiring many volunteer hours because so few rural municipalities have a clinic. Community and parish
nurses routinely serve elderly clients and are often called to aid victims
of farm accidents until the ambulance arrives. Many communities support a volunteer ambulance service that depends on various forms of
fund raising to remain properly equipped. Stores and cafés provide
gathering places for rural residents as well as a social and economic link
between the people of farm towns and their rural neighbors. North
Dakota is dotted with community-owned enterprises like Drucker's
General Store in Esmond and the People's Store in Forbes, all of which
depend on volunteers to manage the grocery and to drive to larger
towns for stock. Women work as volunteers and managers and, of
course, shop in these stores. Their voluntary labor and interest play a
significant role in maintaining fragile rural communities.[5]

Even this cursory look at contemporary farm women suggests the
ultimate failure of professional agriculturists' efforts to remove
women from active roles in farming. Women's contributions remain
as important to today's northern plains farms and farm communities
as they were in 1900, and only a little more visible. Too often, the question asked of these women is "Why don't you quit—leave the long
hours, the hard times, the low income behind—and take your skills to
a city where you can earn some real money?" The answer is best provided by the pioneer women for whom the work, hardships, and sacrifices had immediate value and meaning that transcended their own
lives.[6]

When pioneer women "retired," many continued working, either
on the farm or on a lot in town. Mrs. Christ Ludwig stayed on the farm
well into her seventh decade, doing "a man's work . . . milking cows,
plowing, running a binder." Ragnhild Raaen moved to Hatton in 1920,

keeping a milk cow and making hay on the edge of town. She was eighty-one. Many raised chickens in the yards of their town homes. Elderly pioneer women did not easily relinquish a sense that providing for their own needs was proper, a means of preventing dependency on charity or on children unwilling or unable to share scarce resources. Work signified a worthy life lived within the approving embrace of family and community.[7]

In 1932, when Mary Barnes Williams published her wonderful collection of McLean County pioneer women's biographies, she used a maternalist analysis, muting the voices of her subjects, who talked plainly about their roles in settlement, farming, raising families, and founding new communities, emphasizing instead the "most divine and sublime mission in life—womanhood and motherhood." Their roles seemed too bold, so Williams cloaked them in the dignity of motherhood. But bold they were. Few farm women expressed the desire for a very different life than they had lived on the northern plains. They knew they had been full partners in one of America's last pioneering experiences, and that in the process they had "carried half."[8]

Notes

Notes to Introduction

1. Epigraph: Mrs. V. K. Wilcox, "Home Making," North Dakota Farmers' Institute *Annual* 5 (1905): 98–102. Text: Wilcox, "Home Making."

2. North Dakota Century Code, 14-07-01 and 14-07-03. The marriage code, originally written in 1877, remains intact today. South Dakota, North Dakota's territorial companion, has also retained these sections of the civil code.

3. North Dakota Century Code, 14-07-02. The political subordination of women is defined elsewhere in the state constitution and laws. Women could vote on any local school issue beginning in 1883 but had no other voting rights until 1917.

4. Mary Neth describes the Golden Age of Agriculture as a period of high contrast with the depressed markets of the 1890s and 1920s in *Preserving the Family Farm: Women, Community, and the Foundations of Agribusiness in the Midwest, 1900–1940* (Baltimore, MD: Johns Hopkins University Press, 1995).

5. Peggy R. Sanday, "Toward a Theory of the Status of Women," *American Anthropologist* 75 (October 1973): 1682–1700. Sanday is not the only theorist to explain women's work in relation to social gender systems. For a summary of prominent theories, especially as they apply to women in the American West, see Karen Anderson, "Work, Gender, and Power in the American West," *Pacific Historical Review* 61 (1992): 481–99.

6. Margery Wolf discusses the "three complexly integrated arenas in which rural women are located" in "Rural Women and Feminist Issues," an unpublished essay written in support of the Rockefeller Fellowship at the University of Iowa in 1987.

7. Interviews conducted by Writers' Project workers are housed in the archives of the State Historical Society of North Dakota [hereafter SHSND] in Bismarck as Historical Data Project Records, Pioneer Biography Files [hereafter PBF], 1936–40, North Dakota Writers' Project Records, Ethnic Group Files [hereafter EGF], 1935–42, and North Dakota Writers' Project Records, Hard Wheat Study Files [hereafter HWF], 1935–42. All are available on microfilm.

8. The three unpublished diaries I have used are Mae Roberts Jensen Diary, 1884–1918, SHSND; Julia Gage Carpenter Diary, 1882–1904, copy in Orin G. Libby Manuscript Collection, Elwyn B. Robinson Department of Special Collections, Chester Fritz Library, University of North Dakota, Grand Forks [hereafter Special Collections, UND]; Mary Alma Barrett Still Diary, 1910–14, North Dakota Institute for Regional Studies, North Dakota State University, Fargo [hereafter NDIRS]. Mary Dodge Woodward's diary has been published as *The Checkered Years: A Bonanza Farm Diary 1884–88*, ed. Mary Boynton Cowdrey (Caldwell, ID: Caxton Printers, 1937; Reprint, with introduction by Elizabeth Jameson, St. Paul: Minnesota Historical Society Press, 1989). Published memoirs include Rachel Calof, *Rachel Calof's Story: Jewish Homesteader on the Northern*

Plains, ed. J. Sanford Rikoon (Bloomington: Indiana University Press, 1995); Pauline Neher Diede, *Homesteading on the Knife River Prairies,* ed. Elizabeth Hampsten (Bismarck, ND: Germans from Russia Heritage Society, 1983), and *The Prairie Was Home* (Richardton, ND: Abbey Press and John H. Gengler, 1986); Aagot Raaen, *Grass of the Earth* (Northfield, MN: Norwegian-American Historical Association, 1950; Reprint, with introduction by Barbara Handy-Marchello, St. Paul: Minnesota Historical Society Press, 1994); Era Bell Thompson, *American Daughter* (Chicago: University of Chicago Press, 1946; Reprint, St. Paul: Minnesota Historical Society Press, 1986); Sophie Trupin, *Dakota Diaspora: Memoirs of a Jewish Homesteader* (Lincoln: University of Nebraska Press, 1984); Nina Farley Wishek, *Along the Trails of Yesterday* (Ashley, ND: The Ashley Tribune, 1941); Carrie Young, *Nothing to Do but Stay: My Pioneer Mother* (Iowa City: University of Iowa Press, 1991).

9. See Jane Adams, *The Transformation of Rural Life: Southern Illinois, 1890–1990* (Chapel Hill: University of North Carolina Press, 1994); Marjorie Griffin Cohen, *Women's Work, Markets and Economic Development in Nineteenth Century Ontario* (Toronto: University of Toronto Press, 1988); David B. Danbom, *Born in the Country: A History of Rural America* (Baltimore, MD: Johns Hopkins University Press, 1995); John Mack Faragher, *Women and Men on the Overland Trail* (New Haven, CT: Yale University Press, 1979); Deborah Fink, *Open Country Iowa: Rural Women, Tradition and Change* (Albany: State University of New York Press, 1986) and *Agrarian Women: Wives and Mothers in Rural Nebraska, 1880–1940* (Chapel Hill: University of North Carolina Press, 1992); Dee Garceau, *The Important Things of Life: Women, Work and Family in Sweetwater County, Wyoming, 1880–1929* (Lincoln: University of Nebraska Press, 1997); Wava G. Haney and Jane B. Knowles, eds., *Women and Farming: Changing Structures, Changing Roles* (Boulder, CO: Westview Press,

1988); Julie Roy Jeffrey, *Frontier Women: The Trans-Mississippi West, 1840–1880* (New York: Hill and Wang, 1979); Katherine Jellison, *Entitled to Power: Farm Women and Technology, 1913–1963* (Chapel Hill: University of North Carolina Press, 1993); Joan M. Jensen, *Loosening the Bonds: Mid-Atlantic Farm Women, 1750–1850* (New Haven, CT: Yale University Press, 1986) and *Promise to the Land: Essays on Rural Women* (Albuquerque: University of New Mexico Press, 1991); Joan M. Jensen and Darlis A. Miller, *New Mexico Women: Intercultural Perspectives* (Albuquerque: University of New Mexico Press, 1986); H. Elaine Lindgren, *Land in Her Own Name: Women as Homesteaders in North Dakota* (Fargo: NDIRS, 1991); Donald B. Marti, *Women of the Grange: Mutuality and Sisterhood in Rural America, 1866–1920* (New York: Greenwood Press, 1991); Valerie Matsumoto, *Farming the Home Place: A Japanese American Community in California, 1919–1982* (Ithaca, NY: Cornell University Press, 1993); Sandra L. Myres, *Westering Women and the Frontier Experience, 1800–1915* (Albuquerque: University of New Mexico Press, 1982); Paula Nelson, *After the West Was Won: Homesteaders and Town-Builders in Western South Dakota, 1900–1917* (Iowa City: University of Iowa Press, 1986); Neth, *Preserving the Family Farm;* Nancy Grey Osterud, *Bonds of Community: The Lives of Farm Women in Nineteenth Century New York* (Ithaca, NY: Cornell University Press, 1991); Carolyn Sachs, *The Invisible Farmers: Women in Agricultural Production* (Totowa, NJ: Rowman and Allanhead, 1983); Rebecca Sharpless, *Fertile Ground, Narrow Choices: Women on Cotton Farms of the Texas Blackland Prairies, 1900–1940* (Chapel Hill: University of North Carolina Press, 1999).

10. Rosa Sigurdardottir Gudmundson, in North Dakota Federation of Women's Clubs, Pioneer Mother Project Records [hereafter PMP], 1938–53, SHSND.

Notes to Chapter 1

1. Epigraph: Rosa Sigurdardottir Gudmundson, PMP. Text: Quoted in Axel Tollefson, "Historical Notes on the Norwegians in the Red River Valley," *Collections of the State Historical Society of North Dakota* 7 (1925): 136–57.

2. Ole Balkan, EGF, Griggs County.

3. Elwyn B. Robinson, *History of North Dakota* (Lincoln: University of Nebraska Press, 1966), 6–10; Frank J. Bavendick, *Climate and Weather in North Dakota* (Bismarck, ND: Water Conservation Commission, 1952), 12, 14; Robert P. Wilkins and Wynona Huchette Wilkins, *North Dakota: A Bicentennial History* (New York: W. W. Norton, 1977), 10. A wet cycle beginning in 1993 has severely damaged recent crops.

4. Edgar I. Stewart, ed., *Penny-An-Acre Empire in the West* (Norman: University of Oklahoma Press, 1968), 25, 26, 35, 37, 183.

5. Bureau of Business and Economic Research, University of North Dakota, and North Dakota Federal Aid Coordinator, Office of State and Local Planning, *Statistical Abstract of North Dakota* (Grand Forks: University of North Dakota Press, 1979), 101.

6. U.S. Census Office, *Report on the Production of Agriculture as Returned at the Tenth Census, 1880* (Washington, DC: GPO, 1883), 101.

7. Robinson, *History of North Dakota*, 3.

8. Mary Jane Schneider, *North Dakota's Indian Heritage* (Grand Forks: University of North Dakota Press, 1990), 21, 66–85.

9. Schneider, *North Dakota's Indian Heritage*, 122–40.

10. Marshall Harris, *Origins of the Land Tenure System in the United States* (Ames: Iowa State University Press, 1953), 2.

11. Robinson, *History of North Dakota*, 105–6. Today, the Dakota call their reservation Spirit Lake.

12. Robinson, *History of North Dakota*, 105–6.

13. Schneider, *North Dakota's Indian Heritage*, 104–21.

14. Stanley N. Murray, "The Turtle Mountain Chippewa," in *The Centennial Anthology of North Dakota History,* ed. Janet Daley Lysengen and Ann M. Rathke, 93–100 (Bismarck: SHSND, 1996); Canute LaFrance and Amos Cartier LaFrance, PBF, Rolette County.

15. Christianson in North Dakota Writers' Project Records, Folklore Files, SHSND.

16. On the nature of personal relationships between settlers and Indians, see Timothy Kloberdanz, "In the Land of the Inyan Woslata: Plains Indian Influences on Reservation Whites," *Journal of the American Historical Society of Germans from Russia* 15 (Summer 1992): 15–27; "Jennie T. (Sharp) Robinson" in Mary A. Barnes Williams, *Fifty Pioneer Mothers of McLean County* (Washburn, ND: Privately printed, 1932), 199.

17. The idea that imaginary lines drawn on maps carry political power is developed by Gregory Nobles in "Straight Lines and Stability: Mapping the Political Order of the Anglo-American Frontier," *Journal of American History* 80 (June 1993): 9–35. The southern part of Dakota Territory became South Dakota.

18. Robinson, *History of North Dakota*, 129.

19. Robinson, *History of North Dakota*, 131–32.

20. Robinson, *History of North Dakota*, 127; Linda Slaughter, *Fortress to Farm, or Twenty-three Years on the Frontier,* ed. Hazel Eastman (New York: Exposition Press, 1972), 57; Wilkins and Wilkins, *North Dakota,* 11.

21. Robinson, *History of North Dakota*, 141–42, 227–28; Harold E. Briggs, "The Great Dakota Boom," in Lysengen and Rathke, eds., *Centennial Anthology,* 110–11, 127.

22. Robinson, *History of North Dakota*, 134–36.

23. Briggs, "Great Dakota Boom," 129; Linda Slaughter, *The New Northwest: A Pamphlet Stating Briefly the Advantages of Bismarck and Vicinity* (Bismarck, ND: Burleigh County Pioneer's Association, 1874), 3–4. Slaughter's intensely boomer

piece contrasts sharply with her 1893 memoir, in which she wrote of the "absence of rain, the hot winds, the blinding dust, the scorching sun at noon, the chilling cold at night and the scarcity of wood," *Fortress to Farm,* 56.

24. Robinson, *History of North Dakota,* 153; Powers quoted in Briggs, "Great Dakota Boom," 114.

25. Robinson, *History of North Dakota,* 148–49. Under the Timber Culture Act, the number of trees to be planted, the number of acres planted to trees, the number of surviving trees, and the number of years of survival varied as Congress tried in vain to forest the grasslands by law.

26. Robinson, *History of North Dakota,* 134, 137–39. On bonanza farms see also Stanley N. Murray, *The Valley Comes of Age: A History of Agriculture in the Valley of the Red River of the North, 1812–1920* (Fargo: NDIRS, 1967), and Hiram Drache, *Day of the Bonanza: A History of Bonanza Farming in the Red River Valley of the North* (Fargo: NDIRS, 1964).

27. Robinson, *History of North Dakota,* 154.

28. Robinson, *History of North Dakota,* 152–54; Briggs, "Great Dakota Boom," 125.

29. Robinson, *History of North Dakota,* 235–36; U.S. Department of Agriculture, *Yearbook of Agriculture 1900* (Washington, DC: GPO, 1901). On diversification, see *Biennial Reports of the Commissioner of Agriculture and Labor to the Governor of North Dakota* (Bismarck, ND: The Board, 1892–1924).

30. Elizabeth Solem, EGF, McKenzie County.

31. The Burleigh County Pioneer's Association organized in 1874, one year after the Northern Pacific Railroad reached the brand-new town of Bismarck. Benjamin F. and Linda W. Slaughter Papers, SHSND. The Steele County Pioneer Association was established eight years after the founding of the county seat, but none of the charter members had lived in Steele County for eight years. Records of the Steele County Museum, Hope, ND.

32. Timothy Kloberdanz, "Volksdeut-

sche: The Eastern European Germans," in *Plains Folk: North Dakota's Ethnic History,* ed. William C. Sherman and Playford V. Thorson (Fargo: NDIRS, 1988), 117–56.

33. William C. Sherman, *Prairie Mosaic: An Ethnic Atlas of Rural North Dakota* (Fargo: NDIRS, 1983). Sherman's study demonstrates the persistence of ethnic communities over more than a century.

34. U.S. Department of Commerce, Bureau of the Census, *Fifteenth Census of the United States: 1930,* Population and Agriculture (Washington, DC: GPO, 1932); U.S. Census Office, *Report of the Statistics of Agriculture in the United States at the Eleventh Census 1890* (Washington, DC: GPO, 1895).

35. Henry G. Stoltzenburg, PBF, Adams County; N. Johanna Kildahl, "Reminiscences," 7, N. Johanna Kildahl Papers, 1895–1936, Special Collections, UND; "Clara M. Jensen Peterson," in Williams, *Fifty Pioneer Mothers,* 79.

Notes to Chapter 2

1. Title quotation: unnamed woman, EGF, McLean County. Epigraph: Caroline Gjelsnes to Marius Gjelsnes, 22 June 1892, trans. Orville Bakken, Special Collections, UND.

2. John Geizler, PBF, McIntosh County. A year after Wilhelmina died, John Geizler married her seventeen-year-old cousin, who subsequently bore thirteen children. She was, according to Catherine, good to her stepchildren.

3. Virginia Scharff, "Gender and Western History: Is Anybody Home on the Range?" *Montana: The Magazine of Western History* (Spring 1991): 65.

4. Raaen, *Grass of the Earth,* 134–35; Calof, *Rachel Calof's Story,* 10; Peter Hansen, PBF, Barnes County.

5. Wishek, *Along the Trails,* 243; Jacob Zimmerman, EGF, McIntosh County. Out of respect for the descendants of this woman, I choose to not name her here. The terms "Germans from Russia," "German Russian," and "Black Sea Germans" all refer to ethnic Germans who settled in South Russia near the Black Sea at the invitation of

Catherine the Great in the eighteenth and nineteenth centuries. On their history, see Adam Giesinger, *From Catherine to Khrushchev: The Story of Russia's Germans* (Lincoln, NE: American Historical Society of Germans from Russia, 1981), and Richard Sallet, *Russian German Settlements in the United States,* trans. LaVern J. Rippley and Armand Bauer (Fargo: NDIRS, 1974).

6. Susannah Preece Bonde and Mrs. Douglas Bell, PMP; Lindgren, *Land in Her Own Name,* 111. Statistics compiled from U.S. Census Office, *Compendium of the Eleventh Census 1890,* Population (Washington, DC: GPO, 1892); U.S. Census Office, *Twelfth Census of the United States Taken in the Year 1900,* Population (Washington, DC: The Office, 1902); U.S. Department of Commerce, Bureau of the Census, *Thirteenth Census of the United States Taken in the Year 1910,* Population (Washington, DC: GPO, 1913); U.S. Department of Commerce, Bureau of the Census, *Fourteenth Census of the United States Taken in the Year 1920,* Population (Washington, DC: GPO, 1922); *Fifteenth Census,* Population. Unless otherwise specified, all calculations are drawn from census figures on the population of men and women over the age of fifteen.

7. I have chosen to not use names in this discussion of illegitimacy. In many cases, the descendants of these pioneers continue to live and farm in the same county and township and may not be aware of the information I have found. This necessarily requires that I eliminate all references to PBF records and PMP records, which are organized by county and pioneer's name.

8. *Birth, Stillbirth and Infant Mortality Statistics for the Birth Registration Area of the United States, 1928* (Washington: GPO, 1930), 12. In 1917, the state legislature declared all children legitimate, so the term "illegitimate" is used here in its common definition, meaning children born to unmarried women, rather than as a term denoting legal status.

9. Wishek, *Along the Trails,* 245; U.S. Department of Labor, Children's Bureau,

Publication 160: *Dependent and Delinquent Children in North Dakota and South Dakota* (Washington, DC: GPO, 1926), 64. Many descendants of the state's pioneers have told me that their grandparents were not married before the first, or subsequent, pregnancies. However, few people felt the need to explain discrepancies in marriage and birth dates to Writers' Project interviewers. In many of these interviews, the birth date of the first child simply does not appear.

10. Diede, *Prairie Home,* 144.

11. Cavalier County Sheriff's Report, 24 February 1900 and 29 March 1901; Pembina County Sheriff's Report, 15 April 1901; LaMoure County Sheriff's Report, 22 February 1896. State Governor's Records, Sheriff's Jail Reports, Series 172, State Archives, SHSND. The state does not mandate counties to maintain arrest records, but for a few years sheriffs sent their arrest reports to the governor's office. These records appear to be incomplete.

12. Aagot Raaen Papers, Hatton-Eielson Museum, Hatton, ND.

13. Raaen Papers, Hatton-Eielson Museum.

14. "Mor," Raaen Papers, Hatton-Eielson Museum. I am indebted to John Bye of the NDIRS for information concerning Ragnhild Raaen's premarital pregnancy.

15. Woman's Christian Temperance Union Papers, WCTU (Florence Crittenton Home), Record Book, 1892–94, SHSND.

16. *State v. Peoples* 82 NW 749 (1900); *State v. McKnight* 75 NW 790 (1898). A federal study indicated that in 1921, of 208 unwed mothers, 60 reported their occupation as "domestic servant," 12 as "waitress" or "hotel worker." There were 12 teachers, 12 clerks, 15 "other" occupations, 5 schoolgirls, and 92 occupations not reported. U.S. Department of Labor, Children's Bureau, *Dependent and Delinquent Children,* 63.

17. Calof, *Rachel Calof's Story,* 73.

18. Larry Peterson, "Women in North Dakota: The First Century of Population History, 1890–1990" (paper, Northern Great Plains History Conference, La Crosse WI, 1996); U.S. Census Office, *Twelfth Cen-*

sus, Population, part 2; *Statistical Abstract of the United States, 1930* (Washington, DC: GPO, 1930); Judith Walzer Leavitt, *Brought to Bed: Child-Bearing in America, 1750–1950* (New York: Oxford University Press, 1986), 19–20. The birthrates of the 1920s are probably unrealistically low. Well into the 1930s, the state was still urging parents to register the births of their children. Part of the problem for the historian is to correlate the various mathematical calculations of fertility in some meaningful way. Peterson's figures are a ratio of living children under five to all living women between 15 and 44. Some calculate birthrate as a ratio of births per 1,000 population, but the rate is variously calculated as births per 1,000 women, per 1,000 married women, or per 1,000 women between 15 and 44. Without accurate birth registration data, Peterson's research remains the most accurate across decades.

19. U.S. Bureau of the Census, *Census of Population 1900, North Dakota*, Vol. 7 (Washington, DC: Bureau of the Census Microfilm Laboratory); U.S. Bureau of the Census, *Census of Population 1910, North Dakota*, Vol. 7 (Washington, DC: Bureau of the Census Microfilm Laboratory). In 1900, women in the United States bore an average of 3.56 children.

20. U.S. Bureau of the Census, *Census of Population 1900* and *Census of Population 1910*; Raaen, *Grass of the Earth; Standard Atlas of McIntosh County North Dakota* (Chicago: George A. Ogle and Co., 1911); *Standard Atlas of McLean County, North Dakota* (Chicago: George A. Ogle and Co., 1911).

21. On the diphtheria epidemic, see Wishek, *Along the Trails*, 280, 292. "Summer complaint" commonly struck children in their second summer, when they were no longer nursing. Drinking unrefrigerated cow's milk or contaminated water during warm summer months caused intestinal disorders that were sometimes fatal. Marilyn Irvin Holt discusses causes of infant death, particularly "summer complaint" in *Linoleum, Better Babies and the Modern Farm Woman, 1890–1930* (Albuquerque:

University of New Mexico Press, 1995), 101–2.

22. Schilling in U.S. Bureau of the Census, *Census of Population 1900*.

23. Jeffrey, *Frontier Women*, 57–58; J. O. Meidinger, EGF, McIntosh County. Other immigrants such as Thomas Yecovanko of Ukraine (EGF, McLean County) and Dimetri Simshaw from Russia (EGF, McLean County) also realized that the plan to give substantial farms to their sons at maturity had backfired, leaving the sons without education or land and the parents with debts in their old age.

24. Bertha Steigen Bartz, PBF, Barnes County; Bertha Nystrom (Dronan), PBF, Steele County. Ironically, Nystrom's sister objected to Nystrom working out of the home. She told Nystrom that "American women stayed home and let their men do the work." On the use of the term "sick" for pregnancy, see Elizabeth Hampsten, *Read This Only to Yourself: The Private Writings of Midwestern Women, 1880–1910* (Bloomington: Indiana University Press, 1982), 102–11.

25. Diede, *Homesteading*, 46, 48, 58.

26. Herman Roemmich, *A Conflict of Three Cultures: Germans from Russia in America, A History of the Jacob Roemmich Family* (Fargo: NDIRS, 1991), 44.

27. Calof, *Rachel Calof's Story*, 84, 88–89; Gwendoline Kincaid to Mamie Goodwater, 24 June 1895, and Mary Kincaid to Mamie Goodwater, 28 February 1896, in *To All Inquiring Friends: Letters, Diaries and Essays in North Dakota 1880–1910*, comp. Elizabeth Hampsten (Grand Forks: University of North Dakota, Department of English, 1980), 18–19; Frances Wold, ed., "The Letters of Effie Hanson, 1917–1923: Farm Life in Troubled Times," in Lysengen and Rathke, eds., *Centennial Anthology*, 275.

28. Ben Goodwater to Mamie Goodwater, 4 February 1895, in Hampsten, comp., *To All Inquiring Friends*, 12; *State of North Dakota v. W. E. Longstreth*, 19 ND 268; *State of North Dakota v. E. H. Belyea*, 9 ND 353. Individuals have told me in private conversations that abortifacients were available

through doctors or pharmacists. Though I have not been able to obtain records to confirm these anecdotes, the stories indicate that abortifacients would have been available only in specific urban locations.

29. James Grassick, in Stephen L. McDonough Papers, SHSND.

30. Carpenter Diary, 102–6. Special Collections, UND. Aberdeen is more than sixty miles from the southern edge of LaMoure County.

31. Magdalena Job, interview with author, Medina, ND, 19 October 1990.

32. Calof, *Rachel Calof's Story*, 85.

33. "Thomas Raaen and Ragnhild Rodningen," 4–5, 7, Raaen Papers, Hatton-Eielson Museum.

34. Job, interview, 19 October 1990.

35. Diede, *Homesteading*, 84; S. Joachim, "Toward an Understanding of the Russia Germans," address delivered to the Western Conference of the Dakota District of the American Lutheran Church, Concordia College Occasional Papers 1 (August 1931), Moorhead, MN. Joachim was pastor of Zion Lutheran Church, Beulah, ND. On family violence, see also Paula Nelson, ed., "Memoir of a Country Schoolteacher: Dolly Holliday Clark Meets the Ethnic West, 1919–1920," in Lysengen and Rathke, eds., *Centennial Anthology*.

36. Mary Madden Collins, PMP.

37. "Terrible Case at Granville: Little Girl Died as Result of Inhuman Treatment Says County Coroner: Was Sent for Cows and Did Not Return," *Velva Journal*, 30 October 1919, 1; see also *Velva Journal*, 6 and 20 November and 4 December 1919 and 1, 8, and 15 January 1920; the *Granville Herald* carried untitled articles on 29 October and 5 November 1919 and 14 January 1920. The *Journal* reported that October 1919 was the snowiest on record and the coldest in thirty years. Transcripts of the Zimmerman trial are filed with the Governor's Files in the State Archives, SHSND.

38. "Thomas Raaen and Ragnhild Rodningen," 6–7, Raaen Papers, Hatton-Eielson Museum; Pembina County Sheriff's Records, 2 September 1896; LaMoure County Sheriff's Records, 7 February 1896;

Cavalier County Sheriff's Records, 22 August and 4 September 1902 (both incidents for John Delirs); Linda Gordon, *Heroes of Their Own Lives: The Politics and History of Family Violence* (New York: Penguin Books, 1988), 285–86. North Dakota County Sheriff's Records are incomplete.

39. Elizabeth Pleck, "Challenges to Traditional Authority in Immigrant Families," in *The American Family in Social-Historical Perspective*, ed. Michael Gordon, 504–17 (New York: St. Martin's Press, 1983); Diede, *Homesteading*, 81, and *Prairie Home*, 26.

40. *The Revised Code of the State of North Dakota, 1895*, Chap. 5, Art. 3, Secs. 2737 and 2762; *Laws Passed at the First Session of the Legislative Assembly of North Dakota, 1890*, Chap. 168, Sec. 187; *Laws Passed at the Sixth Session, 1899*, Chap. 75, Sec. 2755 (rev.).

41. *Taylor v. Taylor*, 63 NW 893 (May 1895). Robert L. Griswold has written extensively on divorce in the American West. He notes that farm women were a little less likely than upper- and middle-class women to leave their husbands in late-nineteenth-century California. Griswold, "Apart But Not Adrift: Wives, Divorce, and Independence in California, 1850–1890," *Pacific Historical Review* 49 (May 1980): 265–83.

42. "Mor," Raaen Papers, Hatton-Eielson Museum, and Raaen, *Grass of the Earth*, 126.

43. J. O. Meidinger, EGF, McIntosh County; Ole Lima quoted in Omon B. Herigstad, "Norwegian Immigration," *Collections of the State Historical Society of North Dakota* 2 (1908): 199–200.

44. Mathea Heskin Kringlie, PBF, Steele County.

45. Margaret Barr Roberts, "Margaret Barr Roberts," *North Dakota History* 24 (1957): 129–38. The badlands are located in the far southwestern counties of North Dakota.

46. *Statistical Abstract of the United States, 1926; 1928*, 90; *1929*, 92; *1930*, 92; *1931*, 92.

47. Anna Simonson, EGF, Williams County; Peterson in Williams, *Fifty Pioneer Mothers*, 77.

48. Margaret Nordgaard Brunsdale and Marie Sund Thompson, PBF, Steele County; Isabelle Sinclair Cusator, PMP.

49. Deeby Zine, EGF, Williams County; Mrs. Andrew Severson, EGF, McKenzie County.

50. *Statistics of Women at Work: Based on Unpublished Information Derived from the Schedules of the Twelfth Census: 1900* (Washington, DC: GPO, 1907), 124–26, 180–95.

51. Martine Segalen, *Love and Power in the Peasant Family* (Chicago: University of Chicago Press, 1983), 3.

52. Diede, *Prairie Home*, 25; J. O. Meidinger, EGF, McIntosh County.

53. Rosina Riedlinger, EGF, McIntosh County; Luke Perekrestinko, EGF, McLean County; Guri Sondreal, EGF, Steele County. Norway-born Kathinka Alm, EGF, Griggs County, stated that "it was not so important if the women got a portion of all good food as long as the men got it." I am indebted to Donna Gregory for identifying Mrs. E. M. Sondreal as Guri.

54. Calof, *Rachel Calof's Story*, 43; Elizabeth Solem, EGF, McKenzie County.

55. Mary Ann Nelson Barclay and Johanna Swenson Anderson, PMP. Gwen Fraase, Buffalo, ND, shared with me memories of her grandparents, Ernest and Amanda Norell.

Notes to Chapter 3

1. Title quotation: "Then is the casual or regular labor of women, in assistance volunteered or required in planting, weeding, cultivating, haying, harvesting, and even the care of livestock, be computed at its true value, and its real percentage of our total farm production calculated, how would the figures swell the sum, and magnify the proportion of the wealth wrought from the mine of the farm by the hand of woman!" "Industrial Education of Women," *Report of the Commissioner of Agriculture in the Year 1871* (Washington, DC: GPO, 1872), 337. Epigraph: August Bauer, EGF, McLean County. Text: Elizabeth McQuire, EGF, Grand Forks County.

2. Sachs, *Invisible Farmers*.

3. Mary Meek Atkeson, "Women in Farm Life and Rural Economy," *The Annals of the American Academy of Political and Social Sciences* 143 (May 1929): 191; "Industrial Education of Women," 341.

4. Gilbert Fite, *The Farmers' Frontier: 1865–1900* (New York: Holt, Rinehart, Winston, 1966), 42–43. "Proving up" is the common term for meeting requirements, or proof, on a federal land claim.

5. Anna Carlson, PMP; Anna Kuhlsbraaten Berg, PBF, Steele County; Jensen Diary, 24 and 25 July 1884, SHSND.

6. Luke Perekrestinko, EGF, McLean County; Diede, *Homesteading*, 70.

7. Atkeson, "Women in Farm Life," 188–89. Atkeson compares the "happy situation" of American women who have not had to do field work with that of European farm women who did and suggests that American women should move into farm management.

8. Faragher, *Women and Men on the Overland Trail* and *Sugar Creek: Life on the Illinois Prairie* (New Haven, CT: Yale University Press, 1986); Fink, *Agrarian Women*, 52–53; Gertrude (Mrs. Fingal) Enger, PBF, Steele County.

9. Unnamed Traill County woman, PMP; Helga Aasen Thompson, PBF, Steele County; Olga Zarodney, EGF, McLean County. A stoneboat was a flat, wooden bed on runners built to move stones out of a field. Many settlers used stoneboats for all transportation needs until they could afford a buggy or wagon.

10. Helga Aasen Thompson and Paul Thompson, PBF, Steele County.

11. Mary Hagan Lee and John Lee, PBF, Barnes County. Lily Kritsky cut hay and cured it for a thatched roof with two other women, EGF, McLean County. Fink holds a dimmer view of sod houses in *Agrarian Women*, 31–33.

12. Mrs. Thomas MacPherson, PBF, Steele County; Calof, *Rachel Calof's Story*, 59.

13. Christina Hillius, PBF, McIntosh County; Wishek, *Along the Trails*, 237–38.

14. Unnamed Ukrainian woman, PBF, McLean County; Sarah Gray Braddock, PMP.

15. Among the women who recalled living alone on the claim while their husbands pursued other work are Harriet Cooper Broughton and Sarah Gray Braddock, PMP.

16. Fahlgren in Williams, *Fifty Pioneer Mothers*, 29; Amelia Neveu Chatrand, PMP; Diede, *Prairie Home*, 77, 85, 93.

17. Jeffrey, *Frontier Women*, 4, 26; Erickson in Raaen, *Grass of the Earth*, 125.

18. Olga Zarodney, EGF, McLean County.

19. Karen Bjorlie and Hannah Bell, PMP; Carlson in Williams, *Fifty Pioneer Mothers*, 37.

20. Catherine Geizler, PBF, McIntosh County; Matilda Lushenko, EGF, McLean County; Thingelstad in Raaen Papers, Hatton-Eielson Museum; Diede, *Prairie Home*, 76, 88.

21. Norma E. Berntson, *As the Sod Was Turned* (Fairview, MT: Privately printed, n.d.), 11; Diede, *Prairie Home*, 45–46.

22. Ingaborg Homme, PMP; Kungel in Diede, *Speaking-Out on Sod-House Times* (Richardton, ND: Abbey Press and John H. Gengler, 1985), 43, 57.

23. Julia Sackman to Jodi Nelson, 1995, photocopy in author's possession; Trupin, *Dakota Diaspora*, 61.

24. Link in Diede, *Speaking-Out*, 60.

25. Thersia Bosch, PMP; Kari Stavens, PBF, Steele County; Raaen Papers, Hatton-Eielson Museum.

26. Annie Johnson, HWF.

27. Jensen Diary, 27, 28, and 30 August and 3 and 4 September 1884, SHSND.

28. Jensen Diary, 19–21 and 24–27 October 1887, SHSND. For more on threshing, see Thomas D. Isern, *Bullthreshers and Bindlestiffs: Harvesting and Threshing on the North American Plains* (Lawrence: University Press of Kansas, 1990), 96–99.

29. Isern, *Bullthreshers and Bindlestiffs*, 99; David E. Schob, *Hired Hands and Plowboys: Farm Labor in the Midwest, 1815–1860* (Urbana: University of Illinois Press, 1975), 220. Hobo Chicago worked for George Cole of Steele County, George Cole Diary, 9 September 1898, Steele County Museum, Hope, ND.

30. Knute Pladson and Barbo Pladson, PBF, Steele County; Nelson, ed., "'All Well and Hard at Work': The Harris Family Letters from Dakota Territory, 1882–1888," *North Dakota History* 57 (Spring 1990): 28–29.

31. Berit Erstad and Erich Erstad, PBF, Steele County.

32. Maria Sveinsdottir Benson, PMP; Diede, *Prairie Home*, 19, and *Homesteading*, 39.

33. Calof, *Rachel Calof's Story*, 42.

34. Diede, *Homesteading*, 38, 45–47, 58, 59, 64, 65.

35. Ole Bolkan, EGF, Griggs County; August Bauer, EGF, McLean County. At the time, one hundred pounds of bread flour sold for about two dollars.

36. Irving Gardner, PBF, Steele County. Mortgage agent Seth K. Humphrey also found that the lack of sanitation interfered with his appetite when traveling about the Dakotas. See *Following the Prairie Frontier* (Minneapolis: University of Minnesota Press, 1931), 129–30.

37. Fite, *Farmer's Frontier*, 108–9; *Second Biennial Report of the Commissioner of Agriculture* (1892), 21–22.

38. Ole Overboe, HWF.

39. Bertha Dronan, PBF, Steele County; Jennie Pratt Codding and Mrs. J. C. Fay, PMP.

40. Olson in Williams, *Fifty Pioneer Mothers*, 33; Marian Kramer and Fred Daniels, PBF, Barnes County.

41. Christina Bossart and Frederick Bossart, PBF, McIntosh County.

42. Lizzie Dunn, PBF, Barnes County.

43. Mary Wilma M. Hargreaves, *Dry Farming in the Northern Great Plains, 1900–1925* (Cambridge, MA: Harvard University Press, 1957), 499; Gunhild Oiehus Grimsrud, PMP.

44. Ben Overby, EGF, Griggs County.

45. Andrew Johnson, EGF, McHenry County.

46. Ole Bolkan and Mary Bolkan, EGF, Griggs County.

47. Hanson and Erickson in Williams, *Fifty Pioneer Mothers*, 109, 113.

48. Amanda Noren Bjor and Julia Abbott, PMP.

49. I use the terms "barn" and "barnyard" loosely to differentiate the work of

caring for livestock from the work of caring for family. Many settlement farms had no barn, and the cows were milked where they were caught.

50. U.S. Census Office, *Tenth Census of the United States Taken in the Year 1890, Agriculture* (Washington, DC: GPO, 1893), and *Twelfth Census, Agriculture.*

51. U.S. Census Office, *Tenth Census, Agriculture, Twelfth Census, Agriculture.*

52. Bentz in Diede, *Speaking-Out*, 14; U.S. Department of Commerce, Bureau of the Census, *Thirteenth Census, Agriculture.*

53. Elizabeth Solem, EGF, McKenzie County; Wahl in Williams, *Fifty Pioneer Mothers*, 121.

54. Gottlieb Breitling, EGF, McIntosh County.

55. Jeffrey, *Frontier Women*, 76.

56. Marti, *Women of the Grange*, 73, 80.

57. Woodward, *The Checkered Years*, 168, 175, 217; Wishek, *Along the Trails*, 235.

58. Henry Wallace, "The Relation of the Creamery to Iowa Farming," *Report of the Board of Directors of the Iowa State Agricultural Society 1880* (Des Moines, IA: F. M. Mills, 1881), 97. For a contemporary Iowa woman's perspective on dairying, see Judy Nolte Lensink, ed., *"A Secret to Be Burried": The Life and Diary of Emily Hawley Gillespie* (Iowa City: University of Iowa Press, 1989).

59. Among the historians who have linked insanity to homesteading women on the plains are Walter Webb, *The Great Plains* (New York: Grosset & Dunlap, 1931), Mari Sandoz, *Old Jules* (Lincoln: University of Nebraska Press, 1935), and Raaen, *Grass of the Earth.* Among the novelists who have used this idea are Ole Rølvaag, *Giants in the Earth* (New York: Harper and Brothers, 1927), and Mary Worthy Breneman, *The Land They Possessed* (Brookings: South Dakota Committee on the Humanities and South Dakota Library Association, 1989). However, in *Lark Against the Thunder* (New York: Island Press, 1953) author Bea Aagard created a male character who became violently insane due to his failure at farming in eastern North Dakota.

60. Humphrey, *Following the Prairie Frontier*, 131; Webb, *Great Plains*, 506.

61. Hospital population statistics are summarized in *Ninth Biennial Report of the North Dakota State Hospital for the Insane to the Board of Control of State Institutions* (Bismarck, ND: The Department, 1928), 35. I have taken state population statistics from federal census data. The figures for 1886 are compared with 1885 federal manuscript census county summaries, and the figures for 1928 are compared with 1930 federal census figures. The county sheriff was responsible for transporting people to the state hospital. In the few Sheriff's Jail Reports available, more than twice as many men as women were reported by sheriffs as "insane." Suicides among men range from twenty-one to forty-two per biennium. The federal census of 1900 reported seventeen suicides in North Dakota: sixteen men, one woman. Nationally, men committed suicide at a rate three times greater than that of women. U.S. Census Office, *Twelfth Census, Vital Statistics*, 234, 611.

62. *Ninth Biennial Report of the North Dakota State Hospital for the Insane* (1928).

63. *Ninth Biennial Report of the North Dakota State Hospital for the Insane* (1928).

64. *Ninth Biennial Report of the North Dakota State Hospital for the Insane* (1928).

65. Annie Pike Greenwood, "Growing Things from the Soil Is Bliss," in *Writings of Farm Women 1840–1940: An Anthology*, ed. Carol Fairbanks and Bergine Haakenson (New York: Garland Publishing, 1990), 325.

66. Ella Mae Ruland, EGF, McKenzie County; Bertha Marie Walley, EGF, McHenry County.

67. Judith Brown, "Note on the Division of Labor by Sex," *American Anthropologist* 72 (1970): 1073–78; Patricia Branca, "A New Perspective on Women's Work: A Comparative Typology," *Journal of Social History* 9 (Winter 1975): 129–53; Charlotte Perkins Gilman, *Women and Economics: A Study of the Economic Relation Between Men and*

Women as a Factor in Social Evolution
(Boston: Small, Maynard and Co., 1898).

68. On the effect of urbanization on
women's social roles, see Mary Ryan, *Cradle of the Middle Class: The Family in
Oneida County, New York, 1790–1865*
(New York: Cambridge University Press,
1981), and Jeanne Boydston, *Home and
Work: Housework, Wages, and the Ideology
of Labor in the Early Republic* (New York:
Oxford University Press, 1990). On trade
unionists' objections to female labor, see Alice Kessler Harris, *Out to Work: A History
of Wage Earning Women in the United
States* (New York: Oxford University Press,
1983). On farm women in the eastern industrializing economy, see Osterud, *Bonds
of Community*, and Jensen, *Loosening the
Bonds*.

69. Gilman, *Women and Economics;*
Herbert Quick, "The Women on Farms,"
Good Housekeeping 57 (September 1913):
429. The same issue of *Good Housekeeping*
that carried Quick's article also ran one that
fanned the fears of industrialization: Mary
Alden Hopkins, "New England Mill
Slaves," 323.

70. Lena Bauer and August Bauer, EGF,
McLean County. Though single men and
women homesteaded, they depended on
hiring or exchanging labor to complete the
work. See Erling N. Sannes, "'Free Land for
All': Ei ung snasakvinne som nybyggar i
Nord-Dakota," *Kumur Arsskrift Nr. 11*
(1990): 18–32. Mr. Sannes kindly provided
me with Erik Gran's English translation of
his article. Young, *Nothing to Do but Stay;*
Lindgren, *Land in Her Own Name.*

Notes to Chapter 4
1. Title quotations: Mary Baxter Cannell, PMP, and Annie Julia Schwalier Reuter
in Williams, *Fifty Pioneer Mothers*, 125.
Epigraph: Katie Ulmer Roth quoting her
mother in Diede, *Speaking-Out*, 77.

2. U.S. Census Office, *Twelfth Census,
Agriculture*, 110; U.S. Department of Com-
merce, Bureau of the Census, *Fifteenth
Census, Agriculture*, 1082. The Northern
Pacific Railroad owned most of the land

along the tracks through its land-grant sub-
sidy. Some of this land was sold to settlers
who could afford it. The best land, however,
in the well-watered eastern part of the state
became bonanza farms.

3. Nancy Folbre, *The Invisible Heart:
Economics and Family Values* (New York:
The New Press, 2001), xii.

4. Osterud, *Bonds of Community*, 233;
Seena B. Kohl, "The Making of a Community: The Role of Women in an Agricultural
Setting," in *Kin and Communities: Families
in America*, ed. Allan J. Lichtman and Joan
Challinor, 175–86 (Washington, DC: Smithsonian Institution Press, 1979). Robert V.
Hine, *Community on the American Frontier: Separate but Not Alone* (Norman: University of Oklahoma Press, 1980).

5. On the customs of Black Sea Germans in South Russia, see Giesinger, *From
Catherine to Khrushchev.*

6. Job, interview, 15 September 1990;
Fred Marzolf, EGF, McLean County. On vil-
lage life in South Russia, see Giesinger,
From Catherine To Khrushchev.

7. Mrs. Frank Davison, PBF, Adams
County.

8. Betsy Lekvold Bakke and Elizabeth
Warner Bechtel, PMP.

9. Leidholm in Williams, *Fifty Pioneer
Mothers*, 93; Mrs. Samuel L. Ferguson on
the Esler Ranch, PMP. Seth Humphrey
states that it was ordinary courtesy to leave
fifty cents after dropping in for a meal with
a homesteading family, *Following the
Prairie Frontier*, 110.

10. Alice Ransier Barrington, PMP;
Reuter in Williams, *Fifty Pioneer Mothers*,
125; Christian Klaudt, PBF, McIntosh
County.

11. Jennie Pratt Codding, PMP.

12. Bertha Daniels Brown, PMP;
Humphrey, *Following the Prairie Frontier*,
105–8.

13. Eittah, letter to *McLean County
Mail*, 28 May 1887; Brita Berg, PBF, Steele
County. On women's voluntary organiza-
tions, see Ann Firor Scott, *Natural Allies:
Women's Associations in American His-
tory* (Urbana: University of Illinois Press,

1991); Ryan, *Cradle of the Middle Class;* Nancy Cott, *The Bonds of Womanhood: "Woman's Sphere" in New England 1780–1835* (New Haven, CT: Yale University Press, 1977).

14. Mrs. Abraham Nelson, EGF, Steele County; Jensen Diary, 3 and 4 September 1884, 28 and 29 September 1885, 27, 28, and 29 September and 3, 19, 20, 21, and 27 October 1887, SHSND.

15. Christina Hillius, PBF, McIntosh County.

16. Gunhild Grimsrud, Karen Oien Bjorlie, and Jane Fulton Burnett, PMP; Ingeborg Larson, PBF, Traill County; Mrs. Abraham Nelson, EGF, Steele County. Aagot Raaen wrote that women sometimes secured a mortgage on the farm for a sewing machine, *Grass of the Earth,* 101–2. Commuting a homestead claim meant paying a per-acre fee in order to receive title before the five-year residence requirement had been met.

17. Mary Baxter Cannell and Susannah Preece Bonde, PMP; Jensen Diary, SHSND.

18. Erick Johnson on Williams family, PBF, McHenry County; Lily Kritsky on Eschenko family, EGF, McLean County.

19. Mary Elizabeth Madden Collins and Jerry Collins, PMP.

20. Leavitt, *Brought to Bed,* 97; Bertha Daniels Brown and Minnie Witkop Barr, PMP.

21. Dorotheo Jensen Christofferson and Angeline Peranto Carter, PMP. Jonsdottir's experience is recounted in Thorstina Walters, *Modern Sagas: The Story of Icelanders in North America* (Fargo: NDIRS, 1953), 2, 3.

22. Stokka in Myrtle Bemis Porterville Papers, Box 1, Folder 19, NDIRS; Walters, *Modern Sagas,* 4; Fay in Angela Boleyn, *Quarter Sections and Wide Horizons: A Series of Stories on Pioneer Women of North Dakota* (Bismarck: North Dakota State Library, 1978), 1:47.

23. *Laws Passed at the Thirteenth Session of the Legislative Assembly of the Territory of Dakota, 1879,* Chap. 14, Sec. 30, 33; *Laws Passed at the Fifteenth Session of the Legislative Assembly of the Territory of Dakota, 1883,* Chap. 44, Sec. 66; Robinson, *History of North Dakota,* 299; Bill G. Reid,

"Elizabeth Preston Anderson and the Politics of Social Reform," in *The North Dakota Political Tradition,* ed. Thomas Howard (Ames, IA: North Dakota Centennial Heritage Series, Iowa State University Press, 1981), 175; Myrtle Bemis Porterville Papers, Box 8, Folder 3; Julia Sackman to Jodi Nelson, 1995, photocopy in author's possession.

24. *McLean County Mail,* 18 June 1887; Anna Esby, PBF, Barnes County.

25. Reid, "Elizabeth Preston Anderson"; "North Dakota Woman's Christian Temperance Union," Elizabeth Preston Anderson Papers, NDIRS; Elizabeth Cady Stanton, Susan B. Anthony, and Matilda Joslyn Gage, eds., *History of Woman Suffrage,* Vol. 3, 1876–85 (New York: National American Woman Suffrage Association, 1922), 662, 667–68; Ida Husted Harper, ed., *The History of Woman Suffrage,* Vol. 5, 1900–1920 (New York: National American Woman Suffrage Association, 1922); Flora E. Baker, PMP.

26. Jeanne Tucker, "The History of Woman Suffrage in North Dakota" (unpublished paper, 1951, Special Collections, UND), 36–38, 42; quotation from *Grand Forks Herald,* 27 November 1919.

27. Kim E. Nielsen, "'We All Leaguers by Our House': Women, Suffrage, and Red-Baiting in the National Non-Partisan League," *Journal of Women's History* 6 (Spring 1994): 32, 35–36. Gayle Gullett examines suffragists' roles for the woman voter in California during the same time period in "Constructing the Woman Citizen and Struggling for the Vote in California, 1896–1911," *Pacific Historical Review* 69 (November 2000): 573–93.

28. Raaen, *Grass of the Earth,* 120–22; Oscar Brandon testimony, *State of North Dakota v. Orlaug Aasen,* Coroner's Inquest on the body of Peter P. Lomen, 8 February 1890, Hatton, Traill County Courthouse, Hillsboro, ND; Charles A. Pollock, *Manual of the Prohibition Law of North Dakota 1910* (N.p.: North Dakota State Enforcement League, 1910), 8. My research on this event is developed in "Land, Liquor and the Women of Hatton, North Dakota," *North Dakota History* 59 (Fall 1992): 22–29.

29. Gyda Pladson, a granddaughter of Orlaug Aasen, one of the participants, in a telephone interview with the author indicated that there was widespread approval of the women's actions (25 June 1991). Nicolai Berg, in "The Bergs of Newbergh" (unpublished manuscript, Steele County Historical Society, Hope, ND), noted his family's support of the raid and added somewhat apologetically that his wife, Tonetta, did not participate.

30. Scott, *Natural Allies*.

31. Froen Ladies' Aid Society, Horace, Fargo Circuit; Ladies' Aid Society of Faith Lutheran Church, Williston, American Lutheran Church Women History Project; Christine Ladies' Aid Society, Christine, Fargo Circuit. All sources housed in Women's Missionary Federation [hereafter WMF], North Dakota District, Archives of the Evangelical Church in North Dakota, Luther Seminary, St. Paul, MN.

32. Froen Ladies' Aid Society, Bang Lutheran Church Ladies' Aid Society, WMF records. When cash was scarce in the early years of settlement, churches raised money in various ways. Some congregations charged a fee for baptism or communion. Others asked members to pledge a portion of their harvest to the church. Some congregations used cemetery land to raise a crop. As farms matured and cash became more readily available, members pledged cash contributions from their income. Ladies' Aid funds supplemented these means of supporting the congregation.

33. Froen and Wild Rice Ladies' Aid Societies, Fargo Circuit, and Trondenes Aid, Cooperstown Circuit, WMF records.

34. Froen Ladies' Aid Society, WMF records; Alice Maurer Bartheld, "Reflections of a Pioneer Daughter," in *Assumption of Mary Church Diamond Jubilee 1904–1979* (Starkweather, ND: Privately printed, 1979), 10–11.

35. Goose River Ladies' Aid, Goose River Circuit, WMF records.

36. Ellen Calder DeLong Papers, SHSND.

37. E. Clifford Nelson and Eugene L. Fevold, *The Lutheran Church Among Norwegian-Americans* (Minneapolis, MN:

Augsburg Publishing House, 1960), 1:299, 2:229; Robert C. Ostergren, *A Community Transplanted: The Trans-Atlantic Experience of a Swedish Immigrant Settlement in the Upper Middle West, 1835–1915* (Madison: University of Wisconsin Press, 1988), 19, 212.

38. Trupin, *Dakota Diaspora*, 63–65; Calof, *Rachel Calof's Story*, 32, 72–73; Harriet Rochlin and Fred Rochlin, *Pioneer Jews: A New Life in the Far West* (Boston: Houghton Mifflin Company, 2000), 89. On Jewish farmers in North Dakota, see also W. Gunther Plaut, "Jewish Colonies at Painted Woods and Devils Lake," *North Dakota History* 32 (January 1965): 59–70; Jason Zevenbergen, "Establishing a Jewish Community: A Study of Jewish Immigrant Homesteaders in North Dakota, 1880–1920 (unpublished paper, Special Collections, UND).

39. *Minutes of the North Dakota Mission of the Methodist Episcopal Church*, First Session, 1884, 19, Special Collections, UND; *Minutes of the Sixth Session of the North Dakota Annual Conference of the Methodist Episcopal Church*, 1894, 51, Special Collections, UND; Gol Ladies' Aid Society, Fargo Circuit, and Beaver Creek Ladies' Aid Society, Goose River Circuit, WMF records; *Golden Anniversary of Ebenezer Lutheran Church* (Northwood, ND: Privately printed, 1950), 25–26.

40. Peace Church (Scranton), American Lutheran Church Women History Project, WMF records; *Ostervold Lutheran Church: A Century of Love 1883–1983* (Finley, ND: Privately printed, 1983), 8, 11; church minutes, 22 May 1899 and 1 June 1903, Hebron and New Salem, German Evangelical Colonization Society, Colony Records, Special Collections, UND.

41. Trondenes Ladies' Aid Society, Cooperstown Circuit, WMF records; *Aurdal 1883–1983* (Forbes, ND: Privately printed, 1983), 5.

42. Jon Gjerde, *From Peasants to Farmers: The Migration from Balestrand, Norway, to the Upper Middle West* (New York: Cambridge University Press, 1985), 230.

43. Hol Church Ladies' Aid Society,

Goose River Circuit, and Trondenes Ladies' Aid Society, Cooperstown Circuit, WMF records; *Aurdal 1883–1983*, 5; "Parsonage History for Gran and Mayville Lutheran Ladies' Aid," Goose River Circuit, Heskin in Bruflat Ladies' Aid Society, Goose River Circuit, and Gronlie in Valley Grove Ladies' Aid Society, Cooperstown Circuit, WMF records.

44. Gol Ladies' Aid Society, Fargo Circuit, and Norway Ladies' Aid Society, Cooperstown Circuit, WMF records; Laurel Thatcher Ulrich, *Goodwives: Image and Reality in the Lives of Women in Northern New England, 1650–1750* (New York: Knopf, 1982). In some women's societies, the pastor took a leadership position; in others, he was sometimes invited to attend meetings. In contrast to rural Ladies' Aid Societies, men did hold offices in some urban women's organizations. In Cooperstown, men held offices in the WCTU and Order of the Eastern Star. Myrtle Bemis Porterville Papers, Ms. 296, NDIRS.

45. Raaen, *Grass of the Earth*, 163–64; *Golden Anniversary of Ebenezer Lutheran Church*, 27–28.

46. St. John's Ladies' Aid Society, Fargo Circuit, Crosby Peace Lutheran and Faith American Lutheran Church, East Fork, American Lutheran Church Women History Project, WMF records; Berntson, *As the Sod Was Turned*, 95–96.

47. Williams, *Fifty Pioneer Mothers*, 51–52; Stephanie Abbot Roper, "African Americans in North Dakota, 1800–1940" (master's thesis, University of North Dakota, 1993), 72.

48. Angry Chippewa and Métis confronted fearful settlers over taxation matters, but there was no bloodshed. See Murray, "Turtle Mountain Chippewa," 83–108. I use the terms "Native American" and "Indian" when the tribal affiliation is unknown. In their stories of encounters with Native Americans, pioneers never identified them by tribal affiliation.

49. Mary Madden, PMP; Burg in Williams, *Fifty Pioneer Mothers*, 167.

50. Robinson in Williams, *Fifty Pioneer*

Mothers, 199; Mrs. August Borner, PMP; John Koehn, PBF, Barnes County.

51. Robinson in Williams, *Fifty Pioneer Mothers*, 199; Mrs. Alf Eastgate, PMP.

52. Bridget Burke Cranley, PMP. Cranley's description of what she taught the Indian woman may represent a general exchange of knowledge. It is highly unlikely that an Indian woman living near Pembina—the oldest European American settlement in North Dakota—was not familiar with cloth dresses.

53. Mrs. E. B. Albertson, PMP; Berntson, *As the Sod Was Turned*, 26.

54. Sarah Braddock, PMP.

55. Thompson, *American Daughter*, 383, 387; Roper, "African Americans in North Dakota," 48, 102–5. On African Americans in North Dakota, see also Thomas Newgard and William C. Sherman, "Blacks," in Sherman and Thorson, eds., *Plains Folk*.

56. Roper, "African Americans in North Dakota," 55, 72–73, 113; Thompson, *American Daughter*, 60–63, 72–74, 94.

57. Thomas Yecovanko, EGF, McLean County; Hannah Anderson, PMP.

58. Mrs. Abraham Nelson, EGF, Steele County.

59. Marian Perales, "Empowering the Welder," in *Writing the Range: Race, Class, and Culture in the Women's West*, ed. Elizabeth Jameson and Susan Armitage, 21–41 (Norman: University of Oklahoma Press, 1997).

60. Helga Aasen Thompson and Paul Thompson, PBF, Steele County.

Notes to Chapter 5

1. Epigraph: Rosina Riedlinger, EGF, McIntosh County. Text: Scot Arthur Stradley, *The Broken Circle: An Economic History of North Dakota* (Grand Forks: Bureau of Business and Economic Research, University of North Dakota, 1993), 70.

2. On the role of gender in butter and egg production in other states, see Jensen, *Loosening the Bonds;* Osterud, *Bonds of Community;* Lensink, ed., *"A Secret to Be Burried";* Fred Bateman, "The Marketable

Surplus in Northern Dairy Farming: New Evidence by Size of Farm in 1860," *Agricultural History* 52 (July 1978): 345–63.

3. "A Just Complaint," *The Dakota Farmer*, 15 September 1897, 8.

4. On the effect of industrialization and urbanization on farming, see David B. Danbom, *The Resisted Revolution: Urban America and the Industrialization of Agriculture, 1900–1930* (Ames: Iowa State University Press, 1979). On the importance of women's reproductive role on Norwegian immigrant grain farms, see Gjerde, *From Peasants to Farmers*, 194–201.

5. Nelson, ed., "'All Well and Hard at Work,'" 33; John S. Otto, "Farming in Russia and North Dakota: One German-Russian Family's Experiences," *North Dakota History* 55 (Spring 1988): 26; Andrew Davidson, PBF, Barnes County.

6. Otto, "Farming in Russia and North Dakota," 26; Luke Perekrestinko, EGF, McLean County; Laura Wheeler quoted in Mary-Susan Abelow-King, "The Streets Were Paved with Gold" (paper, Northern Great Plains History Conference, Grand Forks, ND, 1990).

7. Rosina Riedlinger, EGF, McIntosh County.

8. Production quantity figures, egg and poultry sales figures, and butter sales figures are taken from U.S. Census Office, *Twelfth Census*, Agriculture, 110, 178, 615; U.S. Department of Commerce, Bureau of the Census, *Thirteenth Census*, Agriculture, 284, 289, 294, *Fourteenth Census*, Agriculture, 626, 631, 636, *Fifteenth Census*, Agriculture, 1082, 1095, 1100, 1118. Wheat price figures are taken from U.S. Department of Agriculture, *Yearbook 1910*, 518, *Yearbook 1925*, 764, *Yearbook 1930*, 600.

9. Still Diary, 31 December 1911, NDIRS; Thomas Raaen credit account, Raaen Papers, Hatton-Eielson Museum.

10. Mrs. F. Fitzmaurice, "The Dairy," North Dakota Farmers' Institute *Annual* 2 (1902): 32–33.

11. Cohen, *Women's Work*, 63.

12. The landmark years relate to federal agricultural census data. The agricultural census is taken at the same time as the population census (the year ending in zero), but figures recorded are for the previous calendar year (the year ending in 9).

13. U.S. Census Office, *Report on the Productions of Agriculture Tenth Census*, 260, *Report of the Statistics of Agriculture Eleventh Census*, 342, *Twelfth Census*, xxxi.

14. "Neat cattle" is an archaic term for cattle. Oxen and dairy cattle were identified separately, so "neat cattle" were any other bovines, including beef cattle.

15. Oluf Anderson, HWF, Cass County.

16. Mrs. Hans Emmanuel Anderson, EGF, Eddy County.

17. Agnethe Jensen Borreson and Thersia Sherman Bosch, PMP; Herred and Swanson in Williams, *Fifty Pioneer Mothers*, 53, 73.

18. Jensen Diary, 2 August 1884, SHSND.

19. Jacobsen in Axel Axelson, PBF, Barnes County; Tirsten Swenson, PBF, Barnes County.

20. Betsy Halstenson Broton, PMP; Marian Koehn Kramer, PBF, Barnes County; U.S. Census Office, *Statistics of the Population of the United States at the Tenth Census 1880* (Washington, DC: GPO, 1883), 564, *Compendium of the Eleventh Census*, and *Twelfth Census*, Population, 596; U.S. Department of Commerce, Bureau of the Census, *Thirteenth Census*, Population, 343, *Fourteenth Census*, Population, 752, *Fifteenth Census*, Population, 433.

21. Williams, *Fifty Pioneer Mothers*, 49, 61.

22. Caroline Radke Fregein, PBF, McIntosh County.

23. Humphrey, *Following the Prairie Frontier*, 116.

24. Trupin, *Dakota Diaspora*, 59; E. F. Ladd, "Preserving Eggs," North Dakota Agricultural College, Government Agricultural Experiment Station, Bulletin 35, 330–32; M. A. Johnson, *Fifty Years of Country Storekeeping* (Larimore, ND: Privately printed, 1955), 95.

25. Johnson, *Fifty Years of Country Storekeeping*, 12; Alva H. Benton, "Poultry and Egg Marketing in North Dakota,"

North Dakota Agricultural College, Government Agricultural Experiment Station, Bulletin 215 (February 1928), 8, 25–27.

26. Johnson, *Fifty Years of Country Storekeeping,* 87; Benton, "Poultry and Egg Marketing," 8–9.

27. Jensen Diary, 31 May 1884, SHSND; Hans Lindaas to Mathias Lindaas, Bismarck, ND, 22 December 1883, Lindaas Family Papers, Ms. 196, Folder 4, Special Collections, UND; Robinson, *History of North Dakota,* 227.

28. Benton, "Poultry and Egg Marketing," 5–7.

29. Benton, "Poultry and Egg Marketing," 5–7.

30. Hannah Lovass Kjelland, PBF, Barnes County; Johnson, *Fifty Years of Country Storekeeping,* 15.

31. Torkel Fuglestad Papers, Ms. 251, Box 1, Folder 1, Special Collections, UND.

32. Joseph Falerius, PBF, Barnes County.

33. For a thorough discussion of the efforts of the North Dakota Agricultural Experiment Station to establish commercial dairying, see David B. Danbom, "The North Dakota Agricultural Experiment Station and the Struggle to Create a Dairy State," *Agricultural History* 63 (Spring 1989): 174–86.

34. John L. Coulter, "Industrial History of the Valley of the Red River of the North," *Collections of the State Historical Society of North Dakota* 3 (1910): 638.

35. *Third Biennial Report of the Commissioner of Agriculture* (1894), 14–15.

36. *Third Biennial Report of the Commissioner of Agriculture* (1894), 18.

37. Einar Brosten to Brother, 17 June 1888, Cooperstown, Dakota Territory, translator unknown, Myrtle Bemis Porterville Papers, Box 1, Folder 18, NDIRS.

38. Rosina Riedlinger, EGF, McIntosh County; Christina Hills Caldwell, PMP.

39. Sannes, "'Free Land for All,'" 28–29; Otto Monson Lunstrom, "Memoirs." Kristi Groberg kindly shared Lunstrom's papers with me.

40. *Twelfth Biennial Report of the Commissioner of Agriculture* (1912), 120.

41. U.S. Census Office, *Eleventh Census,* 170, 302, *Twelfth Census,* 110, 466, 615.

42. U.S. Census Office, *Tenth Census,* 564, *Eleventh Census,* 634, *Twelfth Census,* 596; U.S. Department of Commerce, Bureau of the Census, *Thirteenth Census,* 343.

43. U.S. Census Office, *Twelfth Census,* 615; U.S. Department of Commerce, Bureau of the Census, *Thirteenth Census,* 289, *Fourteenth Census,* 631, *Fifteenth Census,* 1118.

44. U.S. Department of Commerce, Bureau of the Census, *Fifteenth Census,* 1118; Bethel Herigstad, EGF, Griggs County.

45. Anonymous writer to R. F. Flint, in *Biennial Report of the Dairy Commissioner to the Commissioner of Agriculture and Labor of the Dairy Interests* (N.p., 30 June 1912), 180–81.

46. Timothy McNamara, EGF, Pembina County; Mary Agnes McCann Farley, PMP.

47. Robinson, *History of North Dakota,* 236.

48. Kildahl, "Reminiscences," 2, 6, Special Collections, UND.

49. Bertha Christina Nystrom Dronan, PBF, Steele County.

Notes to Chapter 6

1. Epigraph: Williams, *Fifty Pioneer Mothers,* n.p.

2. On the leadership and thought of the Country Life Movement, see William L. Bowers, *The Country Life Movement in America, 1900–1920* (Port Washington, NY: Kennikat Press, 1974), 4, 28. On the relation of industrial America to agricultural development, see Danbom, *Resisted Revolution.*

3. Bowers, *Country Life Movement,* 24–27, 63.

4. Bowers, *Country Life Movement,* 63–64; Danbom, *Resisted Revolution,* 5.

5. Liberty Hyde Bailey, *The Country Life Movement in the United States* (New York: MacMillan Company, 1911), 85–88. On the interconnectedness of productive and reproductive labor, see also Carolyn Sachs, "The Participation of Women and Girls in Market and Non-Market Activities

on Pennsylvania Farms," in Haney and Knowles, *Women and Farming*, 125, 132, and Rachel Ann Rosenfeld, *Farm Women: Work, Farm, and Family in the United States* (Chapel Hill: University of North Carolina Press, 1985), 52–98.

6. Bailey, *Country Life Movement*, 89, 93.

7. Sally McMurry, *Families and Farmhouses in Nineteenth Century America: Vernacular Design and Social Change* (New York: Oxford University Press, 1988), 95.

8. North Dakota Farmers' Institute Records, Ms. 131, NDIRS; John Hamilton, *Farmers' Institutes in the United States* (Washington, DC: GPO, 1904), 7, 10.

9. Hamilton, *Farmers' Institutes*, 14.

10. Hamilton, *Farmers' Institutes*, 15–16.

11. North Dakota Farmers' Institute Records, NDIRS; *Proceedings of the American Association of Farmers' Institute Managers 1897*, Columbus, OH, 27–28 October 1897 (Lincoln, NE: State Journal Company, 1898), 22–23.

12. North Dakota Farmers' Institute Records, NDIRS.

13. The number of articles signed by men in each edition of the *Annual* ranged from twenty in 1900 to seventy-seven in 1911. The average was thirty-five.

14. H. U. Thomas, "The Institute and the Farmer," North Dakota Farmers' Institute *Annual* 1 (1900): 99.

15. Fitzmaurice, "The Dairy," 30–33; Mrs. G. I. C., "One Year's Experience with Turkeys," North Dakota Farmers' Institute *Annual* 2 (1902): 125–27; Alice M. Sheppard, "Information on Skim Milk," North Dakota Farmers' Institute *Annual* 4 (1904): 53–54, and "A Modern Farm House Built at a Moderate Cost," North Dakota Farmers' Institute *Annual* 4 (1904): 121–23.

16. Mrs. E. T. Curtiss, "Our Farm Life, How to Decrease Its Evils and Increase Its Blessings," North Dakota Farmers' Institute *Annual* 2 (1902): 46–54. Curtiss and Mrs. V. K. Wilcox were probably paid institute speakers but were also farm women who

drew on their experience to substantiate their claims. Sarah Elbert writes about New York farm women who "did not really ever part . . . with their productive skills and their desire for integration of home and work" in "Women and Farming: Changing Structures, Changing Roles," in Haney and Knowles, eds., *Women and Farming*, 251.

17. Wilcox, "Home Making." For a discussion on the use of the word "sphere" and how it has shaped women's history, see Linda K. Kerber, "Separate Spheres, Female Worlds, Woman's Place: The Rhetoric of Women's History" in *Toward an Intellectual History of Women: Essays by Linda K. Kerber* (Chapel Hill: University of North Carolina Press, 1997), 159–99.

18. Wilcox, "Home Making."

19. *Proceedings of the American Association of Farmers' Institute Managers 1897*, 22–23.

20. W. H. Beal, John Hamilton, and G. C. Creelman, *Proceedings of the Ninth Annual Meeting of the American Association of Farmers' Institute Workers*, St. Louis, MO, 18–20 October 1904 (Washington, DC: GPO, 1905), 46–49.

21. Beal, *Proceedings of the Ninth Annual Meeting*, 32.

22. Beal, *Proceedings of the Ninth Annual Meeting*, 32.

23. Jessie B. Hoover, NDAC Professor of Home Economics, referred to homemaking as the "universal profession of women" in "Home Economics in North Dakota Agricultural College," North Dakota Farmers' Institute *Annual* 11 (1911): 237–42.

24. *Annual* 10 (1910): 7; Diede, *Homesteading*, 44–50; Jessie B. Hoover, "White Sauce and Its Uses," North Dakota Farmers' Institute *Annual* 11 (1911): 145–47.

25. Benton, "Poultry and Egg Marketing."

26. U.S. Census Office, *Twelfth Census, Agriculture*, 110; U.S. Department of Commerce, Bureau of the Census, *Fourteenth Census, Agriculture*, 626; *Seventh Biennial Report of the Commissioner of Agriculture* (1902), 50; *Fifteenth Biennial Report of the Commissioner of Agriculture* (1918), 119.

27. Raaen, *Grass of the Earth;* Jensen Diary, SHSND; Young, *Nothing to Do but Stay.*

28. Wilcox, "Home Making," 92; Bowers, *Country Life Movement,* 126; U.S. Department of Commerce, Bureau of the Census, *Fourteenth Census,* Agriculture, 626, *Fifteenth Census,* Population, 423.

29. *Eighteenth Biennial Report of the Commissioner of Agriculture* (1924), 52, 107.

30. Link in Diede, *Speaking-Out,* 60. Author's italics.

31. W. C. Palmer, "The Farmer's Wife," *North Dakota Farmers' Institute Annual* 11 (1911): 88.

32. On the symbolism of farmhouses among North Dakota immigrants, see Fred W. Peterson, "Norwegian Farm Homes in Steele and Traill Counties, North Dakota: The American Dream and the Retention of Roots, 1890–1914," *North Dakota History* 51 (Winter 1984): 4–13, and Otto, "Farming in Russia and North Dakota." On the relation of farmhouses to the social order of rural life, see McMurry, *Families and Farmhouses.*

33. Raaen, *Grass of the Earth,* 90; Trupin, *Dakota Diaspora,* 130.

34. On the movement to improve the farm household, see Holt, *Linoleum, Better Babies,* and Tymchuk in Agnes Palanuk, ed., *North Dakota Ukrainian Oral History Project* (N.p.: Privately printed, n.d.).

35. Boydston, *Home and Work,* 157–58.

36. Boydston, *Home and Work,* 157–58.

37. Williams, *Fifty Pioneer Mothers,* 69.

38. McMurry, *Families and Farmhouses,* 95.

Notes to Conclusion

1. U.S. Department of Commerce, Bureau of the Census, *Fifteenth Census;* "N.D. Posts Biggest Loss in Population," *The Fargo Forum,* 31 December 1998; "Where Are North Dakota's Missing Children?" *North Dakota Geographic Alliance Magazine* 1 (Spring 2002): 7–12.

2. Heidi L. Dyrstad, "'Just As Good As They Are': Voices of Contemporary Women Involved in Farming and Ranching in North Dakota" (PhD diss., University of North Dakota, 2001), 66. Dyrstad did not identify her subjects by their real names. I will follow her pattern and not identify contemporary women unless their names have been in the newspaper or on Internet websites.

3. http://www.patriesraspberries.com (accessed 4 June 2002).

4. Dyrstad, "'Just as Good as They Are,'" 75, 121.

5. Blake Nicholson, "Small Towns Banding Together to Open Needed Grocery Stores," *The Fargo Forum,* 3 December 2000, sec. A, p. 11.

6. Visibility of farm women has increased through publication of several histories and sociological and anthropological studies (see 168 n9). Recent broadcast of *The Farmers' Wife* on Public Broadcasting System stations brought many of the concerns of farm women and their families into public discussion. The question is not a quotation, but implied by many women in the Dyrstad study.

7. Mrs. Ludwig was described by Lizzie Margaret Dunn, PBF, Barnes County; Raaen Papers, Hatton-Eielson Museum.

8. Williams, *Fifty Pioneer Mothers,* 185.

Bibliography

Abbreviations

NDIRS
North Dakota Institute for Regional Studies, North Dakota State University, Fargo.
SHSND
State Historical Society of North Dakota, Bismarck.
Special Collections, UND
Elwyn B. Robinson Department of Special Collections, Chester Fritz Library, University of North Dakota, Grand Forks.

Primary Sources
Manuscript Collections

American Lutheran Church Women History Project. Evangelical Lutheran Church in America, District III. Women's Missionary Federation Records. Luther Seminary, St. Paul, Minnesota.

Anderson, Elizabeth Preston. Papers. NDIRS.

"The Bergs of Newburgh." Unpublished manuscript. Steele County Historical Society. Hope, ND.

Carpenter, Julia Gage. Diary, 1882–1902. Copy in Special Collections, UND.

Cole, George. Diaries. Steele County Museum, Hope, ND.

Delong, Ellen Calder. Papers. SHSND.

Fuglestad, Torkel. Papers. Special Collections, UND.

German Evangelical Colonization Society. Church Minutes. Colony Records. Special Collections, UND.

Gjelsnes, Marius and Caroline. Letters. Trans. Orville Bakken. Special Collections, UND.

Jensen, Mae Roberts. Diary, 1884–1918. SHSND.

Joachim, S. "Toward an Understanding of the Russia Germans." An address delivered to the Western Conference of the Dakota District of the American Lutheran Church, Concordia College Occasional Papers 1 (August 1931). Concordia College, Moorhead, MN.

Kildahl, N. Johanna. "Reminiscences." Papers, 1895–1936. Special Collections, UND.

Lindaas Family. Papers. Special Collections, UND.

Lunstrom, Otto Monson. "Memoirs." Manuscript in possession of Kristi Groberg, Fargo, ND.

McDonough, Stephen L. Papers. SHSND.

Minutes of the North Dakota Mission of the Methodist Episcopal Church. 1884–1908. Special Collections, UND.

North Dakota Church Records. Fargo Diocese Parish Records. 1908. Special Collections, UND.

North Dakota Farmers' Institute Records. NDIRS.

Porterville, Myrtle Bemis. Papers. NDIRS.

Raaen, Aagot. Papers. Hatton-Eielson Museum, Hatton, ND.

Sackman, Julia. Letters to Jodi Nelson. 1995. Copies in author's possession.

Slaughter, Benjamin F. and Linda W. Papers. SHSND.

Still, Mary Alma Barrett. Diary, 1910–14. NDIRS.

Woman's Christian Temperance Union Papers. WCTU (Florence Crittenton Home) Record Book, 1892–94. SHSND.

Zimmerman Trial. Governor's Files. SHSND.

Newspapers

Dakota Farmer
Fargo Forum
Granville Herald
McLean County Mail
Velva Journal

Government Documents

Beal, W. H., John Hamilton, and G. C. Creelman. *Proceedings of the Ninth Annual Meeting of the American Association of Farmers' Institute Workers.* St. Louis, MO, 18–20 October 1904. Washington, DC: GPO, 1905.

Biennial Report of the Dairy Commissioner to the Commissioner of Agriculture and Labor of the Dairy Interests. N.p., 30 June 1912.

Biennial Reports of the Board of Trustees of the Hospital for the Insane at Jamestown to the Governor of North Dakota. Bismarck, ND: The Trustees, 1892–1910.

Biennial Reports of the Commissioner of Agriculture and Labor to the Governor of North Dakota. Bismarck, ND: The Department, 1892–1924.

Biennial Reports of the North Dakota State Hospital for the Insane to the Board of Control of State Institutions. Bismarck, ND: The Board, 1914–28.

Biennial Reports of the State Board of Health to the Governor of North Dakota. Bismarck, ND: The Board, 1908–24.

Birth, Stillbirth, and Infant Mortality Statistics for the Birth Registration Area of the United States, 1928. Washington, DC: GPO, 1930.

Bureau of Business and Economic Research, University of North Dakota, and North Dakota Federal Aid Coordinator, Office of State and Local Planning. *Statistical Abstract of North Dakota.* Grand Forks: University of North Dakota Press, 1979.

Hamilton, John, for the U.S. Department of Agriculture, Office of Experiment Stations. *Farmers' Institutes in the United States.* Washington, DC: GPO, 1904.

"Hardships of Farmers' Wives." *Report of the Commissioner of Agriculture for the Year 1862.* Washington, DC: GPO, 1863.

"Industrial Education of Women." *Report of the Commissioner of Agriculture in the Year 1871.* Washington, DC: GPO, 1872.

Proceedings of the American Association of Farmers' Institute Managers. Columbus, OH, 27–28 October 1897. Lincoln, NE: State Journal Company, 1898.

Report of the Secretary of the Iowa State Agricultural Society, 1879. Des Moines, IA: F. M. Mills, State Printer, 1880.

State Governor's Records. Sheriff's Jail Reports. Series 172. State Archives. SHSND.

Statistical Abstracts of the United States. Washington, DC: GPO, 1927–31.

Statistics of Women at Work: Based on Unpublished Information Derived from the Schedules of the Twelfth Census: 1900. Washington, DC: GPO, 1907.

True, A. C., D. J. Crosby, and G. C. Creelman, eds. *Proceedings of the Sixth Annual Meeting of the American Association of Farmers' Institute Workers.* Buffalo, NY, 18–19 September 1901. Washington, DC: GPO, 1902.

U.S. Bureau of the Census. *Census of Population 1900, North Dakota.* Vol. 7. Washington, DC: Bureau of the Census Microfilm Laboratory.

——. *Census of Population 1910, North Dakota.* Vol. 7. Washington, DC: Bureau of the Census Microfilm Laboratory.

U.S. Census Office. *Compendium of the Eleventh Census 1890.* Pt. 1, Population. Washington, DC: GPO, 1892.

——. *Report of the Statistics of Agriculture in the United States at the Eleventh Census 1890.* Washington, DC: GPO, 1895.

——. *Report on the Productions of Agriculture as Returned at the Tenth Census 1880.* Washington, DC: GPO, 1883.

——. *Statistics of the Population of the United States at the Tenth Census 1880.* Washington, DC: GPO, 1883.

——. *Tenth Census of the United States Taken in the Year 1890.* Pt. 1, Agriculture. Washington, DC: GPO, 1893.

——. *Twelfth Census of the United States Taken in the Year 1900.* Pts. 1–2, Population; Vol. 4.2, Vital Statistics; Vol. 5.1, Agriculture. Washington, DC: The Office, 1902.

U.S. Department of Agriculture. *Report*

103. *Social and Labor Needs of Farm Women.* Washington, DC: GPO, 1915.

———. Report 104. *Domestic Needs of Farm Women.* Washington, DC: GPO, 1915.

———. Report 105. *Educational Needs of Farm Women.* Washington, DC: GPO, 1915.

———. Report 106. *Economic Needs of Farm Women.* Washington, DC: GPO, 1915.

———. *Yearbooks of Agriculture.* Washington, DC: GPO, 1900–1930.

U.S. Department of Commerce. Bureau of the Census. *Fifteenth Census of the United States: 1930.* Vol. 2.1, Agriculture; Vol. 3.2, Population. Washington, DC: GPO, 1932.

———. ———. *Fourteenth Census of the United States Taken in the Year 1920.* Vol. 3, Population; Vol. 6.1, Agriculture. Washington, DC: GPO, 1922.

———. ———. *Thirteenth Census of the United States Taken in the Year 1910.* Vol. 3, Population; Vol. 7, Agriculture. Washington, DC: GPO, 1913.

U.S. Department of Labor. Children's Bureau. Publication 160: *Dependent and Delinquent Children in North Dakota and South Dakota.* Washington, DC: GPO, 1926.

Wallace, Henry. "The Relation of the Creamery to Iowa Farming." *Report of the Board of Directors of the Iowa State Agricultural Society 1880.* Des Moines, IA: F. M. Mills, 1881.

Unpublished Material

Historical Data Project Records. Pioneer Biography Files, 1936–40. SHSND. Microfilm.

Job, Magdalena. Interview with author. Medina, ND. 15 September and 19 October 1990.

North Dakota Federation of Women's Clubs. Pioneer Mother Project Records, 1938–53. SHSND. Microfilm.

North Dakota Writers' Project Records. Ethnic Group Files, 1935–42. SHSND. Microfilm.

———. Folklore Files. SHSND.

———. Hard Wheat Study Files, 1935–42. SHSND.

Pladson, Gyda. Interview with author. 25 June 1991.

State of North Dakota v. Orlaug Aasen. 28 February 1890. Coroner's Inquest on the body of Peter P. Lomen, 8–11 February 1890, Hatton. Traill County Courthouse, Hillsboro, ND.

Published Material

Assumption of Mary Church Diamond Jubilee 1904–1979. Starkweather, ND: Privately printed, 1979.

Aurdal 1883–1983. Forbes, ND: Privately printed, 1983.

Benton, Alva H. "Poultry and Egg Marketing in North Dakota." North Dakota Agricultural College, Government Agricultural Experiment Station. Bulletin 215 (February 1928): 5–27.

Berntson, Norma E. *As the Sod Was Turned.* Fairview, MT: Privately printed, n.d.

C———, Mrs. G. I. "One Year's Experience with Turkeys." North Dakota Farmers' Institute *Annual* 2 (1902): 125–27.

Calof, Rachel. *Rachel Calof's Story: Jewish Homesteader on the Northern Plains.* Edited by J. Sanford Rikoon. Bloomington: Indiana University Press, 1995.

Curtiss, Mrs. E. T. "Our Farm Life, How to Decrease Its Evils and Increase Its Blessings." North Dakota Farmers' Institute *Annual* 2 (1902): 46–54.

Diede, Pauline Neher. *Homesteading on the Knife River Prairies.* Edited by Elizabeth Hampsten. Bismarck, ND: Germans from Russia Heritage Society, 1983.

———. *The Prairie Was Home.* Richardton, ND: Abbey Press and John H. Gengler, 1986.

———. *Speaking-Out on Sod-House Times.* Richardton, ND: Abbey Press and John H. Gengler, 1985.

Fitzmaurice, Mrs. F. "The Dairy." North Dakota Farmers' Institute *Annual* 2 (1902): n.p.

Golden Anniversary of Ebenezer Lutheran Church. Northwood, ND: Privately printed, 1950.

Hoover, Jessie B. "Home Economics in North Dakota Agricultural College." North Dakota Farmers' Institute *Annual* 9 (1909): 237–42.

———. "White Sauce and Its Uses." North Dakota Farmers' Institute *Annual* 11 (1911): 145–47.

Hopkins, Mary Alden. "New England Mill Slaves." *Good Housekeeping* 57 (September 1913): 323.

Humphrey, Seth K. *Following the Prairie Frontier.* Minneapolis: University of Minnesota Press, 1931.

Johnson, M. A. *Fifty Years of Country Storekeeping.* Larimore, ND: Privately printed, 1955.

Ladd, E. F. "Preserving Eggs." North Dakota Agricultural College, Government Agricultural Experiment Station. Bulletin 35 (January 1899): 330–32.

Ostervold Lutheran Church: A Century of Love 1883–1983. Finley, ND: Privately printed, 1983.

Palanuk, Agnes, ed. *North Dakota Ukrainian Oral History Project.* N.p.: Privately printed, n.d.

Palmer, W. C. "The Farmer's Wife." North Dakota Farmers' Institute *Annual* 11 (1911): 88–89.

Pollock, Charles A. *Manual of the Prohibition Law of North Dakota 1910.* N.p.: North Dakota State Enforcement League, 1910.

The Presbyterian Church of Bathgate — 100 Years 1883–1983. N.p.: n.d.

Raaen, Aagot. *Grass of the Earth.* Northfield, MN: Norwegian-American Historical Association, 1950. Reprint, with introduction by Barbara Handy-Marchello, St. Paul: Minnesota Historical Society Press, 1994.

———. *Hamarsbon-Raaen Genealogy.* N.p.: Privately printed, 1954.

Roberts, Margaret Barr. "Margaret Barr Roberts." *North Dakota History* 24 (1957): 129–38.

Sheppard, Alice M. "Information on Skim Milk." North Dakota Farmers' Institute *Annual* 4 (1904): 53–54.

———. "A Modern Farm House Built at a Moderate Cost." North Dakota Farmers' Institute *Annual* 4 (1904): 121–23.

Slaughter, Linda. *Fortress to Farm, or Twenty-three Years on the Frontier.* Edited by Hazel Eastman. New York: Exposition Press, 1972.

———. *The New Northwest: A Pamphlet Stating Briefly the Advantages of Bismarck and Vicinity.* Bismarck, ND: Burleigh County Pioneer's Association, 1874.

Standard Atlas of McIntosh County, North Dakota. Chicago: George A. Ogle and Co., 1911.

Standard Atlas of McLean County, North Dakota. Chicago: George A. Ogle and Co., 1914.

Thomas, H. U. "The Institute and the Farmer." North Dakota Farmers' Institute *Annual* 1 (1900): 91–99.

Thompson, Era Bell. *American Daughter.* Chicago: University of Chicago Press, 1946. Reprint, St. Paul: Minnesota Historical Society Press, 1986.

Trupin, Sophie. *Dakota Diaspora: Memoirs of a Jewish Homesteader.* Lincoln: University of Nebraska Press, 1984.

Ward, Florence E. "The Farm Woman's Problems." *Journal of Home Economics* 12 (October 1920): 437–57.

"Why Young Women Are Leaving Our Farms." *Literary Digest* 67 (2 October 1920): 56–58.

Wilcox, Mrs. V. K. "Home Making." North Dakota Farmers' Institute *Annual* 5 (1905): 91–102.

Williams, Mary A. Barnes. *Fifty Pioneer Mothers of McLean County.* Washburn, ND: Privately printed, 1932.

Wishek, Nina Farley. *Along the Trails of Yesterday.* Ashley, ND: The Ashley Tribune, 1941.

Woodward, Mary Dodge. *The Checkered Years: A Bonanza Farm Diary 1884–88.* Edited by Mary Boynton Cowdrey. Caldwell, ID: Caxton Printers, 1937. Reprint, with introduction by Elizabeth Jameson, St. Paul: Minnesota Historical Society Press, 1989.

Secondary Sources

Aagard, Bea. *Lark Against the Thunder.* New York: Island Press, 1953.

Abelow-King, Mary-Susan. "The Streets Were Paved with Gold." Paper, Northern Great Plains History Conference, Grand Forks, ND, 6 October 1990.

Adams, Jane. *The Transformation of Rural Life: Southern Illinois, 1890–1990*. Chapel Hill: University of North Carolina Press, 1994.

Anderson, Karen. "Work, Gender, and Power in the American West." *Pacific Historical Review* 61 (1992): 481–99.

Armitage, Susan, and Elizabeth Jameson, eds. *The Women's West*. Norman: University of Oklahoma Press, 1987.

Atkeson, Mary Meek. "Women in Farm Life and Rural Economy." *The Annals of the American Academy of Political and Social Sciences* 143 (May 1929): 188–94.

Bailey, Liberty Hyde. *The Country Life Movement in the United States*. New York: MacMillan Company, 1911.

Bateman, Fred. "The Marketable Surplus in Northern Dairy Farming: New Evidence by Size of Farm in 1860." *Agricultural History* 52 (July 1978): 345–63.

Bavendick, Frank J. *Climate and Weather in North Dakota*. Bismarck, ND: Water Conservation Commission, 1952.

Beard, Mary, ed. *America Through Women's Eyes*. New York: MacMillan Company, 1933.

Bennholt-Thomsen, Veronika. "Towards a Theory of the Sexual Division of Labor." In *Households and the World-Economy, Explorations in the World-Economy*, edited by Joan Smith, Immanuel Wallerstein, and Hans-Dieter Evers, 252–71. Publications of the Fernand Braudel Center, vol. 3. Beverly Hills, CA: Sage Publications, 1984.

Boleyn, Angela. *Quarter Sections and Wide Horizons: A Series of Stories on Pioneer Women of North Dakota*. 2 vol. Bismarck: North Dakota State Library, 1978.

Bowers, William L. *The Country Life Movement in America, 1900–1920*. Port Washington, NY: Kennikat Press, 1974.

Boydston, Jeanne. *Home and Work: Housework, Wages, and the Ideology of Labor in the Early Republic*. New York: Oxford University Press, 1990.

Branca, Patricia. "A New Perspective on Women's Work: A Comparative Typology." *Journal of Social History* 9 (Winter 1975): 129–53.

Breneman, Mary Worthy. *The Land They Possessed*. Brookings: South Dakota Committee on the Humanities and South Dakota Library Association, 1989.

Briggs, Harold E. "The Great Dakota Boom." In Lysengen and Rathke, eds., *Centennial Anthology*, 109–31.

Brown, Judith. "Note on the Division of Labor by Sex." *American Anthropologist* 72 (1970): 1073–78.

Brudvig, Glenn Lowell. "The Farmers' Alliance and Populist Movement in North Dakota (1884–1896)." Master's thesis, University of North Dakota, 1956.

Bunkers, Suzanne L. *"All Will Yet Be Well:" The Diary of Sarah Gillespie Huftalen, 1873–1952*. Iowa City: University of Iowa Press, 1993.

Cohen, Marjorie Griffin. *Women's Work, Markets and Economic Development in Nineteenth Century Ontario*. Toronto: University of Toronto Press, 1988.

Conzen, Kathleen Neils. "Peasant Pioneers: Generational Succession among German Farmers in Frontier Minnesota." In *The Countryside in the Age of Capitalist Transformation: Essays in the Social History of Rural America*, edited by Steven Hahn and Jonathan Prude, 259–92. Chapel Hill: University of North Carolina Press, 1985.

Cott, Nancy. *The Bonds of Womanhood: "Woman's Sphere" in New England 1780–1835*. New Haven, CT: Yale University Press, 1977.

Coulter, John L. "Industrial History of the Valley of the Red River of the North." *Collections of the State Historical Society of North Dakota* 3 (1910): 627–41.

Danbom, David B. *Born in the Country: A History of Rural America*. Baltimore, MD: Johns Hopkins University Press, 1995.

——. "The North Dakota Agricultural Experiment Station and the Struggle to Create a Dairy State." *Agricultural History* 63 (Spring 1989): 174–86.

——. *The Resisted Revolution: Urban America and the Industrialization of Agriculture, 1900–1930*. Ames: Iowa State University Press, 1979.

Drache, Hiram. *Day of the Bonanza: A His-*

tory of Bonanza Farming in the Red River Valley of the North. Fargo: NDIRS, 1964.

Dyrstad, Heidi L. "'Just as Good as They Are': Voices of Contemporary Women Involved in Farming and Ranching in North Dakota." PhD diss., University of North Dakota, 2001.

Elbert, Sarah. "Women and Farming: Changing Structures, Changing Roles." In Haney and Knowles, eds., *Women and Farming*, 245–64.

Emmons, David M. "The Influence of Ideology on Changing Environmental Images: The Case of Six Gazeteers." In *Images of the Plains: The Role of Human Nature in Settlement*, edited by Brian W. Blouet and Merlin P. Lawson, 125–36. Lincoln: University of Nebraska Press, 1975.

Faragher, John Mack. *Sugar Creek: Life on the Illinois Prairie*. New Haven, CT: Yale University Press, 1986.

——. *Women and Men on the Overland Trail*. New Haven, CT: Yale University Press, 1979.

Fink, Deborah. *Agrarian Women: Wives and Mothers in Rural Nebraska, 1880–1940*. Chapel Hill: University of North Carolina Press, 1992.

——. *Open Country Iowa: Rural Women, Tradition and Change*. Albany: State University of New York Press, 1986.

Fite, Gilbert. *The Farmers' Frontier: 1865–1900*. New York: Holt, Rinehart, Winston, 1966.

——. "Land and Its Meaning." *South Dakota History* 15 (Spring 1985): 2–25.

Flora, Cornelia Butler. "Rural Women: A Retrospective and a Prospective Thought." Paper, Rural Women/Feminist Theory Conference, Iowa City, IA, 1992.

Folbre, Nancy. *The Invisible Heart: Economics and Family Values*. New York: The New Press, 2001.

Garceau, Dee. *The Important Things of Life: Women, Work and Family in Sweetwater County, Wyoming 1880–1929*. Lincoln: University of Nebraska Press, 1997.

Giesinger, Adam. *From Catherine to Khrushchev: The Story of Russia's Germans*. Lincoln, NE: American Historical Society of Germans from Russia, 1981.

Gilman, Charlotte Perkins. *Women and Economics: A Study of the Economic Relation Between Men and Women as a Factor in Social Evolution*. Boston: Small Maynard and Co., 1898.

Gjerde, Jon. *From Peasants to Farmers: The Migration from Balestrand, Norway, to the Upper Middle West*. New York: Cambridge University Press, 1985.

Gonzalez, Rosalinda Mendez. "Distinctions in Western Women's Experience: Ethnicity, Class, and Social Change." In Armitage and Jameson, eds., *The Women's West*, 237–51.

Gordon, Linda. *Heroes of Their Own Lives: The Politics and History of Family Violence*. New York: Penguin Books, 1988.

Greenwood, Annie Pike. "Growing Things from the Soil Is Bliss." In *Writings of Farm Women 1840–1940: An Anthology*, edited by Carol Fairbanks and Bergine Haakenson, 315–38. New York: Garland Publishing, 1990.

Griswold, Robert L. "Apart But Not Adrift: Wives, Divorce, and Independence in California, 1850–1890." *Pacific Historical Review* 49 (May 1980): 265–83.

Gullett, Gayle. "Constructing the Woman Citizen and Struggling for the Vote in California, 1896–1911." *Pacific Historical Review* 69 (November 2000): 573–93.

Hampsten, Elizabeth. *Read This Only to Yourself: The Private Writings of Midwestern Farm Women, 1880–1910*. Bloomington: Indiana University Press, 1982.

Hampsten, Elizabeth, comp. *To All Inquiring Friends: Letters, Diaries and Essays in North Dakota 1880–1910*. Grand Forks: University of North Dakota, Department of English, 1980.

Handy-Marchello, Barbara. "Land, Liquor and the Women of Hatton, North Dakota." *North Dakota History* 59 (Fall 1992): 22–29.

Haney, Wava G., and Jane B. Knowles, eds. *Women and Farming: Changing Structures, Changing Roles*. Boulder, CO: Westview Press, 1988.

Hansen, Marcus L. "The History of American Immigration as a Field for Research."

American Historical Review 32 (April 1927): 500–518.

Hargreaves, Mary Wilma M. *Dry Farming in the Northern Great Plains, 1900–1925.* Cambridge, MA: Harvard University Press, 1957.

Harper, Ida Husted, ed. *The History of Woman Suffrage.* Vol. 5, 1900–1920. New York: National American Woman Suffrage Association, 1922.

Harris, Alice Kessler. *Out to Work: A History of Wage Earning Women in the United States.* New York: Oxford University Press, 1983.

Harris, Katherine. "Homesteading in Northeastern Colorado, 1873–1920." In Armitage and Jameson, eds., *The Women's West,* 165–78.

Harris, Marshall. *Origins of the Land Tenure System in the United States.* Ames: Iowa State University Press, 1953.

Herigstad, Omon B. "Norwegian Immigration." *Collections of the State Historical Society of North Dakota* 2 (1908): 199–200.

Hillesland, Anton. "The Norwegian Lutheran Church in the Red River Valley." *Collections of the State Historical Society* 7 (1925): 195–283.

Hine, Robert V. *Community on the American Frontier: Separate but Not Alone.* Norman: University of Oklahoma Press, 1980.

Holt, Marilyn Irvin. *Linoleum, Better Babies and the Modern Farm Woman, 1890–1930.* Albuquerque: University of New Mexico Press, 1995.

Hunter, W. C. *Presbyterianism in North Dakota.* N.p.: Synod of North Dakota, 1959.

Isern, Thomas D. *Bullthreshers and Bindlestiffs: Harvesting and Threshing on the North American Plains.* Lawrence: University Press of Kansas, 1990.

Jeffrey, Julie Roy. *Frontier Women: The Trans-Mississippi West, 1840–1880.* New York: Hill and Wang, 1979.

Jellison, Katherine. *Entitled to Power: Farm Women and Technology, 1913–1963.* Chapel Hill: University of North Carolina Press, 1993.

Jensen, Joan M. *Loosening the Bonds: Mid-Atlantic Farm Women, 1750–1850.* New Haven, CT: Yale University Press, 1986.

———. *Promise to the Land: Essays on Rural Women.* Albuquerque: University of New Mexico Press, 1991.

Jensen, Joan M., and Darlis A. Miller. *New Mexico Women: Intercultural Perspectives.* Albuquerque: University of New Mexico Press, 1986.

Jones, Jacqueline. *Labor of Love, Labor of Sorrow: Black Women, Work and the Family from Slavery to the Present.* New York: Vintage Books, 1986.

Kerber, Linda K. "Separate Spheres, Female Worlds, Woman's Place: The Rhetoric of Women's History." In *Toward an Intellectual History of Women: Essays by Linda K. Kerber,* 159–99. Chapel Hill: University of North Carolina Press, 1997.

Kloberdanz, Timothy. "In the Land of Inyan Woslata: Plains Indian Influences on Reservation Whites." *Journal of the American Historical Society of Germans from Russia* 15 (Summer 1992): 15–27.

———. "Volksdeutsche: The Eastern European Germans." In Sherman and Thorson, eds., *Plains Folk,* 117–82.

Kohl, Seena B. "The Making of a Community: The Role of Women in an Agricultural Setting." In *Kin and Communities: Families in America,* edited by Allan J. Lichtman and Joan Challinor, 175–86. Washington, DC: Smithsonian Institution Press, 1979.

Leavitt, Judith Walzer. *Brought to Bed: Child-Bearing in America, 1750–1950.* New York: Oxford University Press, 1986.

Lensink, Judy Nolte, ed. *"A Secret to Be Burried": The Life and Diary of Emily Hawley Gillespie.* Iowa City: University of Iowa Press, 1989.

Lindgren, H. Elaine. *Land in Her Own Name: Women as Homesteaders in North Dakota.* Fargo: NDIRS, 1991.

Lysengen, Janet Daley, and Ann M. Rathke, eds. *The Centennial Anthology of North Dakota History: Journal of the Northern Plains.* Bismarck: SHSND, 1996.

McMurry, Sally. *Families and Farmhouses in Nineteenth Century America: Vernac-*

ular Design and Social Change. New York: Oxford University Press, 1988.

Marti, Donald B. *Women of the Grange: Mutuality and Sisterhood in Rural America, 1866–1920.* New York: Greenwood Press, 1991.

Matsumoto, Valerie. *Farming the Home Place: A Japanese American Community in California, 1919–1982.* Ithaca, NY: Cornell University Press, 1993.

Murray, Stanley N. "The Turtle Mountain Chippewa." In Lysengen and Rathke, eds., *Centennial Anthology,* 83–108.

———. *The Valley Comes of Age: A History of Agriculture in the Valley of the Red River of the North, 1812–1920.* Fargo: NDIRS, 1967.

Myres, Sandra L. *Westering Women and the Frontier Experience, 1800–1915.* Albuquerque: University of New Mexico Press, 1982.

Nelson, E. Clifford, and Eugene L. Fevold. *The Lutheran Church Among Norwegian-Americans.* 2 vols. Minneapolis, MN: Augsburg Publishing House, 1960.

Nelson, Paula. *After the West Was Won: Homesteaders and Town-Builders in Western South Dakota, 1900–1917.* Iowa City: University of Iowa Press, 1986.

Nelson, Paula, ed. "'All Well and Hard at Work': The Harris Family Letters from Dakota Territory, 1882–1888." *North Dakota History* 57 (Spring 1990): 24–37.

———. "Memoir of a Country Schoolteacher: Dolly Holliday Clark Meets the Ethnic West." In Lysengen and Rathke, eds., *Centennial Anthology,* 288–307.

Neth, Mary. *Preserving the Family Farm: Women, Community, and the Foundations of Agribusiness in the Midwest, 1900–1940.* Baltimore, MD: Johns Hopkins University Press, 1995.

Newgard, Thomas, and William C. Sherman. "Blacks." In Sherman and Thorson, eds., *Plains Folk,* 381–88.

Nielsen, Kim E. "'We All Leaguers by Our House': Women, Suffrage, and Red-Baiting in the National Non-Partisan League." *Journal of Women's History* 6 (Spring 1994): 31–50.

Nobles, Gregory. "Straight Lines and Stability: Mapping the Political Order of the Anglo-American Frontier." *Journal of American History* 80 (June 1993): 9–35.

Ostergren, Robert C. *A Community Transplanted: The Trans-Atlantic Experience of a Swedish Immigrant Settlement in the Upper Middle West, 1835–1915.* Madison: University of Wisconsin Press, 1988.

Osterud, Nancy Grey. *Bonds of Community: The Lives of Farm Women in Nineteenth Century New York.* Ithaca, NY: Cornell University Press, 1991.

Otto, John S. "Farming in Russia and North Dakota: One German-Russian Family's Experiences." *North Dakota History* 55 (Spring 1988): 23–30.

Perales, Marian. "Empowering the Welder." In *Writing the Range: Race, Class, and Culture in the Women's West,* edited by Elizabeth Jameson and Susan Armitage, 21–41. Norman: University of Oklahoma Press, 1997.

Peterson, Fred W. "Norwegian Farm Homes in Steele and Traill Counties, North Dakota: The American Dream and the Retention of Roots, 1890–1914." *North Dakota History* 51 (Winter 1984): 4–13.

Peterson, Larry. "Women in North Dakota: The First Century of Population History, 1890–1990." Paper, Northern Great Plains History Conference, La Crosse, WI, 1996.

Plaut, W. Gunther. "Jewish Colonies at Painted Woods and Devils Lake." *North Dakota History* 32 (January 1965): 59–70.

Pleck, Elizabeth. "Challenges to Traditional Authority in Immigrant Families." In *The American Family in Social-Historical Perspective,* edited by Michael Gordon, 504–17. New York: St. Martin's Press, 1983.

Quick, Herbert. "The Women on Farms." *Good Housekeeping* 57 (September 1913): 426–36.

Reid, Bill G. "Elizabeth Preston Anderson and the Politics of Social Reform." In *The North Dakota Political Tradition,* edited by Thomas W. Howard, 183–202. Ames, IA: North Dakota Centennial Heritage Series, Iowa State University Press, 1981.

Robinson, Elwyn B. *History of North Dakota*. Lincoln: University of Nebraska Press, 1966.

Rochlin, Harriet, and Fred Rochlin. *Pioneer Jews: A New Life in the Far West*. Boston: Houghton Mifflin Company, 2000.

Roemmich, Herman. *A Conflict of Three Cultures: Germans from Russia in America, A History of the Jacob Roemmich Family*. Fargo: NDIRS, 1991.

Rølvaag, O. E. *Giants in the Earth: A Saga of the Prairie*. New York: Harper and Brothers, 1927.

Roper, Stephanie Abbot. "African Americans in North Dakota, 1800–1940." Master's thesis, University of North Dakota, 1993.

Rosenfeld, Rachel Ann. *Farm Women: Work, Farm, and Family in the United States*. Chapel Hill: University of North Carolina Press, 1985.

Ryan, Mary. *Cradle of the Middle Class: The Family in Oneida County, New York, 1790–1865*. New York: Cambridge University Press, 1981.

Sachs, Carolyn. *The Invisible Farmers: Women in Agricultural Production*. Totowa, NJ: Rowman and Allanhead, 1983.

——. "The Participation of Women and Girls in Market and Non-Market Activities on Pennsylvania Farms." In Haney and Knowles, eds., *Women and Farming*, 123–34.

——. "Understanding Women's Lives." Paper, Rural Women/Feminist Theory Conference, Iowa City, IA, 1992.

Salamon, Sonya, and Ann Mackey Keim. "Land Ownership and Women's Power in a Midwestern Farming Community." *Journal of Marriage and the Family* 41 (February 1979): 109–19.

Sallet, Richard. *Russian German Settlements in the United States*. Translated by LaVern J. Rippley and Armand Bauer. Fargo: NDIRS, 1974.

Sanday, Peggy R. "Toward a Theory of the Status of Women." *American Anthropologist* 75 (October 1973): 1682–1700.

Sandoz, Mari. *Old Jules*. Lincoln: University of Nebraska Press, 1935.

Sannes, Erling N. "'Free Land for All': A Young Snasean Woman Homesteads in North Dakota." Manuscript in author's possession. Published as "'Free Land for All': Ei ung snasakvinne som nybyggar i Nord-Dakota." Translated by Erik Gran. *Kumur Arsskrift Nr. 11* (1990): 18–32.

Scharff, Virginia. "Gender and Western History: Is Anybody Home on the Range?" *Montana: The Magazine of Western History* (Spring 1991): 62–65.

Schneider, Mary Jane. *North Dakota's Indian Heritage*. Grand Forks: University of North Dakota Press, 1990.

Schob, David E. *Hired Hands and Plowboys: Farm Labor in the Midwest, 1815–1860*. Urbana: University of Illinois Press, 1975.

Scott, Ann Firor. *Natural Allies: Women's Associations in American History*. Urbana: University of Illinois Press, 1991.

Seelye-Miller, Rose. "Women Farmers of Dakota." *The Nebraska Farmer* (3 September 1896 and 10 September 1896).

Segalen, Martine. *Love and Power in the Peasant Family*. Chicago: University of Chicago Press, 1983.

Sharpless, Rebecca. *Fertile Ground, Narrow Choices: Women on Cotton Farms of the Texas Blackland Prairies, 1900–1940*. Chapel Hill: University of North Carolina Press, 1999.

Sherman, William C. *Prairie Mosaic: An Ethnic Atlas of Rural North Dakota*. Fargo: NDIRS, 1983.

Sherman, William C., and Playford V. Thorson, eds. *Plains Folk: North Dakota's Ethnic History*. Fargo: NDIRS, 1988.

Stanton, Elizabeth Cady, Susan B. Anthony, and Matilda Joslyn Gage, eds. *History of Woman Suffrage*. Vol. 3, 1876–85. New York: National American Woman Suffrage Association, 1922.

Stewart, Edgar I., ed. *Penny-An-Acre Empire in the West*. Norman: University of Oklahoma Press, 1968.

Stradley, Scot Arthur. *The Broken Circle: An Economic History of North Dakota*. Grand Forks: Bureau of Business and Economic Research, University of North Dakota, 1993.

Tollefson, Axel. "Historical Notes on the Norwegians in the Red River Valley." *Collections of the State Historical Society of North Dakota 7* (1925): 136–57.

Tucker, Jeanne. "The History of Woman Suffrage in North Dakota." Unpublished paper, 1951. Available: Special Collections, UND.

Ulrich, Laurel Thatcher. *Goodwives: Image and Reality in the Lives of Women in Northern New England, 1650–1750*. New York: Knopf, 1982.

——. *A Midwife's Tale: The Life of Martha Ballard, Based on Her Diary, 1785–1812*. New York: Vintage Books, 1991.

Walters, Thorstina. *Modern Sagas: The Story of Icelanders in North America*. Fargo: NDIRS, 1953.

Webb, Walter. *The Great Plains*. New York: Grosset & Dunlap, 1931.

Wilkins, Robert P., and Wynona Huchette Wilkins. *North Dakota: A Bicentennial History*. New York: W. W. Norton, 1977.

Williams, Mary A. Barnes. *History of the Methodist Church*. Washburn, ND: Privately printed, 1950.

Williamson, Erik. "'Doing What Had to Be Done:' Norwegian Lutheran Ladies Aid Societies of North Dakota." *North Dakota History 57* (Spring 1990): 2–13.

Wilson, Gilbert. *Agriculture of the Hidatsa Indians: An Indian Interpretation*. Minneapolis: University of Minnesota Press, 1917. Reprint, *Buffalo Bird Woman's Garden: Agriculture of the Hidatsa Indians*. St. Paul: Minnesota Historical Society Press, 1987.

Wold, Frances, ed. "The Letters of Effie Hanson, 1917–1923: Farm Life in Troubled Times." In Lysengen and Rathke, eds., *Centennial Anthology*, 268–87.

Wolf, Margery. "Rural Women and Feminist Issues." Unpublished essay, 1987.

Young, Carrie. *Nothing to Do but Stay: My Pioneer Mother*. Iowa City: University of Iowa Press, 1991.

Zevenbergen, Jason. "Establishing a Jewish Community: A Study of Jewish Immigrant Homesteaders in North Dakota, 1880–1920." Unpublished paper, n.d. Special Collections, UND.

Index

Picture Credits

Women of the Northern Plains was designed and set in type by Will Powers at the Minnesota Historical Society Press and was printed by Maple Press, York, Pennsylvania.